CLIMATE ADAPTATION

Accounts of Resilience, Self-Sufficiency and Systems Change

CLIMATE ADAPTATION

Accounts of Resilience, Self-Sufficiency and Systems Change

Edited by Arkbound Foundation

Climate Adaptation
by Arkbound Foundation

© Arkbound Foundation

ISBN: 9781912092123

First published in 2021
by Arkbound Foundation (Publishers)

Arkbound is a social enterprise that aims to promote social inclusion, community development and artistic talent. It sponsors publications by disadvantaged authors and covers issues that engage wider social concerns. Arkbound fully embraces sustainability and environmental protection. It endeavours to use material that is renewable, recyclable or sourced from sustainable forest.

Arkbound
Rogart Street Campus
4 Rogart Street
Glasgow G40 2AA

www.arkbound.com

Contents

Key Contributors   i

Background and Acknowledgements   viii

Key Supporters   xi

Introduction   xiii

Part 1

The Situation   1

Oceans in Peril   30

Our Society   58

Part 2

Towards a Transformative Adaptation Strategy in Nepal   80

Stories from the Blue Continent   92

Droughts in Lamu County   109

Local Agro-ecological Transition in Brazil   121

Climate Migration   135

Earth Rejuvenation   148

Wayfinding in a time of Covid   157

Part 3

From Thinking to Acting   173

Environmental Education   198

PROUT   213

Visioning the Future as an Act of Subversive Democracy   248

Commons-based Monies for an Inclusive and Resilient Future   264

Dodo, Phoenix or Butterfly?   285

Conclusion   300

Key Contributors

Dr Renuka Thakore

Renuka is the founder of Global Sustainable Futures: Progress through Partnership Network, University College of Estate Management, UK, which provides leadership to a global network, administering multidisciplinary activities and research partnerships development platform. Her research interests include sustainability and sustainable development and transformations. Her passion is to investigate the challenges of natural and societal systems and identify emerging trends that are competent in offering sustainable solutions. She contributes to the knowledge by revealing the strategic reality of real-world problems researched through transdisciplinarity and systems thinking.

Dr Morgan Phillips

Morgan is UK co-director of the Glacier Trust, and head of insight at Global Action Plan. He holds a PhD in environmental education and has previously worked as head of Eco-Schools England and lectured on the politics of climate change at Brunel University. Morgan is the author of Great Adaptations: In the Shadow of a Climate Crisis, also published by Arkbound UK.

Dr Janis Steele

Janis was born and raised in Montreal, Canada and earned a BA in human ecology at College of the Atlantic in Maine and her PhD in cultural anthropology at the University of Massachusetts Amherst. She co-founded the non-profit Island Reach to ally with partners in Indigenous and local communities, social movements, and members of civil society to help achieve community-driven biocultural resilience. She has worked in the US, Caribbean and, for the past nine years, in Oceania where she has collaborated with the Pacific Climate Warriors, Vanuatu Climate Action Network and local environmental activists.

Fazeela Mubarak

Fazeela is an accountant by profession but has for the last eight years been volunteering for environmental causes. She started volunteering with Care for the Wild Kenya in the Tsavo Conservation area where she learned the importance of community conservation and the contribution of Indigenous practices to the thriving biodiversity. Her dedication saw her elected twice to the board of Friends of Nairobi National Park where she was part of the Save Nairobi National Park Campaign. Alongside her friend Tiju Aziz, Fazeela has worked on major drought mitigation projects in Lamu where the effects of climate breakdown were catastrophic. Their work saw the implementation of sustainable projects that continue to benefit both wildlife and communities.

Rodrigo Machado Moreira

Rodrigo grew up in a small town in Paraná State, Brazil and studied veterinary medicine in Botucatu, São Paulo. He then did his master's degree at UNICAMP, Campinas State University, and finally at the University of Cordoba in Spain for his PhD in agroecology.

Isobel Thomas-Horton

Isobel is a recent graduate of English literature at Glasgow University. She was part of a course and symposium on the migrant crisis at the Johannes Gutenberg University in Mainz, Germany, in 2018. Meeting migrants and hearing their stories led to her interest in climate migration. She is currently the editor of The World + 3 journal, a student-led exploration of the changes society needs to make to survive a warmer world. More information can be found at plus3degrees.carrd.co.

Carol Manetta

Carol was born in Michigan, USA and traveled extensively to research Virtual Reality in its early stages. This allowed her to form research protocols for other topics, including worker owned cooperatives, farming organically, hydroponics food production and more. Her master's degree in instructional design, development and testing prepared her for community work after her tenure at Ford Motor Company and its subsidiary, Ford Credit, was completed. This degree and work brought her experience to other topics: airline personnel training, prisoners returning to society, hydroponics tower production, worker owned cooperatives functioning, and more. She is Executive Director of Reap Goodness, www.reapgoodness.org, an organization based in Arizona, USA.

Dr Luiza Sarayed-Din

Luiza was born and raised in Belo Horizonte, Brazil. She did her masters in Rio de Janeiro and lived in Oman, Malaysia and Singapore for eight years. Luiza did her PhD at the University of Malaya and is now doing a postdoc at the Federal University of Rio de Janeiro.

Professor Rupert Read

Rupert is an environmental philosopher based in Norwich, and an expert in the Precautionary Principle. He was previously the spokesperson for Extinction Rebellion, and a councillor for the Green Party. He is the co-founder of Green House Think Tank, and the author of This Civilisation is Finished: Conversations on the End of Empire – and what Lies Beyond, and Extinction Rebellion: Insights from the Inside. He has previously written articles for The Guardian, The Independent, and The Conversation. His most recent book is Parents for a Future: How Loving our Children can Stop Climate Collapse, published with UEA Press.

Jane Riddiford

Jane was born in New Zealand and has lived and worked for the past 25 years in London. She studied at Bath University and Ashridge Business School. She founded Global Generation in 2004, an educational charity which connects people living in London to nature. This also creates more integrated, environmentally responsible communities.

Karen Scott

Karen lives in west Wales and trained to facilitate Work That Reconnects (WTR) with Chris Johnstone, Joanna Macy and others in 2012–13. After many years working in the voluntary and community sector ('third sector') development, Karen has more recently been running her own freelance practice, Being in Nature, offering nature-based coaching, nature-connection programmes, and online and in-person WTR spirals. The pilot project that took WTR into the Welsh Government was initially inspired by hearing Joanna Macy tell the Shambhala warrior prophecy. Karen is also a doting grandmother to twin boys, a keen grower, and an explorer of the beautiful Pembrokeshire coast and countryside. For further information, please visit her WTR Network facilitator profile here: https://workthatreconnects.org/user/karenann/
Website: www.beinginnature.net

Vitalie Duporge

Vitalie is a doctorate researcher at the University of Bristol looking at non-formal models of sustainability and environmental education in the context of ecovillages. Vitalie has lived and worked in ecovillages in Spain, New Zealand and Sweden. She is part of the Climate Change Education Research Network (CCERN, Bristol University) and the Global European Ecovillage Network (GEN EU).

Olivia Copsey

Olivia is an education for sustainable development (ESD) specialist with an MSc in education for sustainability. She has worked on sustainable schools strategies in the Channel Island of Jersey, and the Indian Ocean islands of Madagascar, Comoros, Mauritius and Zanzibar. Olivia was a founding member and coordinator of the Eco-Schools African Network, a community of practice for ESD involving 11 African countries, and is technical associate with Community Efforts for Conservation and Development (CECOD) in Uganda. She is currently leading a youth enterprise programme for young adults with learning disabilities in Cornwall, UK.

Dr Ester Barinaga

Ester Barinaga is professor of social entrepreneurship at Lund University, School of Economics and Management. She also holds a professorship (with special responsibilities) at the Copenhagen Business School. She is interested in concepts and strategies that may help us better design organisations for social change. Her current work focuses on community currencies as a method to build more resilient communities and more inclusive cities. The methods she uses are interventionist, actively taking part in the entrepreneurial processes she also studies. Currently, and together with a group of researchers from Gothenburg University, Sweden and JOOUST University, Kenya, she is working with local communities to set up three community currencies in the city of Kisumu, Kenya.

Dr Anne-Kathrin Schwab

Anne-Kathrin has worked as a postdoctoral researcher at the University of Vechta since March 2020 at the department of sustainable economy. During her research for her PhD within the ecovillage Lebensgarten Steyerberg in Germany, she worked at the University of Siegen and accompanied several projects; for instance, on the urban development project Scoutopia. She is engaged in the Global Ecovillage Network (GEN) in Germany within the projects Living in Sustainable Villages such as in the Erasmus Plus project Ecovillage Transition in Action. Within GEN International, she has developed with the GEN research group several formats to promote ecovillage research.

Filippo Basso

Filippo is the overall coordinator and strategic planner of the Ananda Valley conscious local development project and director of the environmental association EcoAtivo. He is passionate about ecology and the environment and has a MSc in mathematics and a science diploma from the Scuola Normale Superiore of Pisa, Italy. He has participated in several European projects related to regeneration, education, awareness-raising, environmental protection, and R&D in technological areas. He is the manager of the R&D department of an IT company, cooperating with the University of Beira Interior, Politecnico of Turin, and other European research centres.

Shriraksha Mohan

Shriraksha is a meditator, an advocate for economic democracy and equity, and a software engineer by profession. Originally from India, she now lives and works in Oregon, USA. Being acutely aware of the social, economic, political and environmental issues in her home country India, and her adopted home, the United States, she strongly believes that systemic changes to pre-existing structures are a dire necessity for all-round elevation of humanity and regeneration of the planet. Inspired by the spiritual and socio-economic philosophy of PR Sarkar, she contributes to creating socio-economic awareness for systems change.

Dada Vedaprajinananda

Dada is yoga-meditation teacher, author, editor and a singer-songwriter. He received a BA in History from Colgate University and also attended Columbia University's School of International Affairs. He is the founding editor of New Renaissance Magazine (www.ru.org) and has been a student of PR Sarkar's progressive utilisation theory (Prout) for over 50 years. His books include Prout Explained, The Wisdom of Tantra and From Brooklyn to Benares and Back. He is the author of numerous magazine articles and has released seven albums of original songs in the past 20 years.

Steven Gorelick

Steven is the Managing Programs Director of Local Futures, where he has worked since 1987. He is the co-director of the documentary film The Economics of Happiness, author of Small is Beautiful, Big is Subsidized, and co-author of Bringing the Food Economy Home. He writes frequently for the Local Futures blog, and his writings have also been published in Counterpunch, Deep Green Resistance, Resilience and other online platforms, as well as The Ecologist and Resurgence magazines.

Dr Ashish Kothari

Ashish is the founder-member of Kalpavriksh, a member of many people's movements. He taught at the Indian Institute of Public Administration; coordinated India's national biodiversity strategy & action plan, served on boards of Greenpeace International & India, ICCA Consortium. He helps coordinate Vikalp Sangam, Global Tapestry of Alternatives and Radical Ecological Democracy. He is also the co-author and co-editor of Churning the Earth, Alternative Futures, and Pluriverse: A Post-Development Dictionary.

Background and Acknowledgements

The genesis for this book can be traced back to late 2019, when we sought to create a legacy to the COP26 climate summit in Glasgow, as part of the Arkbound Foundation's environmental objectives. We realised there were two major gaps in environmental literature: firstly, that most focus is put on mitigating or preventing climate change, either from the top down or by augmenting individual behaviour; secondly, that there was very little coverage of accounts from people who would be most adversely impacted by climate change (or who are already being impacted), invariably those in the Global South. Our exploration in these areas also revealed that most books rarely delve into systemic change – at best merely touching upon it. The more we uncovered about climate change, the greater we realised how important it was for people and communities to be empowered in adapting to it and in building resilience, moving towards wholly different socio-economic structures rather than labouring under the same 'eternal GDP growth' model and being reliant upon national and international entities who have consistently failed to take sufficient action.

After extensive outreach to organisations, communities and environmental leaders across the world, we collated content that addressed these gaps and issues. As many of the authors are from positions of disadvantage, in comparison with their Northern counterparts, we offered small advance royalties to support them and their projects. These payments came in addition to a share of royalties from sales of the book.

The postponement of the COP26 summit in 2020 turned out to be fortuitous, allowing us more time to develop the book and ensure that it kept pace with the latest climate data. Not only that, but we hoped it would allow us time to seek funding. Being a very small charity, we had almost no money – being reliant on voluntary input, as with many other projects we have undertaken. However, despite over 30 funding applications and enquiries, we realised that there exists a substantial barrier to small organisations, who are not part of established networks, in accessing environmental funding. Indeed, the majority of this funding seemed to be disbursed without even the opportunity to apply for it – by invitation only – with the bulk going to large, well connected organisations who operate more of a 'top-down' model in trying to make a difference. Worryingly, we also found a great deal of this money is used internally by these large organisations on high staff salaries, fundraising and administration costs. Not only that, but other funding streams for creative and culture focused projects failed to bridge the divide between 'the environment' and 'society'. In short, we found the vast majority of creative and cultural sector funders regarded climate change as an abstract, separate issue that had little to no bearing on their field. Even for those committed to tackling climate change, this proved to be the case.

This issue is important because it means any environmental project by a small or community-rooted organisation faces huge barriers in getting funding. At the same time, for any project by an organisation which is not exclusively within the 'environmental' sector, their other funding avenues will invariably refuse support because they cannot see the relevance of climate change on wider society and culture. The consequences, for us, is that we were faced with a large budgetary deficit (over £6000). It meant going to our authors and explaining we would have to pay them a lower advance royalty, in cutting back on paid promotional avenues, and being even more reliant on voluntary input.

It is only thanks to these incredible volunteers that the project was able to proceed. Moreover, we are grateful for the understanding of authors who accepted the situation in having to be paid a lower level of advance royalty than we set out to pay, with several choosing to remit their advance royalty altogether. It is also thanks to a grant from Friends Provident that we were able to pay author royalties at all, together with donations from the Edward Hoare Charitable Fund, Climadapt and a number of individuals.

For the complete design and typesetting of this book, Tasmin Briers deserves huge appreciation – working long hours at a far lower rate than what we would have liked to provide. In editing and proofreading chapters, we were likewise reliant on the voluntary input of Jim Dempsey and Steve Mcnaught. The project's overall coordination by Emily Andrews, who put in extra voluntary hours and a great deal of effort, was essential. And for the book's promotion, we are grateful to Elly Donovan, Carolina Carvalho and Gerard O'Hare in offering so much for so little, giving generous discounts and offering their free time to raise awareness.

Key Supporters

We are grateful to the following key supporters for enabling this book to be produced:

Friends Provident Foundation

Friends Provident Foundation is an independent charity that makes grants and uses its endowment towards a fair and sustainable economic system that serves society. They connect, fund, invest and share learning to shape an economy that works for all. Funding from Friends Provident was provided towards the chapters that presented alternative economic systems and models.

Edward Hoare

Edward's interest in the environment was sparked from an early age by the gift from a godfather of a pair of binoculars. Total immersion in Brazil in the late 1960s for 3 years - no previous connections, new language, new job, life learning – also had a major influence. His active involvement with charities and social impact organisations has been a focus, alongside story-telling, jargon busting and global resource management. He helped found Universalrisk.org and Thortspace in the early 2000s – a space that brings together thinking and doing, with cross-silo multi-stakeholder collaboration.

Climadapt

Climadapt is a Scottish based social enterprise dedicated to enabling people and communities to adapt to climate change. Founded in 2020, the organisation provides enhanced EDP certification, climate adaptation assessments and self-sufficiency plans. For further information, visit www.climadapt.co.

Introduction

It is becoming increasingly clear that we live within an inequitable, exploitative socio-economic system. One which extracts things from the environment, processes them via waged workers, and funnels the benefits to a very small minority. It is a system that practically enslaves billions in a robotic cycle of 'work, produce, consume'. In the process, it is destroying our planet.

Despite all the evidence pointing to a swiftly approaching demise of this system, humanity continues on the same trajectory. Some might argue that there are no realistic alternatives; that it may be an 'intrinsic part' of human nature to dominate and exploit. Wealth and power will always be accumulated in the hands of the few, and history has shown they will stop at nothing to hold onto it. And yet there are alternatives. Even though Western, capitalist society has come to span the globe, there have existed other forms of society where humans have lived in harmony with the planet and without exploiting one another. A few still remain: Indigenous communities, dubbed backwardly primitive by colonialist attitudes, whose knowledge and practices are actually far in advance of our own in many respects. Even within post-industrialised nations, there is an increasing number of ecological communities and people seeking to live in a fully sustainable, ethical manner – something that has become impossible within contemporary society. We have reached a stage where every act of consumption and production, no matter how small, can be linked to supply chains that, at some stage, are destructive. The capitalist model of mass production, factory farming, high intensity agriculture, waste and worker exploitation has become embedded. We depend on it to survive. Because of that, any collapse that lies ahead will have severe impacts on billions of people. The poorest and most vulnerable will experience the worst impacts first, while the rich and powerful will be insulated – at least for a time. Suffering and death on a scale never seen before in history is what future generations could now face.

The aim of this book is to set out the possibility of a different future. We do not try to run away from what all scientific evidence points towards, and indeed will set it out clearly so the magnitude of the crisis facing our planet and species can be understood. Nor do we take the approach of entrusting upon some technological innovation to miraculously reverse emissions and restore ecosystems. Rather, we take the perspective that socio-economic collapse is probable, and rather than giving up hope seek instead to outline ways people and communities can adapt to it.

The case studies herein demonstrate how adaptations can be made in hostile environments – from fire ravaged regions to flood-prone settlements. Each also demonstrates how humans can return to living sustainably – not only surviving but developing and discovering. From more equitable economic models to systems that focus on enhancing wellbeing and long-term opportunities, the future can be very different if we set out to create it.

Part 1:
Overview

Where are we – and where are we going?

The Situation

An overview

Steve Mcnaught, Dr Mairi Shaw, Dr Morgan Phillips,
Dr Justin Stevens

Where are we now, how did we get here, and what lies ahead?

The purpose of this chapter is to provide a background on climate change, but it is not a comprehensive overview. Rather, we present snapshots that offer a window into the size of the issue, the scale of the crisis, and the options humanity faces over the coming decades. Certain things we do not touch upon, even though, in some countries, they are contested: for example, that humans are responsible for accelerating global temperatures. Likewise, we endeavour to present a wholly factual, broad account, rather than favouring a particular perspective. It is also important to bear in mind that climate data is constantly being updated and models can change.

* * *

Climate change is a reality and the extent and speed of it is becoming ever more evident: temperatures are increasing; rainfall patterns are shifting; sea ice, glaciers and snow are melting, and sea levels are rising. There are significant impacts on ecosystems, economic sectors, infrastructure and human health. The Paris Agreement of 2015 represented a step forward – with signatories aiming to limit global warming to well below 2°C and pursue efforts to limit it to 1.5°C above pre-industrial levels. However, it is clear that these commitments, even if realised, are not enough: on current trajectories, climate scientists estimate that the planet is heading for a 3.2°C rise by 2100[1].

While climate change is only a relatively recent public concern, it has been known about in scientific circles for much longer. Eunice Foote and John Tyndall knew the heating potential of an atmosphere heavy in carbon dioxide as early as the 1850s. By the 1950s, oceanographer Roger Revelle was briefing the United States Congress on the issue and lobbying for funds to build an atmospheric carbon dioxide monitoring station at Mauna Loa in Hawaii. Evidence supporting these early theories and findings has been building ever since.

Today, we are experiencing human-made global *heating*, with temperature rises actually becoming noticeable. The truth is that climate change can still be limited, possibly tamed, but it is going to loom over humanity for many decades, if not centuries. In fact – if current political, social and cultural trends persist – and it continues to be fed, it is going to get bigger and uglier. Soon it might fully mature, become unleashed and start feeding off itself.

The biggest challenge is to continue to prosper in spite of the crisis that surrounds us. This is what billions of people are already busy trying to do. They are doing what they can to try to prevent climate change, but they are also striving to continue prospering – each with their own definitions (and re-definitions) of what prosperity means. Local and national governments are also doing this, as are businesses and institutions; they look at the impacts of climate change as barriers to the progress they each seek. They search for ways to lower their contribution to the crisis, but also for ways to manoeuvre a path through it. They deal with climate change the same way as the road engineer deals with a mountain range. The options are to: (a) stop, give up; or (b) struggle on and find the most efficient, most intelligent way through. Most choose option 'b'; humans are not typically into declaring that they've reached a dead end.

However, there is a big difference between climate change and a mountain range: climate change lacks an obvious 'other side'; it is an elongated storm, an interminable mountain range. We won't climb over and descend to hospitable valleys and open plains; not any time soon. As noted by the United Nations:

> 'There is inertia in the climate system. While some changes in the natural system, such as ocean acidification, can be detected almost immediately and can be clearly attributed to anthropogenic influence, other effects, such as sea level rise, will gradually but inexorably reveal themselves over the next several centuries. They are equally attributable to climate change, but the connection is less obvious to non-scientific observers because of the delay. Ice loss from the Greenland and Antarctic ice sheets is already contributing to sea level rise. The unstable retreat of some Antarctic and Greenland glaciers may further accelerate sea level rise, possibly abruptly. Mass loss from the Greenland Ice Sheet could be irreversible in the foreseeable future. Risks of biodiversity loss and extinction increase greatly both for terrestrial and marine species as warming increases, with large increases for warming levels between 1.5 and 2°C (see section 3.2) and further increases in risk beyond 2°C warming. Ocean warming, acidification and deoxygenation, permafrost degradation, and the extinction of species are phenomena that are highly relevant to human societies and ecosystem integrity but are effectively irreversible on century time scales.' [2]

Going through climate change (successfully) will require huge transformations in the way societies, economies and everyday life operates. This mountain range requires us to reimagine ourselves into beings who are capable of traversing very rocky ground. We are entering undiscovered territory as a civilisation: only in the last few decades have average temperatures risen enough to generate noticeable effects. Like a mutating giant with a sore head, climate change is flexing its muscles and getting active, with the world starting to tremble.

* * *

In just a few hundred years, humans have made changes to the climate, oceans, land and other species on a scale that has never been seen before. Indeed, so great are these changes that many geologists consider humans to have created a unique geological epoch, called the Anthropocene[4]. We are witnessing a sixth mass extinction event, with an estimated 150 species going instinct every day. Across Earth's history, there have been five previous mass extinction events, all resulting in catastrophic biosphere and geosphere changes, while also giving rise to new species in the aftermath. Indeed, we can observe a kind of ying and yang between origin and extinction: rather than being a constant, gradual evolution of life, it instead consists of periods of stability, as well as sudden upheavals.

Unlike other planets we know, Earth has surface and atmospheric conditions that are influenced and determined by a complex biosphere. Plants and animals, evolving together, maintain a careful balance of nitrogen, oxygen, carbon dioxide and other gases that keep the planet at a relatively stable temperature and in conditions that support life. What all mass extinction events have in common is a major destabilising of the biosphere, geosphere and atmosphere, with changes in one having impacts on the others. The extinction event that is currently underway is unique in that it is being driven by the actions of the human species. Overfishing, deforestation, expansion of agriculture, air and water pollution, are all having an effect. Climate change is exacerbating all of these factors. To understand why that is the case, we need to take a look at the relation between greenhouse gases and temperature.

There are two main culprits driving climate change right now: carbon dioxide and methane. Both trap heat in the atmosphere, and indeed we depend upon them to keep the Earth's surface temperature warmer rather than a frigid -18°C. However, in the last 120 years (a tiny slither of time in geological terms), the concentration of both these gases in the atmosphere has shot up to unprecedented levels and global average temperatures have risen as a result (see figures 1-3).

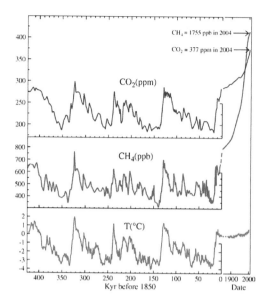

Figure 1: These charts show the levels of CO₂, methane (CH₄) and temperature going back over 400,000 years. Higher temperatures almost exactly correlate with increases in CO₂ and CH₄. (Source: https://history.aip.org/climate/xMethane.htm)

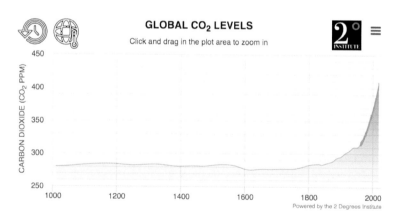

Figure 2: Carbon dioxide graph – the last time these levels of CO₂ were seen was 3 million years ago. At that time, sea levels were 25 metres higher than they are now.[5] (Source: https://www.CO₂levels.org/)

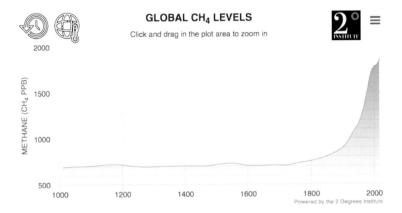

Figure 3: Levels of methane. (Source: https://www.methanelevels.org/)

The increase in the atmospheric concentration of both carbon dioxide and methane began in 1800s as the Industrial Revolution gathered pace and humanity started to burn fossil fuels – coal, then oil and gas – to power factories, heat homes, and drive early forms of motorised transport. Fossil fuel use accelerated for over a century, with the graphs started to take on their famous 'hockey stick' shape from the 1950s onwards as the post WWII baby boom combined with the birth of modern consumer capitalism to accelerate demand for food, energy and material goods.

The release of carbon dioxide, methane and other greenhouse gases into the atmosphere is only one part of the story. Higher temperatures are also eroding the planet's *ability to re-absorb* these gases. This is especially problematic in our marine environments. Oceans are one of the planet's largest 'carbon sinks'. However, as the ocean absorbs more carbon, it becomes more acidic, which, in turn, reduces its ability to hold oxygen (a process known as hypoxia). Should this continue, the oceans will keep getting warmer and become much less efficient at absorbing carbon.[6]

In a similar way, higher temperatures also make it harder for vegetation to act as a carbon sink. For example, the Amazon rainforest – already under intense pressure due to deforestation – is projected to turn into savannah if temperatures increase by over 2°c[7]. Likewise, more intense and widespread droughts, caused by global warming, will result in further wildfires – to the point where in some areas vegetation will actually become a source of carbon dioxide rather than a sink[8]. The devastating 2020 wildfires in California and Australia are, in essence, a taste of the future.

Figure 4: Californian wildfires 2020: even the richest societies are not immune to climate change (Source: https://www.cnet.com/how-to/updates-on-wildfires-ravaging-california-oregon-and-west-and-how-to-help/)

Finally, even though higher levels of carbon dioxide can be beneficial to plant growth, higher temperatures can also reduce the ability of plants to photosynthesise and act as a carbon sink. One study predicts that by as early as 2040, the ability of land systems to absorb carbon will be reduced by half.[9]

* * *

In the public discourse on climate change, CO_2 is the most frequently cited greenhouse gas; it has a lifespan of several hundred years and is considered the most problematic. The other greenhouse gases receive a lot less attention and are often bundled together as 'CO_2e' (Carbon Dioxide equivalent), but one deserves special attention: methane. Methane lasts an average of 12 years in the atmosphere – a comparatively short time – but it is significantly more potent, intensifying the greenhouse effect by at least 28 times more than CO_2.[10]

Methane is also more susceptible than CO_2 to rising temperatures. As the Earth warms, it destabilises the geologic formations where methane is naturally stored. This means that as well as being released from livestock animals and processes of food waste management, methane is also escaping in increasing volumes from natural stores in the higher latitudes and altitudes. Rising temperatures are causing permafrost thaw, which allows previously trapped pockets of methane to seep out of the (formerly frozen) organic material and into the atmosphere.[11] There is evidence of this in Russia, north of the Arctic circle, where the Batagaika crater, which originally formed in 1960, is expanding at a rate of 10 metres per year.[12] It is also happening in the Himalayas, where permafrost thaw in the periglacial environment is triggering landslides, threatening lives and releasing more methane into the atmosphere.[13]

Figure 5: The growing maw of the Batagaika Crater in Siberia. (Source: http://www.bbc.com/earth/story/20170223-in-siberia-there-is-a-huge-crater-and-it-is-getting-bigger)

Towards the poles, huge swathes of the Arctic circle are at risk of melting and are already showing signs of doing so. Regions like Siberia are experiencing record heat waves – reaching an unprecedented 48°C in June 2021.[14] At a global level, if temperatures rise by around 10°C, methane actually begins to be released from the ocean floor. This causes a runaway global warming effect, which is thought to have occurred during the Permian Extinction, the largest mass extinction event the Earth has seen.[15] By the end, around 80% of life on Earth had been wiped out, and it took a further 10 million years to get back to prior levels of biodiversity.[16] Although such a huge rise is highly unlikely to occur in the near future, it is important to keep close track of methane emissions, while continuing to search for ways to stop them from being released into the atmosphere.

In summary, greenhouse gases emitted by human activities are trapping heat and adding unprecedented amounts of energy to the Earth's system, pushing it out of balance. Indeed, the flow of additional energy is roughly equivalent to that of four nuclear bombs of the size dropped on Hiroshima, every second.[17] It should come as no surprise to learn that Earth's temperatures are shooting upwards.

* * *

The above impacts of CO_2 and methane are examples of positive feedback loops, which occur if one input produces more of a second system output, which then feeds back to produce more of the first input. Eventually, a chain of reinforcing reactions may gain sufficient momentum to throw a system permanently out of balance.

Such positive feedback loops are very important in predicting temperature rises, but there are also a range of other mechanisms, often interconnected. The below diagram provides an overview of some of the many factors that need to be considered. This is what makes it so hard to be certain of exactly how much temperatures will rise, coupled with the difficulty of predicting what kind of policies nations will adopt and the issue of 'tipping points' (which we shall look at in more detail further on).

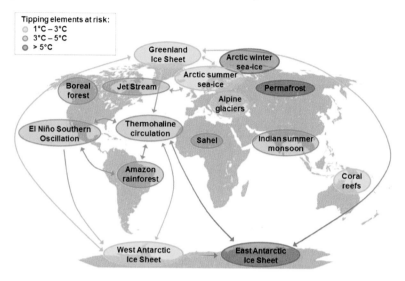

Figure 6. Credit: https://www.pnas.org/content/115/33/8252.

Because of these things, we may in fact be looking at a higher temperature rise than 3.2 degrees by 2100, unless radical steps are taken to address emissions. Almost all signatories to the Paris agreement are not fulfilling their commitments, of which there is no present mechanism to hold them to account.[18] Indeed, since the date the Agreement was signed, global carbon emissions *increased* by 3%.[19] Secondly, as we have seen, higher temperatures cause increasing levels of methane and CO_2 – a problem compounded by positive feedback loops and eroding the effectiveness of natural carbon sinks.

The IPCC has developed 4 main emission trajectories, labelled 'representative concentration pathways' (RCPs) – shown below:

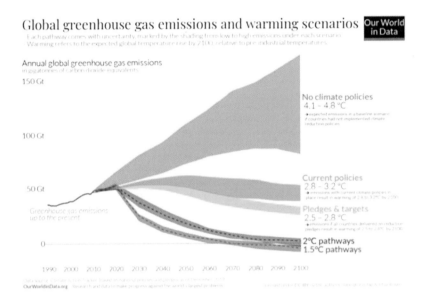

Figure 5 and 6: Projected atmospheric GHG emissions in different scenarios, up to 2100. (Source: https://ourworldindata.org/future-emissions and https://www.ipcc-data.org/guidelines/pages/glossary/glossary_r.html)

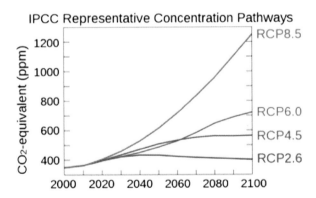

There is much debate among climate scientists as to which RCP we are actually on. Some still hold out hope that it is possible to keep within a 1.5 degree rise, or certainly under 2 degrees. Others conclude that such a rise is all but inevitable.[20] In 'Deep Adaptation' by Rupert Read and Jem Bendell, it is argued that the IPCC estimates of global heating always steer on the lower side.[21] The authors go on to say (citing research by McLaren and Markusson, 2020) that *'climate policy makers and the IPCC have often co-created scenarios in which future, unproven technological solutions have provided justification for delaying action.'*

Whatever the case, present measurements can only be de described as worrying. For example, the rate at which glacial ice is melting (one of the most reliable measurements of climate change) accelerated by 57% from 1990 to 2017.[22] A similar situation is being observed with Arctic sea ice: since 1981, NASA has observed a 13% decline per decade – meaning that, by the 2030s, it would be entirely ice-free in summer.[23] This, in turn, makes it easier for heat to be absorbed rather than reflected, due to the loss of ice and snow (the albedo effect) – an example of yet another positive feedback loop and potential tipping point. Dr Rachael Treharne, writing in a paper by the Woodwell Climate Research Centre, noted: *'Based on what we already know about abrupt thaw and wildfire, these feedback loops are likely to substantially exacerbate the permafrost thaw feedback and resulting carbon emissions.'*[24] Meanwhile, on the other side of the world, researchers have uncovered the potential for an irreversible tipping point in Antarctica by 2060, should temperatures go above 2°C.[25] Once that point is crossed, sea level rises will not only be greater but occur much faster. This will happen regardless of whether we later succeed in removing large quantities of CO_2 from the atmosphere (with technologies which do not currently exist).[25]

Such data demonstrates how each degree (or indeed tenth of a degree) entails huge, far-reaching impacts that are not always taken into account. 2020 observations of oceanic methane bubbles, along with widespread permafrost thaw (noted above), continue to remind us that urgent action is needed.

It is important to bear in mind that the Paris Agreement seeks to cap warming to below 1.5 degrees because temperatures over this start to create very significant impacts, along with the risk of positive feedback loops causing irreversible planetary tipping points. To contemplate higher rises is to face the prospect of enormous societal changes – the kind that prevent re-elections – alongside widespread devastation, which few governments are willing to prepare for. It is something that can frighten and overwhelm the public, causing many climate scientists to 'steer on the side of less drama'. Indeed, to present a more accurate picture is to stand the risk of being labelled a 'doomist'.

Let us suppose, however, that the rise in temperatures will be 3.2 degrees by 2100. Indeed, let us go a bit further, and say that – by vigorous, swift, effective policies, alongside implementation of carbon extraction technologies and significant lifestyle changes for the highest consuming nations – temperatures are kept to a 'well below 2 degrees' rise. And the point we are trying to make is, *even then*, there is a need for adaptation. A world 2 degrees warmer above pre-industrial levels may not sound a disaster. Actually, this is the *average* global temperature rise – in some places, such as the Arctic, it is known to be much higher (which brings us back to the point about positive feedback loops). But if somehow we prevent further warming, the impacts of a 'world +2 degrees' include even higher incidences of intense storms, disruption to staple crops, up to 1 billion environmental refugees by 2050 and extinctions for many more species. That, unfortunately, is the most optimistic scenario before us. For the sake of accuracy, we have to move a little further into the danger zone, because that is exactly where the world is presently heading. Simultaneously, we need to consider the prospect of some kind of societal collapse: a possibility that other texts are only now starting to consider in detail.·

Whatever the amount of rise, the contributions in this book impart how humanity can endure and even advance by putting in place sufficient resilience and adaptation. It would be wrong to pretend such a world would be pleasant, comfortable and full of opportunities. However, nor does it have to be insufferable, chaotic and devoid of chances to start afresh.

Tipping points

'Climate change is accelerating and its impacts increasing. Human actions are estimated to be causing the planet's climate to change 170 times faster than natural forces.'

Joana Castro Pereira, Global Catastrophic Risks 2020 Annual Report, NOVA University of Lisbon

Figure 7: Glacier melt

We have already explored some positive feedback mechanisms and, in many cases, they can cause the crossing of critical 'tipping points'. These occur when a system is pushed irreversibly out of balance, regardless of further inputs.

Example 1: higher temperatures from CO_2 > melting Arctic ice, causing less reflection of sunlight (reduced albedo) > higher temperatures > total absence of Arctic ice.

Example 2: higher temperatures from CO_2 > reduced ability of plants to photosynthesise > less CO_2 absorbed, causing even higher temperatures > forests become source of CO_2 rather than a sink.

Due to the complexity of feedback mechanisms, which span the entire globe, tipping points are one of the hardest factors to account for. Climate scientists cannot be sure when they may occur or, when they do, or the exact impact they may have. Furthermore, there are often delays between an input factor like CO_2 and an output like higher temperatures. This is why, even though current concentrations of CO_2 are equivalent to the Earth 3 million years ago, we are not seeing sea levels 25 metres higher. That takes time, and there may be other processes that take place which reduce or increase the impacts. For example, a significant weakening in the Gulf Stream, caused by melting ice, may cause temporary reformation of ice in some regions. It is in some ways like predicting the weather in a month's time: we know the processes and the general trajectory, but working out the exact details is problematic. Nonetheless, we can be certain of one thing: tipping points are bad news. There is also growing evidence that they may be more likely than previously thought, have higher impacts and threaten long-term irreversible changes.'

To understand why tipping points are so important, we need to return to how climate change is not just driven by the emissions of greenhouse gases, but also by the ability of systems to absorb CO_2. The land and oceans represent significant carbon sinks and we are now looking at a situation where this function is being eroded. Photosynthesis rates degrade significantly above 28 degrees in tropical forests, while in temperate zones it drops at above 18 degrees. In a similar way, the ocean's ability to absorb carbon is gradually undermined as the Earth warms. This means that even if emissions are reduced, we have to look at ways to counteract the loss and reduced efficiency of carbon sinks.

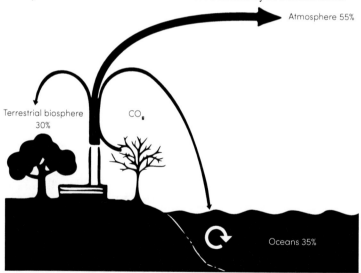

Figure 8: Source: https://guardian.ng/features/science/carbon-sink-detected-underneath-worlds-deserts/

It may be possible to avoid some tipping points, but the risk of them being triggered increases exponentially with higher temperatures. It is like the way that the Earth's weather system becomes super-charged with excess energy. Moreover, since the biosphere and geosphere are inherently interconnected, the crossing of a tipping point in one system can rapidly cause more to topple in other places. So, the prospect of a greater than 2 degrees rise gives rise to an even greater probability of higher temperatures; it is, in many ways, a vicious domino effect.

Due to the prevalence of tipping points across the Earth system, some climate scientists are concerned that we are close to a planetary threshold that, when crossed, would result in 'hothouse Earth' scenario. Preventing this requires 'a coordinated, deliberate effort by human societies to manage our relationship with the rest of the Earth System, recognizing that humanity is an integral, interacting component of the system.'[36]

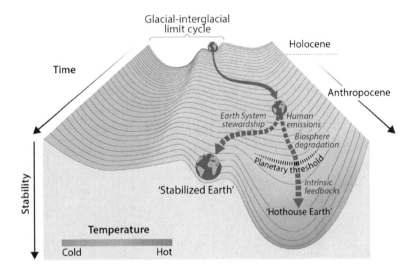

Figure 9: There is a risk that if multiple 'tipping points' are triggered, it will cause a runaway greenhouse effect – 'Hothouse Earth' – resulting in much higher temperatures over a shorter space of time. Currently, while global temperatures stay under 2 degrees, we are still in a 'Stabilized Earth' trajectory. (Source: https://www.pnas.org/content/115/33/8252)

The dangers of passing irreversible tipping points are acknowledged within an IPCC report, due for publication in February 2022 but leaked to the media. With average global surface temperatures already exceeding 1.1°C above pre-industrial levels, it takes only 0.4 more degrees before 1.5 degrees is reached. Even that threshold could lock in 'progressively serious, centuries-long and, in some cases, irreversible consequences', according to the report. The findings drive home the importance of far-reaching structural change, rather than untested technological 'fixes' and half-solutions like carbon credits. Indeed, in order to prevent the current trajectory it is noted that 'we must redefine our way of life and consumption', with 'transformational change operating on processes and behaviours at all levels: individual, communities, business, institutions and governments'.

Population and consumption

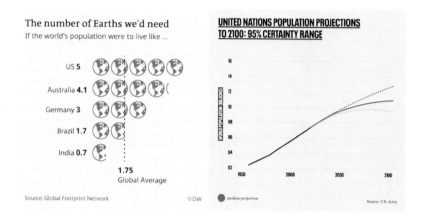

Figure 10: From Global Footprint Network and UN

Before the 1950s, the Earth's human population was always below 2 billion people but, since then, we have seen an increase to just below 8 billion – expected to rise to 10 billion by 2057. Afterwards, the UN predicts a gradual slowing and eventual stabilisation.

Population is often linked to the Earth's natural 'carrying capacity' – how many humans it can support without resources being depleted. As shown above, people are currently exceeding this by 0.75: effectively, humans are in need of two planets, instead of just one. However, the issue is also more nuanced, because of varying consumption levels between (and within) countries. The average American adopts a lifestyle that would require the resources of 5 Earths, while the average Indian could actually increase their levels of consumption slightly. Some consider 'over population' to be the core problem behind environmental problems, including climate change, yet it is not so much numbers but rather the way people live.

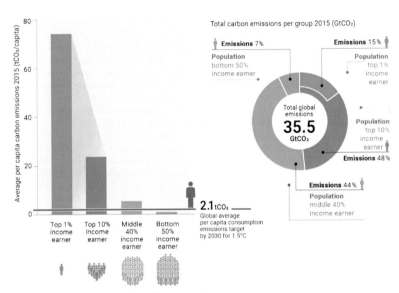

Figure 11: From UNEP Emissions Gap Report, 2020

The richest 10% accounted for 52% of global CO$_2$ emissions between 1990 and 2015. Strikingly, the carbon emissions of the world's richest 1% were also *more than double* the emissions of the *poorest half* of humanity (representing 3.1 billion people).[42] These statistics highlight how the burden of reducing emissions should not be spread equally. It is also important to bear in mind that consumption levels are spreading rapidly across and within different countries: it is estimated that the global middle class exceeded half the global population in 2018. In the 'emerging economies' like India, Brazil and China we are seeing demand for formerly luxury consumer goods, cars and meat-based diets showing no signs of stopping. Of course, it is inherent in human nature to strive for more, especially when there are examples around them, or made visible in popular culture, showing a high consumption lifestyle. From Africa to South America; from India to Australia – all around the world, younger generations are striving for the best mobile phones, fastest cars, biggest houses and most expensive clothes. It is emblematic of globalised capitalism, which places no value on the impacts caused to nature or indeed to local communities.

To reduce consumption levels would require a reconfiguring of our socio-economic model – a subject covered in chapter 4 – but there is also a need to consider the causes around post-1950s population growth. Although many of these are linked to better healthcare and reduced mortality rates, women's empowerment also plays a vital role. Currently the greatest population increases are seen in the poorest countries, which reflect social inequalities and lack of opportunities. Women are expected to produce children, rather than be empowered to pursue education and employment opportunities. Families fight day and night to survive. Rather than being able to access opportunities to pursue individual development, younger generations are seen as future bread winners, taught to do their upmost to make money, care for their elders, and create more offspring. When girls stay at school longer and are given access to reproductive health services, along with equal work opportunities as men, they delay having children until later in life and generally have fewer. Currently, an estimated 65 million do not get that opportunity – not counting a continuing level of inequality even in the richest nations, especially for managerial tier roles. Gender equality, far from being an exclusively social need, is also an environmental one.

If women are truly empowered, the impact goes even further. As noted by Zo Randriamaro of the WoMin African Alliance: *'Those at the forefront of inequality and oppression are best placed to find alternatives. Systemic change should be led from below by rural and working class women who are directly affected by the extractive, colonialist and patriarchal model.'*

Where next?

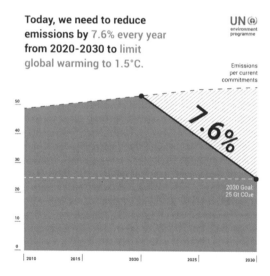

Figure 12: Emission reduction required per year (Source: https://www.un.org/en/climatechange/science/key-findings)

The United Nations requirements to limit climate emissions to below catastrophic levels are clear and yet, as of writing, we are nowhere near making the necessary cuts. Even the outbreak of COVID-19, which caused national lockdowns across the world, flight bans and massive drops in industrial output, resulted in emission reductions no more than 7%. Not only that, but immediately after the 'first wave', emissions swiftly rebounded, with a similar effect observed for the 'second wave'. This, perhaps, is not surprising: our current socio-economic system is built upon negative environmental by-products, of which CO_2 is just one. From individual lifestyle choices (diet, fashion, holidays) to larger infrastructure (housing, transport, energy), simply being part of society entails some degree of emissions. Nevertheless, to keep within the required emissions reductions is certainly necessary and possible. At the moment, however, it does not seem probable – not without a radical change in how our society and economy functions. Consider, for example, the United Nations 'Production Gap' report, which measures the gap between Paris Agreement goals and countries' planned production of fossil fuels. The 2020 report found that countries were 'aiming to produce 120% more fossil fuels by 2030 than would be consistent with limiting global warming to 1.5°C'.

It is also important to bear in mind that reported CO_2 emissions may be higher than is actually the case, as documented by a team of climate scientists in 2021. They found that countries tended to under-report their actual CO_2 emissions, to such a degree that it was equal to what the United States emitted annually (roughly 5.7 million metric tonnes, representing 15% of global emissions).

Despite this, some people and communities across the world have demonstrated how it is *possible* to live with vastly reduced emissions and even none at all. A great deal of this book covers their experiences. It would be easy to push the onus of action onto governments, and it is indeed unfortunate that in many countries people have had to persuade governments to take climate change seriously and take action, rather than vice versa. People cannot afford to continue just waiting for such 'governments' to take the required steps, as emissions fail to go down enough and the planet gets warmer.

Structural changes

'We have to act like our house is on fire... the [UK] government's target is like dialling 999 and asking the fire brigade to come in 30 years' time.'
– Caroline Lucas MP at COP26 Coalition Event, November 2020

Adjusting our behaviour to be more environmentally friendly is one step on the journey; there are many more. Consider, for example, how society has lost connection to nature. We do not realise the link between our consumption and its environmental impacts, which often take place thousands of miles away. This, some argue, is at the root of environmental destruction. In his book, 'How to Thrive in the Next Economy', John Thackara identifies our increasing disconnection from nature as a 'metabolic rift' – caused by 'a combination of paved surfaces and pervasive media that has rendered us cognitively blind to the health of the living systems of which we are a part.' Children are taught in tight, enclosed spaces and play on concrete yards, learning little about growing their own food or the ecology; young people come to understand the world in a segregated, compartmentalised way, pushed towards a function that resembles a cog in a giant machine; adults have jobs with roles that are rarely, if ever, measured by the value they add to society and the environment, but rather the money they make. Every day, messages from culture and media bombard us: buy more; consume more; strive to own more than your peers. It is a throwaway culture, with no better example than the 368 million tons of plastic waste produced in 2019. Indeed, we are now even drinking and eating the waste we have produced – from micro-plastics to toxic chemicals.

Figure 13: Our world today: Shanghai Port. Consumer goods and food can be shipped thousands of miles, including back and forth between countries as it gets manufactured and processed. (Source: https://www.beltandroad.news/business/maritime/top-10-busiest-ports-in-the-world-chinese-seaports-dominate-list/)

Figure 14: A tiny fraction of the world's plastic waste – in this case, from richer nations being shipped to the Maldives. (Source: https://datatopics.worldbank.org/what-a-waste/tackling_increasing_plastic_waste.html)

A zero-carbon society would not have such things. Indeed, despite the challenges, it brings many benefits to our health, wellbeing and innate potential. One of the first steps is to decouple 'prosperity' from environmental damage, embracing economic 'degrowth', localisation and a circular economy (topics covered later on). It involves a reshaping from the bottom up, rather than continuing pursuit of endless growth that is imposed from above on a national and international level, mostly so that huge amounts of wealth keep flowing to a tiny minority.

There is increasing awareness that globalised capitalism is not sustainable, both socially and environmentally, with several books covering the issue. As noted by Dr Gil Penha-Lopes and her colleagues:

'Above all, the global climate crisis has shattered the idea that economic growth can be perpetuated indefinitely on a finite resource base. The number of people materially benefiting from the economic and political system driven by these assumptions has grown over time, with the global financial crisis of 2008 either a brief interruption or sign of things to come. However, this expansion has been at the expense of all who are still outside the circle of material beneficiaries – whether oceans, soils, forests, and atmosphere; people being torn from their lands and working long hours for a pittance or unemployed and desperate; or the future for our own and other species on this planet.'

The connotations behind 'structural change' may seem daunting and unrealistic, yet, right now, we can start making a real impact on climate change. In the documentary '2040', released in 2019, Damon Gameau explores decentralised solar grids that can be shared between homes and communities (as in Bangladesh); 'on-demand' transport instead of mass ownership of cars, allowing the conversion of roads and parking spaces into affordable homes, cycle networks and urban food farms; a shift away from meat, with agriculture that restores the ability of soils to sequester carbon. These are just a few, significant things that could be undertaken immediately – each having an array of positive social and environmental benefits.

There are signs that, slowly, we are moving in the right direction. Renewable energy production across the European Union in 2018 was 18%, double what it was in 2010. The United States re-joining of the Paris Agreement and enactment of climate policies could encourage other countries to take a similar direction. Younger generations are also taking a leading role in fighting back, recognising that it is their future at stake. Movements inspired by Swedish teenager Greta Thunberg have seen coordinated events in cities around the world. A landmark case at the European Court of Human Rights brought by 6 young people from Portugal seeks to hold European nations to account in continuing to produce dangerous levels of emissions. In the USA, the youth-led Sunrise Movement has raised the need for meaningful action on climate change amongst federal and state officials. Awareness and concern about climate change is higher than ever before: all that's missing is the necessary actions to address it.

We can only hope this momentum gathers pace, and rapidly; that people, communities and governments will urgently implement – rather than endlessly debate and delay – the changes necessary. Should that happen, we are still looking at a world with unprecedented levels of greenhouse gases in the atmosphere, reduced efficiency of natural carbon sinks, and increasingly likely crossing of tipping points. The only way to address that is to end the combustion of fossil fuels and industrial scale livestock agriculture, together with finding ways to remove carbon from the atmosphere. We may even need to turn to unproven techniques like cloud seeding and ocean iron fertilisation. Such 'geo-engineering' is highly contentious, and the scale at which it needs to be implemented is immense. In addition, there are real risks of causing unforeseen side effects on the environment. Strengthening and increasing natural carbon sinks could represent a 'lighter' way to reduce atmospheric CO_2 (e.g. planting more forests; better ocean conservation), although it is likely that some form of carbon extraction technology is necessary. Despite increased hopes being placed in this area, the best technology we have currently (atmospheric CO_2 capture machines) consumes a huge amount of energy and costs trillions of dollars to be built at a scale that meaningfully reduces atmospheric CO_2. Needless to say, the costs of allowing such high levels of carbon to remain in the atmosphere will be significantly more in the long run.

The idea of reaching 'net zero' emissions mid-century is what nations strive towards, yet if we place too much emphasis on unproven technology to draw down atmospheric CO_2 then it risks creating 'a cavalier 'burn now, pay later' approach'. Likewise, placing undue reliance on natural carbon sinks and carbon 'offset' schemes can only result in an acceleration of environmental destruction: ecosystems take hundreds of years to be properly established and act as efficient carbon sinks, so we cannot simply rely on creating them at will and expecting this to justify continuing high emissions.

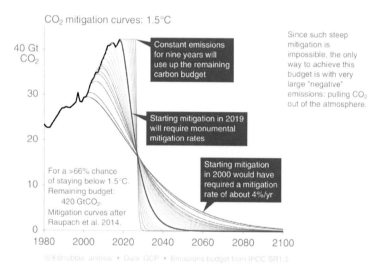

Figure 15: The amount of mitigation efforts required if commenced at different dates. (Source https://theconversation.com/climate-scientists-concept-of-net-zero-is-a-dangerous-trap-157368)

The simple fact is that humanity has a vertical climb on one side and a sheer precipice on the other. The climb of sweeping behavioural and societal changes – however arduous – is far preferable than the precipice of catastrophic climate change.

From denial to action

Given the situation before us, it may be wondered why the vast majority of humanity is not galvanised in preventing it from happening. As things stand, there is increasing awareness of climate change, but few actions that logically follow from that awareness. People are still eating, consuming and going about their lives in ways that differ little from a decade ago, save from a few technological quirks like greater reliance on mobile apps and similar things. However, perhaps the situation is comparable to a family who really want to eat more healthily. They know it is good for them, other people and the environment. But the added costs, preponderance of less healthy foods and accustomed taste to fat and sugar make the transition a constant challenge. Imagine if they found it easy to access healthy food, which was affordable, and they were not bombarded by messages from various sources tempting them back to their old diet. The transition would be much easier. Simply put, individual and systemic changes need to happen simultaneously for climate action to be effective. We cannot place all the blame with individuals, but nor can individuals sit back and wait for 'the system' to change.

At the moment one of the major obstacles is on a cognitive and educational level, woven into many years of fabricated discourse by vested interests to prevent action. Cambridge University published a study in 2020 that looked at different discourses of climate delay – using surveys, community workshops, media sources and political lobbying analysis. The data they collated revealed a range of reasons, some grounded in placing blame elsewhere and others that just push ineffective 'solutions':

Individualism
Individuals and consumers are ultimately responsible for taking actions to address climate change.

Whataboutism
Our carbon footprint is trivial compared to [...]. Therefore it makes no sense for us to take action, at least until [...] does so.

The 'free rider' excuse
Reducing emissions is going to weaken us. Others have no real intention of reducing theirs and will take advantage of that.

Technological optimism
We should focus our efforts on current and future technologies, which will unlock great possibilities for addressing climate change.

Someone else should take actions first: **redirect responsibility**

Change is impossible
Any measure to reduce emissions effectively would run against current ways of life or human nature and is thus impossible to implement in a democratic society.

All talk, little action
We are world leaders in addressing climate change. We have approved an ambitious target and have declared a climate emergency.

It's not possible to mitigate climate change: **surrender**

Discourses of climate delay

Disruptive change is not necessary: **push non-transformative solutions**

Fossil fuel solutionism
Fossil fuels are part of the solution. Our fuels are becoming more efficient and are the bridge towards a low-carbon future.

Doomism
Any mitigation actions we take are too little, too late. Catastrophic climate change is already locked-in. We should adapt, or accept our fate in the hands of God or nature.

No sticks, just carrots
Society will only respond to supportive and voluntary policies, restrictive measures will fail and should be abandoned.

Change will be disruptive: **emphasize the downsides**

Policy perfectionism
We should seek only perfectly-crafted solutions that are supported by all affected parties; otherwise we will waste limited opportunities for adoption.

Appeal to well-being
Fossil fuels are required for development. Abandoning them will condemn the global poor to hardship and their right to modern livelihoods.

Appeal to social justice
Climate actions will generate large costs. Vulnerable members of our society will be burdened; hard-working people cannot enjoy their holidays.

On a deeper level, all these things have forms of cognitive denial linked to how we perceive ourselves and the 'enduring' role of the society we have become accustomed to. A complimentary analysis can be found with the Indigenous rooted organisation 'Gesturing Towards Decolonial Futures' (see page 25), who outline four kinds of denial that prop up the dominant socio-economic system:

- the denial of systemic violence and complicity in harm (the fact that our comforts, securities and enjoyments are subsidised by expropriation and exploitation somewhere else),
- the denial of the limits of the planet (the fact that the planet cannot sustain exponential growth and consumption),
- the denial of entanglement (our insistence in seeing ourselves as separate from each other and the land, rather than 'entangled' within a living wider metabolism that is bio-intelligent), and
- denial of the depth and magnitude of the problems that we face.

The problem is then not just how we act but also how we think and perceive the world. Moreover, we have to come to terms with the fact that, even if humanity changes course and climate change is brought under control, temperatures will rise and action on adaptation (complementary to mitigation) is urgently required. Without this, it will not be possible to prevent or minimise the severest impacts of a warmer world.

We hope, as you read through this book, you will realise what the cognitive, structural and systemic challenges are that prevent real action to tackle the climate emergency and all its linked injustices, together with those which are genuinely effective and build a zero emissions society. There are a multitude of approaches to learn from – some more focused on adaptation and others more on mitigation – but all touch upon how people and communities can build resilience to climate change. We can look to these as real causes for hope, both in how humanity can adapt and how fresh alternatives for a sustainable world can be created.

	Violence	Unsustainability	Entanglement	
Deep denial *Refusal to engage the critique*	No recognition of racial/colonial violence	No recognition of ecological unsustainability	No recognition of entanglement	No recognition of serious problems of concern
Interpretive Denial *Selective acceptance of the critique*	Racial/colonial violence is a product of exclusion from opportunities and institutions, and should be addressed through inclusion and access	Ecological unsustainability (climate change, biodiversity loss, habitat destruction, ecological degradation, pollution) is a product of inefficiency and wastefulness, and should be addressed through technological innovations, renewable energy	Relationality and responsibility are established through individual choices regarding (social, familial, political) association	The problems we face can be adequately addressed with minor changes to policy and practice, and technological solutions
Implicative denial *Acceptance of the critique, but not the full implications*	Racial/colonial violence is a product of the existing system, and should be addressed through systemic changes, e.g., redistributing resources and centering marginalized voices	Ecological unsustainability is a product of corporate greed and political corruption, and should be addressed through collective public action and mass movements to create green energy/jobs/policies	Relationality and responsibility operate within collective structures that exceed individual choices and should be therefore addressed with regard to the relevant power relations and obligations	We will need to take concerted collective action and mobilize political will in order to enable the kind of transformations that can adequately address the serious problems we face
No denial *Full acceptance of critique and implications*	Racial/colonial violence is the condition of possibility for the existing system and while changes to the system in the short term can be important for harm reduction, in the long-term harm will not cease until the system itself is either dismantled or falls on its own	Ecological unsustainability is a product of the economic and ecological logics of the existing system (i.e., extractivist capitalism), and while green energy/jobs/technologies are important for mitigation, we will ultimately need to surrender this way of life and enact another mode of existence	Relationality and responsibility operate at many layers, including an existential layer before will (unconditional), and a political layer that recognizes systemic violence and tries to mitigate harm (in the short term) and cease the harm to ensure collective well-being (in the long term)	The depth and magnitude of the problems we face will make impossible the continuity of our existing ways of knowing, being and relating; we will need to disinvest from dominant problem-solving strategies and tap into exiled capacities to addresses these challenges

Source: https://decolonialfutures.net/

References

1. United Nations (2019). UN emissions report: World on course for more than 3 degree spike, even if climate commitments are met. (https://news.un.org/en/story/2019/11/1052171)

2. United Nations Environment Programme (2021). *Making Peace with Nature: A scientific blueprint to tackle the climate, biodiversity and pollution emergencies*, Nairobi. (https://www.unep.org/resources/making-peace-nature)

3. Subcommission on Quaternary Stratigraphy (2019). *Working Group on the Anthropocene: Results of binding vote by AWG.* (http://quaternary.stratigraphy.org/working-groups/anthropocene/)

4. United Nations Sustainable Development Goals (2019). *UN Report: Nature's Dangerous Decline 'Unprecedented'; Species Extinction Rates 'Accelerating'*, Paris. (https://www.un.org/sustainabledevelopment/blog/2019/05/nature-decline-unprecedented-report/)

5. Lindsey, R. (2020). *Climate Change: Atmospheric Carbon Dioxide. Climate.gov.* (https://www.climate.gov/news-features/understanding-climate/climate-change-atmospheric-carbon-dioxide)

6. Li, G. et al. (2020). *Increasing ocean stratification over the past half-century. Nature Climate Change, 10*(12), pp.1116-1123.

7. Bush, M.B. (2020). New and Repeating Tipping Points: *The Interplay of Fire, Climate Change, and Deforestation in Neotropical Ecosystems1. Annals of the Missouri Botanical Garden, 105*(3), pp.393-404.

8. Hubau, W. et al. (2020). *Asynchronous carbon sink saturation in African and Amazonian tropical forests. Nature, 579,* pp.80-87.

9. Duffy, K.A. et al. (2021). *How close are we to the temperature tipping point of the terrestrial biosphere?. Science advances, 7*(3).; Smith, E. (2020). *Land Ecosystems Are Becoming Less Efficient at Absorbing Carbon Dioxide. NASA's Jet Propulsion Laboratory.* (https://climate.nasa.gov/news/3057/land-ecosystems-are-becoming-less-efficient-at-absorbing-carbon-dioxide/)

10. United Nations Economic Commission for Europe Sustainable Development Goals (2021). *The Challenge.* (https://unece.org/challenge)

11. National Geographic. *Arctic permafrost is thawing fast. That affects us all.* (https://www.nationalgeographic.com/environment/article/arctic-permafrost-is-thawing-it-could-speed-up-climate-change-feature)

12. Vadakkedath, V., Zawadzki, J. and Przeździecki, K. (2020). *Multisensory satellite observations of the expansion of the Batagaika crater and succession of vegetation in its interior from 1991 to 2018. Environmental Earth Sciences, 79*(6), pp.1-10.

13. International Centre for Integrated Mountain Development. *What is permafrost?* (https://www.icimod.org/mountain/permafrost/)

14. Golembo, M. (2021). *Heat wave in Russia brings record-breaking temperatures north of Arctic Circle. abc News,* 23 June. (https://abcnews.go.com/International/heat-wave-russia-brings-record-breaking-temperatures-north/story?id=78446355)

15. Hickey, H. (2018). *What caused Earth's biggest mass extinction?,* Washington. *Stanford Earth Matters.* (https://earth.stanford.edu/news/what-caused-earths-biggest-mass-extinction#gs.79eo3s)

16. Song, H., Wignall, P.B. and Dunhill, A.M. (2018). *Decoupled taxonomic and ecological recoveries from the Permo-Triassic extinction. Science Advances, 4*(10).

17. King, D et al. (2015). *Climate Change: A Risk Assessment. UK Foreign and Commonwealth Office.*

18. SEI, IISD, ODI, E3G, and UNEP (2020). *The Production Gap Report: 2020 Special Report.* (http://productiongap.org/2020report)

19. 2 Degrees Institute (2021). *Global CO$_2$ Levels.* (https://www.CO$_2$levels.org/)

20. Australian Academy of Science (2021). *The risks to Australia of a 3°C warmer world.* (https://www.science.org.au/files/userfiles/support/reports-and-plans/2021/risks-australia-three-deg-warmer-world-report.pdf)

21. Bendell, J. and Read, R. (2021). *Deep Adaptation: Navigating the Realities of Climate Chaos,* Cambridge. Polity Press.

22. Slater, T et al. (2021*). Earth's Ice Imbalance. The Cryosphere.*

23. Borunda, A. (2020). *Arctic summer sea ice could disappear as early as 2035. National Geographic.* (https://www.nationalgeographic.com/science/article/arctic-summer-sea-ice-could-be-gone-by-2035)

24. Natali, S.M. et al. (2021). *Permafrost carbon feedbacks threaten global climate goals. Proceedings of the National Academy of Sciences, 118*(21).

25. DeConto, R.M. et al. (2021). *The Paris Climate Agreement and future sea-level rise from Antarctica. Nature, 593*(7857), pp.83-89.

26. Stockholm University (2020). *The ISSS-2020 Arctic Ocean Expedition.* (https://www.aces.su.se/research/projects/the-isss-2020-arctic-ocean-expedition/)

27. Brysse, K., Oreskes, N., O'Reilly, J. and Oppenheimer, M. (2013). *Climate change prediction: Erring on the side of least drama?. Global environmental change, 23*(1), pp.327-337.

28. Post, E. et al. (2019). *The polar regions in a 2 C warmer world. Science advances, 5*(12).

29. Buis. A. (2019). *A Degree of Concern: Why Global Temperatures Matter. NASA's Global Climate Change Website.* (https://climate.nasa.gov/news/2865/a-degree-of-concern-why-global-temperatures-matter/#:~:text=If%20warming%20reaches%202%20degrees,on%20humans%20and%20ecological%20systems;%20https://www.nytimes.com/interactive/2020/07/23/magazine/climate-migration.html)

30. Phillips, M. (2021). *Great Adaptations.* Arkbound.

31. Bendell, J. and Read, R. (2021).

32. Lenton, T.M. et al (2019). *Climate tipping points—too risky to bet against.*

33. Wunderling, N., Donges, J.F., Kurths, J. and Winkelmann, R. (2021). *Interacting tipping elements increase risk of climate domino effects under global warming. Earth System Dynamics, 12*(2), pp.601-619.

34. Duffy, K.A. et al. (2021).

35. Sakai, J. (2011*). Climate change reducing ocean's carbon dioxide uptake.* University of Wisconsin-Madison. (https://news.wisc.edu/climate-change-reducing-oceans-carbon-dioxide-uptake/)

36. Steffen, W. et al. (2015). *Planetary boundaries: Guiding human development on a changing planet. Science, 347*(6223).

37. Harvey, F. (2021). *IPCC steps up warning on climate tipping points in leaked draft report. The Guardian*, 23 June. (https://www.theguardian.com/environment/2021/jun/23/climate-change-dangerous-thresholds-un-report)

38. Dasgupta, P. et al. (2015). *Climate change and the common good: A statement of the problem and the demand for transformative solutions*, Vatican City.

39. Worldometer (2021). *World Population*. (https://www.worldometers.info/world-population/#:~:text=7.9%20Billion%20(2021),currently%20living)%20of%20the%20world.)

40. United Nations Department of Economics and Social Affairs (2019). *Growing at a slower pace, world population is expected to reach 9.7 billion in 2050 and could peak at nearly 11 billion around 2100*, New York. (https://www.un.org/development/desa/en/news/population/world-population-prospects-2019.html)

41. Elizabeth Dunbar (2019). *Climate Curious: How much does population growth contribute to climate change?. MPR News*, 11 December. (https://www.mprnews.org/story/2019/12/11/climate-curious-how-much-does-population-growth-contribute-to-climate-change)

42. Gore, T. (2020). *Confronting Carbon Inequality: Putting climate justice at the heart of the COVID-19 recovery.*

43. Bradshaw, C.J. et al. (2021). *Underestimating the challenges of avoiding a ghastly future. Frontiers in Conservation Science, 1*, p.9.

44. Population Matters (2021). *Climate Change.* (https://populationmatters.org/climate-change)

45. Population Matters (2021). *Women's Rights.* (https://populationmatters.org/womens-rights)

46. United Nations Women. *Facts & Figures.* (https://www.unwomen.org/en/news/in-focus/commission-on-the-status-of-women-2012/facts-and-figures)

47. Le Quéré, C. et al. (2020). *Temporary reduction in daily global CO_2 emissions during the COVID-19 forced confinement. Nature Climate Change, 10*(7), pp.647-653.

48. Huebi, B. (2021). *Global carbon emissions: the world keeps polluting after Covid-19.* (https://eandt.theiet.org/content/articles/2021/06/global-carbon-emissions-the-world-keeps-polluting-after-covid-19/)

49. SEI, IISD, ODI, E3G, and UNEP (2020).

50. Grassi, G. et al. (2021). *Critical adjustment of land mitigation pathways for assessing countries' climate progress. Nature Climate Change, 11*(5), pp.425-434.

51. Union of Concerned Scientists (2008). *Each Country's Share of CO_2 Emissions.* (https://www.ucsusa.org/resources/each-countrys-share-of-CO_2-emissions)

52. Sanchez, E., Sullivan, M. and Dupart, L. (2017). *In Symmetry with Nature*, Chicago. *Center for Humans & Nature.* (https://www.humansandnature.org/what-happens-when-we-see-ourselves-as-separate-from-or-as-a-part-of-nature-in-symmetry-with-nature)

53. Thackara, J. (2015). *How to thrive in the next economy (Vol. 1)*, London. Thames & Hudson.

54. Statista (2021). *Annual production of plastics worldwide from 1950 to 2020.* (https://www.statista.com/statistics/282732/global-production-of-plastics-since-1950/)

55. Petersen, K.S. (2021). *There is an Alarming Amount of Microplastics in Farm Soil—and Our Food Supply. Civil Eats.* (https://civileats.com/2021/01/27/there-is-an-alarming-amount-of-microplastics-in-farm-soil-and-our-food-supply/); Miller, M. (2017). *Toxic Exposure. UCSF Magazine.* (https://magazine.ucsf.edu/toxic-exposure)

56. Henfrey, T. (2017). *Resilience, Community Action and Societal Transformation: People, Place, Practice, Power, Politics and Possibility in Transition.* Permanent Publications.

57. European Environment Agency (2019). *Share of renewable energy in gross final energy consumption in Europe.* (https://www.eea.europa.eu/data-and-maps/indicators/renewable-gross-final-energy-consumption-4/assessment-4)

58. Global Legal Action Network (2021). *AN EMERGENCY LIKE NO OTHER.* (https://youth4climatejustice.org/)

59. Revkin, A. (2019). *Most Americans now worry about climate change—and want to fix it. National Geographic.* (https://www.nationalgeographic.com/environment/article/climate-change-awareness-polls-show-rising-concern-for-global-warming)

60. Evans, S. (2019). *Direct CO_2 capture machines could use 'a quarter of global energy' in 2100. Carbon Brief.* (https://www.carbonbrief.org/direct-CO_2-capture-machines-could-use-quarter-global-energy-in-2100)

61. Galey, P. (2019). *Climate impacts 'to cost world $7.9 trillion' by 2050. Phys.org.* (https://phys.org/news/2019-11-climate-impacts-world-trillion.html)

62. Dyke, J., Watson, R., Knorr, W. (2021). *Climate scientists: concept of net zero is a dangerous trap. The Conversation.* (https://theconversation.com/climate-scientists-concept-of-net-zero-is-a-dangerous-trap-157368) (79)

63. Thackara, J. (2015).

64. Lamb, W.F. et al. (2020). *Discourses of climate delay. Global Sustainability*, 3. Cambridge University Press.

65. Decolonial Futures. *Gesturing Towards Decolonial Futures.* (https://decolonialfutures.net/4denials/)

Oceans in Peril

The global state of the ocean

Dr Jessica Gier, Amahle Cole and Dr Renuka Thakore

Figure 1: Sunset over the Pacific Ocean seen from the International Space Station

'The Apollo 8 photographs taken on Christmas Eve 1968 revealed our world as the blue planet, finite and beautiful in the dark void of space. Back then, few could have imagined the impact we are now having on this ocean world. The ocean [...] is now becoming more acidic, is heating up with virtually every year, and is losing its life-giving oxygen. The concern is how much longer the ocean can continue to function as it is, whilst subject to the pressures of climate change and other impacts.'

International Programme of the State of the Ocean (IPSO), State of the Ocean Report[1]

Our planet is a huge and finely balanced ecosystem. Change one part and there are knock-on consequences for other parts.'[i,2] The ocean, which represents 97% of the Earth's water and covers 70% of the surface, is an essential element of our global ecosystem. From the oxygen we breathe to the food we eat, much is derived from the seas. The carbon, water and thermohaline cycles all originate there. Without these things, the Earth would be uninhabitable – yet we are witnessing unprecedented changes.

---

i   The 'dynamic, complex, and interdependent' principle of systems-thinking theory stresses the fact that things change all the time, and everything is connected. Essentially, this points out that the ecosystem is dynamic, complex and interdependent. The principle also advocates that simplification, structure and linear thinking have their own limitations and thus consideration should be given to a system's relationships both within the system and with the external environment (Anderson and Johnson, 1997).

Year after year, oceans are getting hotter (see Figure 1 and 2). The rate of warming between 1987-2019 was four and a half times that of 1955-1986, with the pace increasing 500% since the late 1980s[3]. As they absorb more carbon, oceans also soak up 93% of the Earth's excess heat. Hotter oceans translate to more extreme storms, intensive droughts in some areas and flooding in others. The ocean's stored thermal energy is released catastrophically in the form of a more intensive El Niño and contributes significantly to global temperatures.[4] There is a steepening decline of oxygen levels, already impacting multiple species of fish and apex species like dolphins and whales. The Bay of Bengal is one startling example, where increasing temperatures have changed currents and monsoon cycles at the same time as a build-up of agrochemical and sewage levels, pushing this entire ecosystem towards ocean basin anoxia (effectively a 'dead zone').[5]

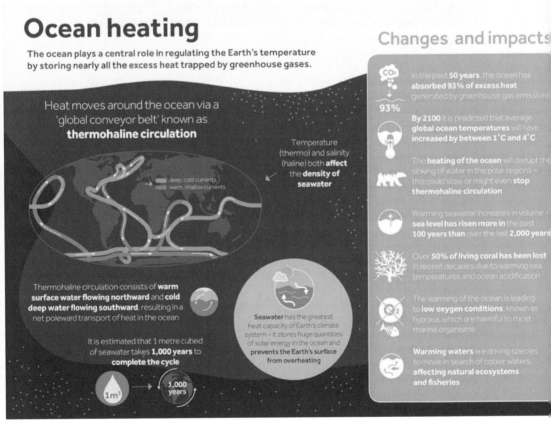

Figure 2: Ocean heating[6]

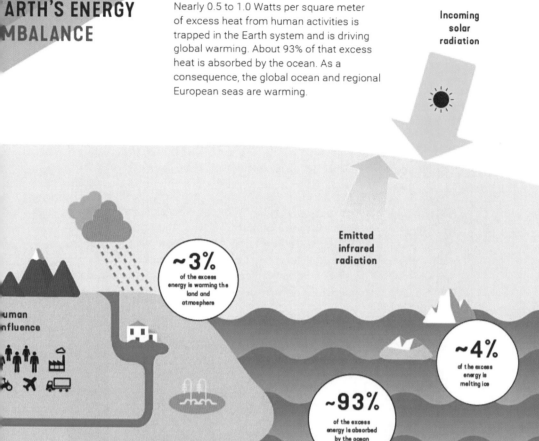

ARTH'S ENERGY MBALANCE

Nearly 0.5 to 1.0 Watts per square meter of excess heat from human activities is trapped in the Earth system and is driving global warming. About 93% of that excess heat is absorbed by the ocean. As a consequence, the global ocean and regional European seas are warming.

Incoming solar radiation

Emitted infrared radiation

~3%
of the excess energy is warming the land and atmosphere

~4%
of the excess energy is melting ice

~93%
of the excess energy is absorbed by the ocean

Human influence

Figure 3: Schematic representations of the flow and storage of energy in the Earth's climate system and related consequences. [7,8]

The causes of these changes are down to more than just CO_2. Simply cutting emissions alone is not enough, but rather a sweeping package of changes – ranging from reducing fishing to stopping undersea resource exploitation and establishing oceanic reserves. The consensus is that such steps must be done by 2029. After that, it is believed many processes will be irreversible.

Ocean acidification – a direct result of increased atmospheric CO_2 – is rapidly changing seawater chemistry. One of the impacts, coupled with rising temperatures, is the annihilation of once-thriving coral reefs.[9] We are now at a stage where 90% of these incredibly diverse and beautiful underwater worlds will vanish from the face of the planet – regardless of any steps we now choose to take. Areas once teeming with life are already barren, leeched expanses. It is an echo of the acres of once pristine Amazonian and East Asian rainforests, cut down to make way for cattle and export crops, in turn producing more greenhouse gas. And yet with the ocean's immensity and depth comes the illusion of inviolability – an illusion that scientists affirm stands at a crucial juncture.

Commenting on the release of a 2019 situation update report, lead author

Professor Dan Laffoley of the International Union for Conservation of Nature (IUCN) said:

> 'Marine life is threatened with suffocation, starvation, overheating and acid corrosion under current climate impacts. The situation is only getting worse. We need to act on climate change but also, urgently build resilience. All life on the Earth is at risk from ocean collapse.'

Aside from their critical foundation in the Earth's global ecosystem, the oceans also represent a reliable historical indicator of what the future may hold. Studies of the Earth's geological past all show that warming, acidification, and hypoxia are three key signals of disruption to the carbon cycle, linked to the previous five mass extinctions. With many oceanic changes exceeding the IPCC's worse case scenarios, we have much to be worried about – and very little time to address it.

IPSO's key findings

- **Human actions have resulted in warming and acidification of the oceans and are now causing increased hypoxia.**
- **The speeds of many negative changes to the ocean are near to or are tracking the worst-case scenarios from IPCC and other predictions. Some are as predicted, but many are faster than anticipated, and many are still accelerating.**
- **The magnitude of the cumulative impacts on the ocean is greater than previously understood.**

Interactions between different impacts can be negatively synergistic (negative impact greater than sum of individual stressors) or they can be antagonistic (lowering the effects of individual impacts). Examples of such interactions include:

- Combinations of overfishing, physical disturbance, climate explosions of these invasive species – including harmful algal blooms – and dead zones;
- Increased temperature and acidification increasing the susceptibility of corals to bleaching and to acting synergistically to impact the reproduction and development of other marine invertebrates;
- Changes in the behaviour, fate and toxicity of heavy metals with acidification – acidification may reduce the limiting effect of iron availability on primary production in some parts of the ocean;

- Increased uptake of plastics by fauna, and increased bioavailability of pollutants through adsorption onto the surface of microplastic particles;
- Feedbacks of climate change impacts on the oceans (temperature rise, sea level rise, loss of ice cover, acidification, increased storm intensity, methane release) on their rate of carbon dioxide uptake and global warming.

- **Timelines for action are shrinking.**
- **Resilience of the ocean to climate change impacts is severely compromised by the other stressors from human activities, including fisheries, pollution and habitat destruction.**
- **Ecosystem collapse is occurring as a result of both current and emerging stressors**

  Stressors include chemical pollutants, agriculture run-off, sediment loads and over-extraction of many components of food webs, which singly and together severely impair the functioning of ecosystems. Consequences include: the potential increase of harmful algal blooms in recent decades; the spread of oxygen-depleted or dead zones; the disturbance of the structure and functioning of marine food webs, to the benefit of planktonic organisms of low nutritional value such as jellyfish or other gelatinous-like organisms; dramatic changes in the microbial communities, with negative impacts at the ecosystem scale; the impact of emerging chemical contaminants in ecosystems.

  This impairment damages or eliminates the ability of ecosystems to support humans.

- **The extinction threat to marine species is increasing rapidly.**

Colder winters, warmer summers

The role of the oceanic system in heat regulation, such as through the Gulf Stream, can impact terrestrial temperatures by several degrees. This means, in some parts of the world, higher global temperatures may paradoxically lead to colder winters. In the case of Western Europe, temperatures are made higher throughout winter due to the gulf current. However, with the melting of Arctic ice, this current is weakened. Already, since the mid-19th century, it has reduced by around 15% – an amount not seen for 1500 years.[10] With more ice melting, the effect is only increasing.[11]

As well as creating colder winters, such oceanic changes are modelled to result in warmer winters for other parts of the word. Heatwaves in Europe have been correlated with colder Northern Atlantic ocean temperatures, causing the channelling of warm winds from the south.[12] At the same time, rainfall in other parts of the world is pushed to other zones – heightening the risk of flooding in one area and drought in another. The world essentially becomes a *planet of extremes*, with survival becoming even harder for multiple species.

This mechanism is an example of how complex the global climate system is, with the changes ahead being far more nuanced than just a rise in temperature. It is also one of the things that can mislead people about 'global warming', with colder winters being mistaken as evidence that it is not in fact occurring (as cited by the former US president, Donald Trump).

Sea levels

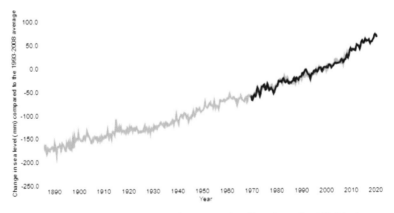

Figure 3: Global mean sea level. Global mean sea level has risen about 8–9 inches (21–24 centimetres) since 1880, with about a third of that coming in just the last two and a half decades. The rising water level is mostly due to a combination of meltwater from glaciers and ice sheets and thermal expansion of seawater as it warms. In 2019, global mean sea level was 3.4 inches (87.6 millimetres) above the 1993 average — the highest annual average in the satellite record (1993-present). From 2018 to 2019, global sea level rose 0.24 inches (6.1 millimetres).[13]

Of course, higher temperatures also mean rising sea levels. Since 1900 (see Figure 3), sea levels have increased on a global scale by about 19 centimetres. This is due to the direct effect of ocean warming causing thermal expansion of seawater, which accounts for about 40% of this increase. The other 60% comes from increased freshwater input from the melting of continental glaciers. Sea level rise projections based on the IPCC's different scenarios (see Figure 5) show that they may be as high as 1 metre by 2100.

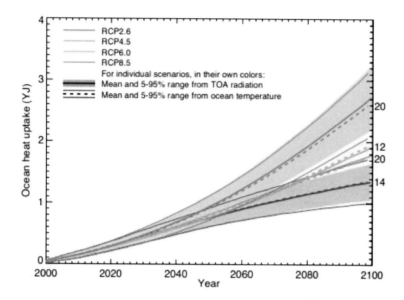

Figure 4: Projected rise in global mean sea level (IPCC, 2013)
Source: Figure 13.8 | Heat uptake by the climate system during the 21st century relative to 1986–2005 projected by CMIP5 Atmosphere–Ocean General Circulation Models (AOG-CMs) under RCP scenarios (1 YJ = 1024 J).[14]

The world's major cities are on the coast, so many are threatened by increases in sea level. With a metre rise by 2100 (see Figure 4), about 40% of the global population living in coastal zones is threatened. One example is New Orleans in the USA, which was already affected by hurricane Katrina in 2005. This was not a direct consequence of global warming per se but rather a storm surge event, yet climate change is going to increase the ferocity and frequency of similar events in the future.

If we look beyond 2100 and to the risk of cascading tipping points being triggered (see chapter 1), this could quite literally be the tip of the iceberg. From Glasgow to London; New York to Rio de Janeiro; Cairo to Capetown; Mumbai to Shanghai – all these cities, and many more, would experience widespread flooding or total inundation. Engineering solutions can only go so far when the world is looking at a global average temperature rise of above 3 degrees.

In many places, the impacts of rising sea levels have already become irreversible. Some low-lying Pacific islands are urgently building more coastal protection and preparing mass evacuation plans[15]; vast swathes of coastal Bangladesh are vanishing into subsistence, causing ongoing migration inland[16]; salinisation of cropland and freshwater supplies has become extremely high risk in over 12 coastal countries and storm surges threaten numerous cities.[17, 18] The good news is this can take centuries to happen; the bad news is it almost definitely will happen – unless we can find a way to stop temperatures from increasing. In the long term, we need to start thinking about a gradual retreat from coastlines, rather than ceaselessly trying to build ever-bigger sea defences.

Overfishing and its consequences

'Many terrestrial, freshwater and marine species have shifted their geographic ranges, seasonal activities, migration patterns, abundances and species interactions in response to climate change, and this trend will continue. Half of all warm-water coral reefs have already been lost due to such combined effects. A third of marine fish stocks have declined as a consequence of overharvesting. Fertilisers entering coastal ecosystems have produced more than 400 ocean 'dead zones' with a total area greater than 245,000 km² – more than the land area of the United Kingdom.' [20]

Overfishing is compounded with nutrient pollution (eutrophication) entering through the food-web interaction and establishment of invasive species.[21, 22] This requires working on reducing fish mortality, increasing the biomass on reefs and making fishing sustainable to maintain ecosystem health and to allow it to continue the provision of the goods and services that humanity requires.[23, 24]

Addressing human impacts on the ocean and developing practical approaches to reduce degradation of the marine ecosystems requires looking at how social and ecological systems intersect.[25] The integrated nature of ecosystems, natural resources and the complex ways these interactions affect overall governance of the marine environment (especially fishing) can be investigated using systems theory.[26] The major synthesis that emerges is the concept of resilience: an ability of a system to persist. In terms of fishing, this includes embedding resilience in all the components of the system, including ecosystem, fishing communities, socio-economic structure and governance institutions.[27]

Marine governance

Marine ecosystem and ocean management require good governance (decision-making). Conventional decision-making typically involves government and a top-down approach, which creates fragmented, uncoordinated outcomes, especially environmental impacts on the marine ecosystem and providing management strategies for complementary systems of the fishery, shipping, tourism and other related sectors.[28,29]

Modern good governance is about going beyond decision-making. This includes thinking of who makes the decisions and for whom they are made, along with the processes used for making decisions and what needs to be considered. Good governance is all about decision-making through engaging multiple stakeholders using participatory processes and co-creating integrated management solutions for environmental and marine protection.[30] We can see such governance as having two main attributes: (i) a multi-level perspective, i.e., decisions that are taken at the local level should be in harmony with those at the higher level, and (ii) capturing the specific reality of a place, i.e., decisions must be made that incorporate local values – what people care about and their aspirations.[31,32] Equally important attributes of good governance are considering 'capital' and 'well-being' in the broadest way. This means all five types of capitals – physical, social, human, natural and financial – are treated equally.[33] The well-being of stakeholders, individuals, households and communities is considered in the context of both resource sustainability and ecosystem health.[34] Finally, good governance should take into account the dynamics of livelihoods and the complexities of well-being. Such decision-making mechanisms can offer the most resilient social-ecological systems.

Climate change makes governance of these systems more challenging due to the crucial interactions taking place between the world's ocean and the projected impacts on the coastal areas.[35] But by enabling governance systems to be more flexible, participatory and precautionary it allows for swifter and more appropriate means of adaptation.[36]

Specific strategies

As covered by IPSO, the scale of problems facing the ocean are immense. If left, these problems could spiral out of control, with runaway impacts on terrestrial habitats. We need to start straight away in fixing the damage caused, utilising nature's own mechanisms of correction and resilience. For example, brown seaweed can grow up to half a metre per day, and by sowing seaweed beds in areas it can rapidly help circulation, water quality and fish stocks – as well as creating a carbon sink and reducing acidity levels.[37] Stimulating the growth of seaweeds in the form of seagrasses or kelp forests is a form of macro-algae cultivation that represents one means of tackling the wider climate emergency.[38] In both cases, the idea is to enhance the production of organic material through the absorption of CO_2 to have organic material buried in the sediment. In the case of kelp forests, there is a chance of circulating some of that organic material through to the deep oceans, which are decoupled from the surface oceans.[39] Such solutions, which can be started by coastal communities straight away, also create new opportunities: seaweed can be used as a biofuel, natural fertiliser and even as a food supplement. Thus an escalating problem with dire impacts can be turned around into an opportunity, for people and the environment they live in.

The scope of responses at our disbursal can help turn the tide and prevent total degradation of the marine environment. A full analysis of each response is beyond the bounds of this chapter, but other examples include:-

- Increasing the number of Marine Protection Areas and the strength of protection in existing areas.
- A global ban on extractive practices: deep sea mining, bottom trawling, blast fishing, chemical fishing, factory fishing vessels, etc.
- Reduction of fish consumption: changing diets towards vegetable replacements.
- Coastal restoration: mangrove plantation, reducing input of chemicals and pollutants from land sources, responsible tourism, etc.
- A global ban on single-use plastics (responsible for widespread ecosystem destruction and circulation of micro-plastics across the marine and terrestrial foodchains).
- Robust activism: the ocean is notoriously hard to monitor and prevent destructive activities, but organisations like Sea Shepherd, Greenpeace and Take 3 can help fill the gap, working in partnership with communities and governments.

Other methods border on geoengineering, which is defined as the deliberate large-scale manipulation of the planetary environment to counteract anthropogenic climate change.[40] The two notable strategies are:-

Ocean iron fertilisation

As noted before, oceans takes up around a third of carbon emitted by human activities. Having a high capacity to sequester carbon, enhancing carbon sequestration[ii], could be a way to mitigate climate change. Several techniques that have been proposed for this relate to ocean iron fertilization.[41] If the ocean is supplied with iron then the growth of phytoplankton can be stimulated. Phytoplankton is at the base of the food chain – absorbing CO_2 and converting it into organic matter.[42] However, such a strategy could also have unexpected impacts. Large-scale manipulations of the environment don't always go as plannened.[43]

---

ii   A natural or artificial process by which carbon dioxide is removed from the atmosphere and held in solid or liquid form.

Enhancing ocean alkalinity

Enhancing ocean alkalinity is another way to control oceanic CO_2. Alkalinity is the capacity of a solution to neutralise the acid[iii]. In terms of enhancing ocean alkalinity, if calcium hydroxide or calcium oxide is added to the ocean and reacts with carbon dioxide, the end product would be calcium carbonate and CO_2. This ends up reducing two molecules of carbon dioxide into one. Geoengineering of marine cloud brightening, or seeding marine stratocumulus clouds, can help to enhance ocean alkalinity.[44] In addition, it is possible for incoming solar radiation to be reflected by ships spraying seawater mist.[45] In some cases, experiments are being carried out to look at adding calcium carbonate to the stratosphere.[46] Nonetheless, as with the case for ocean iron fertilisation, there can be unexpected side impacts and such large-scale strategies can often be reflective of poor governance structures, with little involvement or consent from local communities. As such, they should be regarded as options of last resort, with other methods that work more in harmony with natural processes and which prevent destructive anthropocentric practices being preferable.

---

iii The key anions in seawater are bicarbonate, carbonate and to some extent hydroxides, so enhancing ocean alkalinity raises the carbonate saturation state of the oceans and that can help reverse the effects of ocean acidification.[47]

References

1. Laffoley, D. et al. (2020). *Eight urgent, fundamental and simultaneous steps needed to restore ocean health, and the consequences for humanity and the planet of inaction or delay. Aquatic Conservation: marine and freshwater ecosystems, 30*, pp. 194-208.

2. Anderson, V. and Johnson, L. (1997). *Systems thinking basics,* Cambridge, MA. Pegasus Communications, pp. 1-14.

3. Cheng, L. et al. (2020). *Record-Setting Ocean Warmth Continued in 2019. Adv. Atmos. Sci., 37*, pp. 137–142.

4. Xie, S.-P. et al. (2013). *El Niño modulations over the past seven centuries. Nature Climate Change, 3*(9), pp. 822-826.

5. Brierley, G.J., Li, X., Cullum, C. and Gao, J. eds. (2016). *Landscape and ecosystem diversity, dynamics and management in the Yellow River source zone.* Springer International Publishing, pp. 1-369.

6. OneOcean Infographics (2019). (https://www.oceanprotect.org/resources/assets/infographics/)

7. von Schuckmann, K. (2018) *Copernicus Marine Service Ocean State Report. Journal of Ope.*

8. von Schuckmann, K. et al (2016). *An imperative to monitor Earth's energy imbalance. Nature Clim Change, 6*, pp. 138–144.

9. Heron, S.F. et al. (2017). *Impacts of climate change on World Heritage coral reefs: a first global scientific assessment.*

10. Thornalley, D. et al. (2018). *Anomalously weak Labrador Sea convection and Atlantic overturning during the past 150 years. Nature, 556*, pp. 227–230.

11. Caesar, L. et al (2018). *Observed fingerprint of a weakening Atlantic Ocean overturning circulation. Nature, 556*, pp. 191–196.

12. Thornalley, D. et al. (2018).

13. Lindsey, R. (2021). *Climate Change: Global Sea Level. Climate.gov.* (https://www.climate.gov/news-features/understanding-climate/climate-change-global-sea-level)

14. Church, J.A. et al. (2013). *Sea Level Change,* London and New York. *Climate Change 2013: The Physical Science Basis. Contribution of Working Group I to the Fifth Assessment Report of the Intergovernmental Panel on Climate Change.* Cambridge University Press.

15. Guilford, G. (2014). *An entire island nation is preparing to evacuate Fiji before they sink into the Pacific. Quartz.* (https://qz.com/228948/an-entire-island-nation-is-preparing-to-evacuate-to-fiji-before-they-sink-into-the-pacific/)

16. Park, W. (2019). *Rising sea levels are making traditional ways of life impossible. Rural Bangladeshis are having to adapt to survive. BBC Global News.* (https://www.bbc.com/future/article/20190829-bangladesh-the-country-disappearing-under-rising-tides)

17. Saline Agriculture Worldwide. *Salinization: A Global Challenge.* (https://www.salineagricultureworldwide.com/salinization#:~:text=Salinization%20of%20farmland%20is%20a,not%20suitable%20for%20growing%20crops.)

18. Rahmstorf, S. (2017). *Rising hazard of storm-surge flooding. Proceedings of the National Academy of Sciences, 114*(45), pp. 11806-11808.

19. The Royal Society (2020). *How fast is sea level rising?* (https://royalsociety.org/topics-policy/projects/climate-change-evidence-causes/question-14/)

20. United Nations Environment Programme (2021). *Making Peace with Nature: A scientific blueprint to tackle the climate, biodiversity and pollution emergencies,* Nairobi. (https://www.unep.org/resources/making-peace-nature)

21. Daskalov, G.M., Grishin, A.N., Rodionov, S. and Mihneva, V. (2007). *Trophic cascades triggered by overfishing reveal possible mechanisms of ecosystem regime shifts. Proceedings of the National Academy of Sciences, 104*(25), pp.10518-10523.

22. Doney, S.C. et al. (2012). *Climate change impacts on marine ecosystems. Annual review of marine science, 4,* pp. 11-37.

23. Cinner, J.E. et al. (2009). *Linking social and ecological systems to sustain coral reef fisheries. Current Biology, 19*(3), pp. 206-212.

24. Thrush, S.F. and Dayton, P.K. (2010). *What can ecology contribute to ecosystem-based management?. Annual Review of Marine Science, 2,* pp. 419-441.

25. Charles, A. (2012). *People, oceans and scale: governance, livelihoods and climate change adaptation in marine social–ecological systems. Current Opinion in Environmental Sustainability, 4*(3), pp. 351-357.

26. Garcia, S.M. and Charles, A.T. (2007). *Fishery systems and linkages: from clockworks to soft watches. ICES Journal of Marine Science, 64*(4), pp. 580-587.

27. Berkes, F. and Seixas, C.S. (2005). *Building resilience in lagoon social–ecological systems: a local-level perspective. Ecosystems, 8*(8), pp. 967-974.

28. Grafton, R.Q. et al. eds. (2010). *Handbook of marine fisheries conservation and management.* OUP USA.

29. Charles, A.T. (2008). *Sustainable fishery systems.* John Wiley & Sons.

30. Sumaila, U.R. et al. (2011). *Fisheries, investing in natural capital,* New York. *Towards a green economy: Pathways to sustainable development and poverty eradication: a synthesis for policy makers. United Nations Environment Programme,* pp. 77-109.

31. Armitage, D.R. et al. (2009). *Adaptive co-management for social–ecological complexity.* Frontiers in Ecology and the Environment, 7(2), pp. 95-102.

32. Charles, A. (2010). *Integrated management: a coastal community perspective.* Policy Research Initiative (PRI), Government of Canada.

33. Bavinck, M. and Vivekanandan, V. (2011). *Conservation, conflict and the governance of fisher wellbeing: analysis of the establishment of the Gulf of Mannar National Park and Biosphere Reserve. Environmental Management, 47*(4), pp. 593-602.

34. Coulthard, S., Johnson, D., and McGregor, J.A. (2011). *Poverty, sustainability and human wellbeing: a social wellbeing approach to the global fisheries crisis. Global Environmental Change, 21*(2), pp. 453-463.

35. Parry, M. et al. eds. (2007). *Climate change 2007-impacts, adaptation and vulnerability: Working group II contribution to the fourth assessment report of the IPCC, 4.* Cambridge University Press.

36. Charles, A. (2012). *People, oceans and scale: governance, livelihoods and climate change adaptation in marine social–ecological systems. Current Opinion in Environmental Sustainability, 4*(3), pp. 351-357.

37.   Duarte, C. et al. (2017). *Can Seaweed Farming Play a Role in Climate Mitigation and Adaptation?*. Frontiers in Marine Science.

38.   Duffy, J.E. et al. (2019). *Toward a coordinated global observing system for seagrasses and marine macroalgae. Frontiers in Marine Science, 6*, p. 317.

39.   Filbee-Dexter, K. et al. (2020). *Ocean temperature controls kelp decomposition and carbon sink potential.*

40.   The Royal Society (2009). *Geoengineering the climate: Science, governance and uncertainty.* (https://royalsociety.org//media/Royal_Society_Content/policy/publications/2009/8693.pdf)

41.   Buesseler, K.O. et al. (2008). *Ocean iron fertilization—moving forward in a sea of uncertainty. atmosphere, 1*, p. 2.

42.   Basu, S. and Mackey, K.R. (2018). *Phytoplankton as key mediators of the biological carbon pump: Their responses to a changing climate. Sustainability, 10*(3), p. 869.

43.   Shine, R., Ward-Fear, G., and Brown, G.P. (2020). *A famous failure: Why were cane toads an ineffective biocontrol in Australia?*. Conservation Science and Practice, 2(12), p. 296.

44.   Cao, L., Duan, L., Bala, G. and Caldeira, K. (2017). *Simultaneous stabilization of global temperature and precipitation through cocktail geoengineering. Geophysical Research Letters, 44*(14), pp. 7429-7437.

45.   Lockley, A. et al. (2020). *Glacier geoengineering to address sea-level rise: A geotechnical approach. Advances in Climate Change Research, 11*(4), pp. 401-414.

46.   Robock, A. (2020). Benefits and risks of stratospheric solar radiation management for climate intervention (geoengineering). *Bridge, 50*(1), pp. 59-67.

47.   Albarede, F., Thibon, F., Blichert-Toft, J., and Tsikos, H. (2020). *Chemical archeoceanography. Chemical Geology, 548.*

The Planetary Biosphere

Climate change impacts and adaptation
in terrestrial and freshwater ecosystems

Dr Andy Suggitt

Every second of every day, global meteorological networks record the weather conditions at thousands of monitoring stations on the Earth's surface, supported by satellites orbiting the poles. And once per year, usually around Christmas, scientists at the world's three major climate monitoring centres summarise these data, telling us just how much the world has warmed. We are often alarmed, but not surprised, by what they report. Last year – 2020 – became the joint-hottest on record, alongside 2016. We also broke the +1.2°C warming barrier for the first time – Earth's average temperature is now 1.2°C warmer than it was at the end of the 19th Century.[1]

So much change in a relatively short period of time is having a profound effect on the planet, and nowhere is this more obvious than in the natural world. Often it's the stories of charismatic species that really hit home, or so-called 'indicator' species that are representative of broader groups, habitats or even ecosystems. Whether it's the polar bear clinging to a last chunk of sea ice (more on that in Box 1 below), a hyperdiverse coral reef bleached by increasingly warmer oceans, or photographs of glaciers in retreat, these example impacts colour the story and make it somehow more real. They also remind us of exactly what is at stake.

This chapter will introduce a number of example impacts of climate change as they increasingly manifest on the Earth's surface, from the highest mountains to far-flung coral islands. We'll take in the broad effects on whole ecosystems, and we'll also cover the minutiae: those slight shifts in the timing of ecological processes or life cycle events that can lead to wholesale changes in the makeup of the terrestrial or freshwater realms. When you reach the end, we hope you'll share our view that the list of species or phenomena unimpacted by climate change is much shorter than the list of those that are.

Figure 1: Famous face? In the Disney Pixar film 'Finding Nemo', the eponymous star Nemo, and his parents Marlin and Coral, are clownfish (Amphiprion) – probably Ocelaris clownfish (*Amphiprion ocellaris*). These iconic species form mutualistic relationships with Sea anemones in the family Stichodactylidae. They each depend very closely on the other for survival (Frisch et al.,, 2016), and so warming-driven increases in the frequency and duration of bleaching events for the sea anemones also threaten the clownfish[2]. **Credit:** Goo (Pixabay).

The biological impacts of climate change

Figure 2: The Bramble Cay nelomys (*Melomys rubicola*), the first mammal to go extinct as a direct result of climate change. What Australians used to call their 'little brown rat' lived on a small, 4 hectare island known as a 'Cay' in the Torres Strait, between Australia and Papua New Guinea. It's thought that rising sea levels and the increasing frequency of storm events – both caused by anthropogenic climate change – combined to drive the last few individuals extinct sometime between 2009 and 2014. **Credit:** an Bell (Wikimedia commons).

Climate change is often described as the next big problem facing the world, yet the unfortunate fact is that many of its impacts on our planet are being felt in the here and now. We have already had our first reported mammalian casualty of climate change: the Bramble Cay melomys (Melomys rubicola, Figure 2), an island-dwelling endemic driven extinct by rising sea levels inundating its low-lying habitat.[3] While climate-driven extinctions like this one are still relatively rare, it remains the case that most species on the planet will have to undertake some sort of migration to track the climates they can survive in, a phenomenon known as geographic range-shifting. Indeed it is a species' particular ability to successfully undertake this task that will define its fate in our warming world, with an estimated one in six species facing extinction by the end of the century, should our current commitments on greenhouse gas mitigation be fulfilled.[4]

Let that sink in: one in six of all the species on Earth could face extinction by the end of the century. The latest edition of the Catalogue of Life (2019) has 1.8 million entries in it, and we think – of course, we can't possibly know – that we have described only 20% of all life on Earth. So a simple ballpark calculation suggests that as many as 1.5 million species are threatened by climate change. Over 1 million of the estimated 8 million plant and animal species on Earth are at substantially increased risk of extinction in the coming decades and centuries as a direct or indirect consequence of human activities. Only a quarter of their original habitat is largely still functioning in a semi-natural way, and more than a third of terrestrial global plant production is now appropriated by humans for their own use and the use of domesticated species. In 2020, less than a quarter of the global land surface still functions in a nearly natural way, with its biodiversity largely intact. This quarter is mostly located in dry, cold or mountainous areas, and thus far has a low human population and has undergone little transformation.

And that number is largely in addition to those species already threatened by other drivers of loss, such as habitat change, or the various types of pollution. To put these drivers into context, a recent global assessment concluded that approximately 1 million species are already threatened by human activity.[5] It's findings like these that have led geologists to conclude that we have entered a new epoch known as 'the Anthropocene' – a period where humans (*Anthro* = human) now dominate and define the planet.

Although extinctions are presented as the be-all and end-all (literally) of our impact on the natural world, there is an amazing plethora of other ways that climate change is affecting life on our green planet – from the influence it wields on particular genes up to continental-scale shifts in the worlds biomes. Even with just 1°C of warming so far – and even if we achieve the Paris goals we can expect double that – we now know that climate change influences some 82% of the ecological processes that support ecosystems, and by extension, the people that depend on them.[6] This includes almost all terrestrial processes and two thirds of processes in the freshwater realm, with warming influencing anything from the timing of fish spawning seasons to the sex ratios of offsprings in species like the green sea turtle (*Chelonia mydas*). In fact you'd be hard pressed to find an aspect to life on Earth that *hasn't* been impacted by climate change, as studies that conclude 'no effect' often do so due to an absence of evidence, rather than clear evidence of absence.

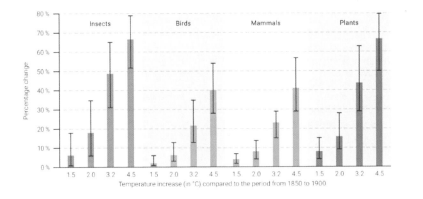

Figure 3.7: Species projected to lose over 50% of their climatically determined geographic range. The proportions of species in four broad groups of organisms that are projected to lose over half of their climatically determined geographic range by

2100 under climate change scenarios in which global warming reaches 1.5°C, 2°C, 3.2°C or 4.5°C above pre-industrial levels by that time. The models used to make these projections assume that species move at realistic rates while attempting to track their geographically shifting climate envelope. The uncertainty range is the 10–90% confidence interval across the various regional climate patterns explored. This study is based on the assessment of 19,848 insect species, 12,429 vertebrate species and 73,224 plant species. Data source: IPCC 2018a, SR1.5, 3.4.3

We can safely say that looking for the fingerprints of climate change in the natural world is both easy and difficult at the same time: easy, because we never have to look far to find them, but also hard, because it requires a fuller understanding of the factors affecting a study species or system before we can successfully attribute an effect to a particular cause. Take the example of the great tit (*Parus major*), a garden bird common in large parts of Eurasia. It has taken many years of long-term monitoring and painstaking observation to determine the ecological 'mismatch' between the peak availability of the caterpillar food source – which is advancing earlier in the year due to climate change – and the timing of egg laying, which is not (Box 2). The results of such experiments emphasise the sore need for more detailed, long-term monitoring programmes for 'indicator' or otherwise 'key' species, particularly in the tropics and/or the Global South, where we know even less about the changes that warming has wrought.

We also know less about the future for freshwater systems under climate change, which face a further (and unique) set of complicating factors of their own. Warming temperatures have led to a reduction in winter ice coverage on lakes; a recent estimate suggested that just 2°C of warming would affect security of water supply for an estimated 400 million people.[7] This increase in intermittency is also replicated in river systems, with a projected shift away from perennial and towards transitional or intermittent flow regimes (Döll & Schmied, 2012); this is of course on top of the growing number of the world's rivers that are now intermittent due to human modification – most prominently the Nile, Indus, Yellow and Colorado Rivers.[8] This effect will be keenly felt by species in desert or arid regions, where increased droughting are more likely to lead to negative effects on freshwater ecosystems.[9] Another key constraint facing the freshwater biota is the extent to which rivers and streams are connected along thermal gradients – this makes the all-important attempts at range shifting more likely to succeed. Successful migration of fish, either seasonal or longer-term shifts towards the poles, can sometimes be impeded by hard engineering structures like dams, many of which were built without mitigation measures like fish ladders to allow species to pass up or down stream (Figure 3).

Figure 3: Pacific salmon (Oncorhynchus) make use of a fish ladder on their way back to spawning grounds on Issaquah Creek, Washington State, USA. The mature salmon use a combination of the Earth's magnetic field and their acute sense of smell to return to the same river, and often even the same spawning ground, that they themselves first spawned at, years earlier. Fish ladders allow salmon and other fish to pass obstacles like dams and proceed up or down stream. **Credit:** John Pavlish (Wikimedia Commons).

Given how pervasive and dominant the impacts of climate change on the natural systems are, the obvious question is: 'what, if anything, can we do to help?' The answer lies in a relatively young field of research known as climate change adaptation.

Box 1
Is climate change increasing the likelihood of polar bears (Ursus maritimus) going extinct?

Polar bears live in the Arctic, and are the largest land carnivores on Earth, with the larger males weighing anything up to 700kg. But their scientific name – *Ursus maritimus* – is a reference to the fact that they also depend on the sea for their survival, and in particular, the sea ice floating on top, where they forage for their main prey item – seals. Because the total area of Arctic sea ice has been in decline for as long as we have been able to measure it, and is now probably at its smallest extent for at least 1,500 years (Kinnard et al., 2011), it follows that Polar bears are certainly a species of concern as warming continues this century.[10]

Yet the polar bear is an extremely difficult species to get good demographic data on, due to the extreme remoteness of its habitat and the dynamic nature of this habitat – the pattern of perennial and seasonal sea ice extents changes every year. Observations may actually increase in number as bears are increasingly spotted on land, yet this can simply be a response to the lack of sea ice offshore. And the status of some subpopulations improved after an international agreement to stop large-scale hunting of bears in the 1970s.

Figure 4: A female polar bear (*Ursus maritimus*) and her cub on dense drift ice in Hinlopen strait, Svalbard. Cubs are dependent on their mothers' energy reserves from birth until exiting maternity dens a few months later, in the spring. **Credit:** AWeith (Wikimedia Commons).

This all means that for almost half the subpopulations of the polar bear, we cannot say with certainty whether numbers are increasing, decreasing or remaining stable.[11] Of those subpopulations that we do have good data for, one has increased in number (M'Clintock Channel), three have declined (Baffin Bay, Kane Basin, and Southern Beaufort Sea) and the remainder have been stable.

It's also likely that the decline in sea ice is not fully reflected in polar bear numbers as yet, because many of the effects of this loss are not felt immediately. For example, we know that polar bears have a remarkable ability to fast for months without food, and to an extent this has made them resilient to losses in foraging habitat. This resilience may be enough for adults to survive in the short term, but not enough to ensure that the bears can successfully reproduce in the long term, because cubs are dependent on their mothers' energy reserves.[12]

Nevertheless, a recent study that related polar bear numbers to sea ice extent (Regehr et al., 2016) determined that a 30% decline in numbers over the next 30 years was more likely than not, and in fact this is sufficient cause for the species to be classified as 'Vulnerable' to extinction as per the so-called IUCN Red List Criteria ('Vulnerable' is one step down from 'Endangered' in the three categories of threatened species).[13]

Similar to other climate-threatened species, scientists will continue to keep an eye out for opportunities to intervene and improve the likelihood of individual subpopulations adapting to the changes that will come (see *Adaptation to climate change* below). But ultimately the best route to successful conservation for this species in the long term is mitigation of greenhouse gas emissions.

Box 2:
Ecological mismatching, species interactions, and the impacts of climate change in your back garden

In combination with one another, climate change effects that are already known to be negative can be much more destructive than most realise. For example, warmer temperatures tend to lead to advancements in the timing of annual life cycle events –such as an earlier timing of budburst in deciduous trees, or the earlier arrival of summer migrants. Taken in isolation, these changes to phenology may not seem deleterious, and in some cases can even be beneficial – such as an extended growing season for agriculture.

But it is only when changes in the timing of ecological events are taken together that the ultimate outcome for biodiversity becomes more apparent. In fact it is becoming increasingly clear that not all species are changing at the same rate. Because most ecosystems consist of intricate ecological networks or webs of co-dependency, should the synchrony between two or any number of species be disrupted, then those species can become mismatched, with knock-on consequences for the condition and ultimately continued survival of affected species.

In a ground-breaking experiment in the Netherlands, researchers examined this question using a long-established experiment on predator-prey dynamics. The researchers observed the egg laying dates of the great tit (*Parus major*, Figure 5) – a garden bird common in northwest Europe – and compared them to the peak emergence dates of the caterpillars it preys on when rearing chicks.[14] They found that the caterpillars had broadly been keeping up with climate change, with peak biomass of caterpillars advancing 9 days over 22 years of spring warming. But there had been no change in the laying dates of the great tits over the same period, leading to an ecological mismatch between them. This mismatch has reduced the weight and success of the resulting fledglings (Visser et al., 2008), which means that the great tit now faces an evolutionary race to respond to the rapid changes in the availability of its prey.[15]

More broadly, an analysis of the climate sensitivity in over 10,000 species showed that, by the middle of this century, primary consumers (like the caterpillars) will be advancing their phenology at over twice the rate of species at other trophic levels (like the great tit) – 6.2 versus 2.5 to 2.9 days earlier, on average.[16] So we should expect to see more examples of mismatching as warming accelerates.

Figure 5: A great tit (*Parus major*) foraging for caterpillars in northeastern Turkey. **Credit:** Zeynel Cebeci (Wikimedia commons)

Climate change adaptation in natural systems

Given how pervasive climate change impacts are, it might be tempting to believe that there is little we can do for the natural world, beyond simply mitigating our greenhouse gas emissions as much as we can. But just as we humans will try to adapt to the changes that have come and will come, so too will other members of the planet's biota. The key to reducing the negative impacts of climate change will be identifying, protecting and ideally facilitating any beneficial adjustments that can be made by or for those systems – whether that is at the level of whole ecosystems or an individual gene.

What are these so-called 'beneficial adjustments'? In the broadest terms, they are changes to a system, a species, or even an individual, that helps it negotiate the change in circumstances. They can be as simple as a lizard shifting its activity pattern to avoid hotter daytime maximum temperatures, or involve more complex mechanisms like evolution towards individuals that can range-shift more quickly, such as certain species of grasshopper or cricket.[17] You could even argue that range-shifting in itself is an adjustment to the changed climate.

Can we do anything to improve the prospect of natural systems making beneficial adjustments to climate change? Whether it's merely the initial effects of climate change being experienced (Figure 1), or the final blow for a species that is already at risk due to other pressures (Figure 2), the answer is often complex, intricate, and at times quite elusive. Detailed investigations of the link between polar bears (*Ursus maritimus*) and climate change are a typical example of this (Box 1). We know the direction of travel, but we don't yet know the destination, and given the continuing uncertainty over if we'll reach the Paris goals, or indeed if those goals are sufficient in themselves, it is likely that we'll have to make some decisions about how best to conserve and manage these systems in the presence of considerable uncertainty.

Another feature of adaptation efforts will be an acceptance of some level of change as an inevitable consequence of the Anthropocene. While there will always be situations in which the conservation of species, populations or individuals in a particular place is paramount, the idea that we can manage or return the landscape to how it was – or rather, how we perceived it to be – prior to human disturbance is probably a thing of the past.[18] Actions taken to help natural systems adapt to climate change will target the fundamental processes and functions that keep ecosystems healthy, whilst recognising that the mix of species that perform these roles may change.

Coming to accept that we are now the main shapers of the natural world actually gives us more ways in which we could act. For example, rather than passively hope that species will be able to successfully range-shift across continents, what if we intervened to ensure that habitats and ecosystems were in the right place to facilitate this, creating suitable habitat along the way? We could ensure that tree planting was targeted in areas where corridors or stepping stones were required, augmenting those old-growth forests most likely to provide migration routes towards cooler climes. And where species may struggle to successfully shift, we may consider moving populations or individuals ourselves – to alternative, cooler spots, or across hostile terrain.[19] We might even choose the more climate-resilient individuals or populations to move when we do so, so that they stand the best chance of survival when they get there.[20]

Conclusion

Climate change is impacting our green planet in a myriad of ways, some of them strikingly obvious – from continental-scale migrations and an elevated risk of extinction for many taxa, to the more subtle changes like the slow decline in condition and foraging ability in species like the polar bear. Throughout them all is the sense that Earth is facing more change than it has for millennia. It is the huge influence of human-caused climate change – and all the other effects we have upon almost every square inch of the planet's surface – that have led to the realisation that we have entered a whole new geological epoch. But with that realisation comes opportunities to intervene more actively in ecosystems, helping natural systems to negotiate the changes in store.

Thankfully we also know that the more extreme scenarios of what will happen to the planet can still be avoided if we stick to, and ideally improve on, the Paris climate goals.

References

1. NASA. (2021). *2020 Tied for Warmest Year on Record, NASA Analysis Shows..* (https://www.nasa.gov/press-release/2020-tied-for-warmest-year-on-record-nasa-analysis-shows).

2. Cortese, D. et al. (2021). *Physiological and behavioural effects of anemone bleaching on symbiont anemonefish in the wild. Functional Ecology,* 35(3), pp. 663-674; Frisch, A.J. et al. (2016). A*nemonefish depletion reduces survival, growth, reproduction and fishery productivity of mutualistic anemone–anemonefish colonies. Coral reefs,* 35, pp. 375-386.

3. Smith, M. (2016). *Climate change claims its first mammal.* Science, 15 June. (https://www.sciencemag.org/news/2016/06/climate-change-claims-its-first-mammal)

4. Urban, M. (2015). *Accelerating extinction risk from climate change.* Science, 348(6234), pp. 571-573.

5. IPBES. (2019). *Global assessment report on biodiversity and ecosystem services,* Bonn, Germany. IPBES secretariat.

6. Scheffers, B.R. (2016). *The broad footprint of climate change from genes to biomes to people.* Science, 16 December. (https://science.sciencemag.org/content/354/6313/aaf7671.full).

7. Sharma, S. et al. (2019). *Widespread loss of lake ice around the Northern Hemisphere in a warming world.* Nature Climate Change, 9(3), pp. 227-231.

8. Döll, P. and Schmied, H.M. (2012). How is the impact of climate change on river flow regimes related to the impact on mean annual runoff? A global-scale analysis. *Environmental Research Letters,* 7(1), pp. 1-11; Datry, T. et al. (2014). *Intermittent Rivers: A Challenge for Freshwater Ecology.* BioScience, 64(3), pp. 229-235.

9. Ledger, M.E. & Milner, A.M. (2015). Extreme events in running waters. Freshwater Biology, 60(12), pp. 2455-2460.

10. Kinnard, C. et al. (2011). *Reconstructed change in Arctic sea ice over the last 1,450 years.* Nature, 479(7374), pp. 509–512.

11. Wiig, Ø. et al. (2015). *Ursus maritimus.* The IUCN Red List of Threatened Species 2015. (https://www.researchgate.net/publication/305992631_Ursus_maritimus_The_IUCN_Red_List_of_Threatened_Species_2015).

12. Molnár, P.K. et al. (2020). *Fasting season length sets temporal limits for global polar bear persistence.* Nature Climate Change, 10(8), pp. 732–738.

13. Regehr, E.V. et al. (2016). *Conservation status of polar bears (Ursus maritimus) in relation to projected sea-ice declines. Biology Letters,* 12(12), p. 20160556.

14. Visser, M.E. et al. (1998). *Warmer springs lead to mistimed reproduction in great tits (Parus major). Proceedings of the Royal Society B: Biological Sciences* 265(1408), pp. 1867-1870.

15. Visser, M.E. et al. (2006). *Shifts in caterpillar biomass phenology due to climate change and its impact on the breeding biology of an insectivorous bird. Oecologia 147*(1), pp. 164–172.

16. Thackeray, S. et al. (2016). *Phenological sensitivity to climate across taxa and trophic levels. Nature,* 535(7611), pp. 241-245.

17. Angilletta, M.J. (2009). *Thermal Adaptation: A Theoretical and Empirical Synthesis.* Oxford University Press Scholarship; Beckmann, B.C. et al. (2015). *Two Species with an Unusual Combination of Traits Dominate Responses of British Grasshoppers and Crickets to Environmental Change. PLoS ONE, 10*(6), pp.1-25.

18.   Thomas, C.D. (2011). *Translocation of species, climate change, and the end of trying to recreate past ecological communities. Trends in Ecology & Evolution, 26*(5), pp. 216-221.

19.   Bellis, J. et al. (2019). *Identifying factors associated with the success and failure of terrestrial insect translocations. Biological Conservation, 236*, pp. 29-36.

20.   Rinkevitch, B. (2019). *The Active Reef Restoration Toolbox is a Vehicle for Coral Resilience and Adaptation in a Changing World. Journal of Marine Science and Engineering, 7*(7), p. 201.

Our Society

Dr Justin Stevens, Dr Anne Chapman and Chris Skinner

On the brink of collapse?

Facing the challenges and future predictions of the situation outlined at the beginning of this book, some have concluded that we are heading towards some kind of societal collapse. That would not be a new phenomenon: across history, numerous societies have risen and fallen. In many cases, their fall was based upon environmental factors. But the world today is different in many respects, with a single 'global village' spanning from continent to continent. We see this in how our networks of food and consumer goods are produced and distributed; in how a handful of dominant nations set the pace of global finance, and even with how the cultures of multiple nations align (from the clothes people wear to the music they listen to and films they watch). As noted by Paul and Anne Ehrlich:

> 'Virtually every past civilization has eventually undergone collapse, a loss of socio-political-economic complexity usually accompanied by a dramatic decline in population size. Some, such as those of Egypt and China, have recovered from collapses at various stages; others, such as that of Easter Island or the Classic Maya, were apparently permanent. All those previous collapses were local or regional; elsewhere, other societies and civilizations persisted unaffected. Sometimes, as in the Tigris and Euphrates valleys, new civilizations rose in succession. In many, if not most, cases, overexploitation of the environment was one proximate or an ultimate cause. But today, for the first time, humanity's global civilization—the worldwide, increasingly interconnected, highly technological society in which we all are to one degree or another, embedded—is threatened with collapse by an array of environmental problems.' [1]

In the same way the biosphere and geosphere are interlinked, we now have a third element to consider: 'the sociosphere'. Just as societies are based upon the stability of environment, so too is the environment – even the world itself – shaped by the dynamics of our civilisation. Due to this civilisation, we are now heading towards a world that is several degrees warmer than it would be if humans chose not to pump huge amounts of greenhouse gases into the atmosphere.

We know that a 'plus 2 degrees world' is catastrophic to multiple species and nations. With temperatures just 1 degree higher than pre-industrial levels, many nations face crop loss, desertification, increased fires and droughts as it is. Others, such as those living on the low-lying Pacific Island of Kiribati, are looking at a situation where their entire nation will disappear.[2] With whole swathes of land made inhospitable, up to 1 billion environmental refugees are predicted with a 2 degree rise by 2050.[3] A 'plus 3 degrees world' tilts things even further out of balance: melting of both poles, causing the start of massive sea level rises, and formerly forested regions turning to plains and desert. The storms and heat waves of today will look mild in comparison. A plus 3 degrees world is one where it is much easier to become plus 4 degrees, even without the emissions of man. And where do we go from plus 4 degrees...?

We can look to the past as an indication of what may happen to the planet if pushed too far out of balance. 252 million years ago, in the Permian Extinction, temperatures rose by 10 degrees centigrade, caused by the release of methane or other toxic chemicals caused by volcanic activity. Once it began there was nothing to hold it back. Only when sunlight was blocked from reaching the Earth by massive cloud cover did temperatures drop.

There is no two ways about it: humanity, and most of the Earth's complex life forms, face extinction. This is not pessimism. This is not scaremongering. It is a cold, hard fact. The warning of over 450 scientists and scholars from 30 countries at the end of 2020 – including more than 60 climatologists – speaks for itself:

> Some of us believe that a transition to a new society may be possible. That will involve bold action to reduce damage to the climate, nature and society, including preparations for disruptions to everyday life. We are united in regarding efforts to suppress discussion of collapse as hindering the possibility of that transition. We have experienced how emotionally challenging it is to recognize the damage being done, along with the growing threat to our own way of life. We also know the great sense of fellowship that can arise. It is time to have these difficult conversations so we can reduce our complicity in the harm and make the best of a turbulent future.[4]

We can choose to turn away from the truth. There is still time, after all – even if things are harder for the next generation, the chances are they will at least survive. *We'll* be fine...

The challenge of structural change

'You're captives of a civilizational system that more or less compels you to go on destroying the world in order to live.'

– from 'Ishmael' by Daniel Quinn

Governments have known about the science behind climate change for decades. A report warning of the risks from continuing CO_2 emissions could be written in 1985, 1995, 2005 or 2015 – whatever the date, no substantive changes have been made. In countries across the world, the prospecting and extracting of even more fossil fuels continues. At best, governments are reacting to the situation – rather than proactively setting out a new course, based on a fundamentally different economy. Emissions continue unabated and even the outbreak of COVID-19, which saw widespread lockdowns, only resulted in the same 'business-as-usual' approach.[5]

Why is this? When presented with the facts and huge widespread risk of societal breakdown – if not outright extinction – the logical conclusion would be that sufficient action would take place to prevent it. After all, the problem is not something beyond our control, such as a massive solar flare or breakdown in the Earth's magnetosphere. Indeed, the problem is of humanity's own making. So why – year after year, warning after warning – is it being left unsolved?

The simple answer is that it is not possible for the present society to take effective action. Our way of life and functioning of governments is *built upon* the necessity of producing emissions. The blood of economies is carbon. Eating, drinking, consumption, accommodation, travelling – every aspect of society is based on extractive modes of production. Whatever the pace of technological innovation, it is still predicated on the pursuit of profit. Governments the world over are led by politicians who are bound by short-term thinking. They are elected based on their impacts within a few years, not by how their decisions affect people in a few decades, let alone how they relate to the prospects of future generations. In most nations, rising to power is not about providing a realistic vision and commitment that benefits people in the long term, but instead about securing influential and wealthy backers. Trace where the money comes from and you can predict how policies will be shaped.

For society to stop using fossil fuels is a bit like withdrawing from a drug addiction to heroin or cocaine. We are talking about more than just shutting down the fossil fuel firms – Exxon, Shell, BP, Chevron and such like. Banks are the links between fossil fuel firms and the future. They walk the line between funding climate disaster and providing climate hope. If banks can turn off fossil fuel funding then that's great – yet, equally, they cannot stop funding fossil fuel firms in one go. Switch them off overnight and some of the world stops: companies and countries alike. It has to be done gradually.

However, since the 2015 Paris Climate Agreement, the world's biggest 60 banks have given fossil fuel firms almost $4 trillion of funding.[6] So how slow can we go? Add more to this equation: even if you stopped banks funding fossil fuel firms, who else would fund them? There are plenty of other places to find funding: hedge funds, private equity, shadow markets, and friends.

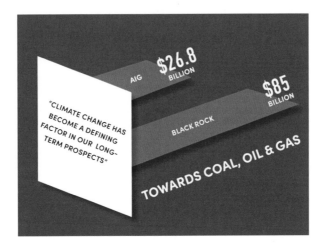

At the same time, powerful investment entities like Black Rock are able to erect a façade of being committed to fighting climate change, while continuing to pour staggering amounts into supporting fossil fuels. Indeed, Black Rock alone was responsible for £85 billion investments to coal companies in 2021, even as it promised to divest from such funds.[77] Likewise, insurance titans like AIG prop up fossil fuel companies to the tune of $26.8 billion, with no plans to reduce such investments.[8] It is no understatement to say that the entire global financial system is really the driving cause of climate change, with private companies making huge profits from the destruction of the planet. Meanwhile, instead of enacting legislation to bring an end to this, governments throw trillions of dollars a year towards such companies in bail-outs, investments and subsidies: the 'G11' alone (top 11 economies) were estimated to provide $189 billion towards coal, oil and gas between January 2020 and March 2021.[9] The United Nations estimates that global subsidies to fossil fuels, non-sustainable agriculture and fishing, non-renewable energy, mining and transportation exceed US$5 trillion annually.[10]

TOP 11 ECONOMIES
UNITED STATES, CHINA, JAPAN, GERMANY, INDIA, UNITED KINGDOM, FRANCE, ITALY, BRAZIL, CANADA, RUSSIA

TOWARDS oɪ̈L & GAS COAL,

There are no signs of the kind of emergency reversal needed to prevent catastrophic climate change from happening. Nonetheless, it is possible. The first step is to track and trace fossil fuel funding in the same way as COVID spreaders. In this way, we can see funding flows from banks and other financial providers through the system to companies who are involved in things that destroy our planet. By utilising a mixture of artificial intelligence, cloud computing, open systems and smartphones, we could link everything happening everywhere to a network of checks and balances. The problem is avoiding a version of Orwell's '1984' – yet, if we network everything with checks and balance, with the right metrics regarding health of the planet versus health of the person, we could create a 1984 in 2022 that actually works.

Alongside this, we need to envision a completely different socio-economic model – and with this comes other challenges. An increasingly polarised and unequal society means that there is a powerful minority who control access to both information and resources. It is the same minority that benefit from the existing system, so they stand the most to lose if it changes. They can and do actively resist attempts to meaningfully reduce emissions, which by nature require a radical change in how society functions and would topple their positions of privilege. They have obfuscated, ridiculed and undermined efforts to tackle climate change since the 80s – and it continues, in various ways, to this day.

One might think 'the 1%', the elite, would realise they exist on the same planet, so cannot avoid the fate of the majority. However, their wealth and power is so huge that it can create the illusion of being shielded from the future impacts of climate change – just like everything else. Since 2019 there has been a surge of 'luxury' bunkers and isolated retreats where the world's elite can escape in the event of a crisis.[11] With access to knowledgeable insider networks and advisers, it goes without saying that they are unlikely to be in the dark about what the future really holds. So too are they disproportionately culpable for this crisis we are facing. As reported by the Cambridge Sustainability Commission on Scaling Behaviour Change in 2021, 'the combined emissions of the richest

1% of the global population account for more than the poorest 50%'.[12] It is no surprise, therefore, that the elite resist the scale of changes required, and instead focus on how *they* will survive beyond the impacts of their actions.

Even people in the West are to some extent guilty of the same mentality. Does the average middle-class shopper radically change their habits to avoid the destruction of habitats halfway around the world? Do they stand shocked at the knowledge that Kiribati in the Pacific and several other low-lying island nations are within years of being completely submerged? The wealthier a person is and the society in which they live, the more protected they will be from climate change. And this same protection lends them the mentality that the impending threats are too remote and far ahead to be concerned with. Besides, they tell themselves, when these threats eventually do arrive, 'technology' will have solved the problem. In other words, they think not much differently than the billionaires above them.

The 'ostrich mentality' of ignoring, minimising or turning away from climate change is still prevalent across much of society.

Simple denial is also very much the norm. The anthropologist Jared Diamond looked at why so many societies make disastrous decisions and he uses the example of people living in a narrow river valley below a high dam. If the dam burst, their homes would be swept away and most of them would drown. People further downstream were less concerned about the dam bursting than those closest to it – but then a strange effect occurs. Just a few miles below the dam, where fear of it breaking is highest, people's concern suddenly falls to zero. This is down to a form of psychological denial: to preserve their sanity, they had to deny the possibility that the dam could burst, even as it loomed down upon them. Just as such denial has been established by psychologists to occur for individuals, it also seems to occur among groups.[13]

Politicians are aware of this. The few that take a stand and try to argue for the widespread, deep changes needed are simply not holding the reins of government. And the elite, with their dominance of the media and culture, will pull out all stops to keep it that way.

This is not to say that the need for individual change cannot be set aside, but in counterpart to it we also need to push for structural change. Back in 2017, it was estimated that just 100 companies were responsible for 72% of emissions.[14] To this day, those same companies have maintained the same model of fossil fuel extraction and dependency – despite the Paris Agreement; despite the knowledge that present emissions put the world on a track of catastrophe; despite the pressing urgency to change course. It is these same companies that fund and lobby the political system and which governments, in turn, support with subsidies and investments.

At present, simply by participating in the current socio-economic system – based on unsustainable extraction, production and consumption – there will *always* be environmental damage, whether we intend it or not. Just as to feed ourselves involves having to buy packaged (plastic) food grown from far away via an industrial agriculture system, people need real alternatives for meaningful change to be possible. And not just alternatives: options that don't involve contributing to the climate crisis should be easier, cheaper and widely available – instead of the opposite.

Such options are not compatible with quickly enriching a minority; of treating the environment as a limitless expanse to draw upon and pollute; of needing to control and own that which does not really belong to anyone. Nor do they fit with the model of acquisition, greed and constant pursuit of material 'upgrades'. We must emulate nature and natural systems: zero waste, circular economies, interconnecting with each other and other species, ensuring the constant rejuvenation of resources. This has been the model since life began and even humans (up until the last few hundred years) followed it. There is no law that we cannot advance, progress and develop only through the present economic system we know.

People are starting to realise this. Movements and organisations are popping out calling for genuine change, with even governments recognising the need to drastically reduce emissions (if only paying lip service to the idea). The change required is nothing less than a fundamental societal transformation, as noted by the United Nations:

> 'Transformation towards sustainability involves significant and mutually reinforcing changes in behaviour, culture, material flows and systems of management and knowledge transmission. With successful transformative change, the consumption of resources would decrease in wealthy contexts and increase sustainably elsewhere. People would be empowered to express and act in accordance with values of environmental responsibility without undue difficulty or self-sacrifice. Human opportunities and outcomes would be more equitable across dimensions of social difference including gender, ethnicity, race and region. Trade and other economic activities including resource extraction and

production of goods and services would yield net-positive effects, resulting in a substantial reduction in negative consequences. Systems of innovation and investment would yield technologies that enable net-positive environmental effects. Education and knowledge transmission would enable everyone to participate in well-functioning societies and new practices of stewardship and sustainability. Human ambitions for a good life would no longer be centred around high levels of material consumption, but around rich relationships involving people and nature, in keeping with diverse traditions throughout the world.' [15]

The restructuring and movement away from greenhouse gases is nowhere near to being realised, because it all goes back to the same challenge: fundamental socio-economic change. Until that is achieved, we are looking face on at our extinction.

Other ways

The Earth is littered with the physical remains of human folly and human hubris. We seem condemned as a species to drive ourselves and our societies toward extinction, although this moment appears be the denouement to the whole sad show of settled, civilized life that began some 5,000 years ago. There is nothing left on the planet to seize. We are now spending down the last remnants of our natural capital, including our forests, fossil fuel, air and water. This time when we go down it will be global. There are no new lands to pillage, no new peoples to exploit. Technology, which has obliterated the constraints of time and space, has turned our global village into a global death trap. The fate of Easter Island will be writ large across the broad expanse of planet Earth. – **Chris Hedges**

Do we take urgent steps away from the precipice, or just shut our eyes pretending it does not exist? Unfortunately, it seems the second option is what most people aware of the facts around climate change choose to adopt. It is not blameworthy, nor irresponsible, but perfectly understandable. After all, the question arises: *what exactly can be done, anyway?*

We must try to answer the question.

In order to answer it, we must first understand how the present situation arose.

Today's society is one where our connection with other species and the ecosystem has been severed. Adults spend their entire lives in the pursuit of money, an illusion created from nothing. Those with money use it to buy luxury goods, things that add nothing to their core wellbeing, and are ever restless for more. Children grow up believing that food comes from machines. In many ways it even does – a model of mass production, with herbicides at one end and pesticides at the other. Land is carved up into segments and sold for private benefit. People are enriched based on how much they profit from the work of others. Underlying it all is extraction, exploitation and destruction of the environment on a globalised scale.

Yet it has not always been this way.

We may have forgotten, but there remain a few pockets of people who can remind us of the other ways: Indigenous communities who see the interconnection between everyone and everything; who view themselves as belonging to the land, rather than vice versa.

An Indigenous village in South America. It is significant that for such Indigenous territories, which represent less than 20 percent of the Amazon, only 1.3 percent of total deforestation occurs.[16]

The present society arose as a Middle Age European phenomenon, which saw powerful nations spread across the globe through colonialism and conquest, using their superior warfare technology to enslave or massacre other societies. Rooted in a philosophical and religious outlook of patriarchy and private ownership, these Europeans held that man is separate and special from other species, with a right to use them – and other non-European peoples – as he saw fit. Even on an academic level, things came to understood in terms of breaking them apart into components, creating artificial separations and specialisms, with the aim of control and domination. As noted by Penha-Lopes et al:

> 'Removal of commons regimes serves several purposes. Denial of the existence of other ways of organising bolsters the ideological power of states and markets. Appropriation of land for other (profit-generating) purposes and the people on it as sources of cheap labour both boosts industrial systems and makes land and people more tractable to central regulation and control. This transfer of people, goods and services from the common pool into the monetary realm, initially via enclosures and land clearances in seventeenth century Britain, was central to capitalism's early establishment and subsequent, ongoing, worldwide expansion. A Yarralin Aboriginal man, Hobbles, described how following the massacre of over 95% of Yarralin people in the Victoria River Delta between 1883 and 1939, the survivors were forced into slave labour at the cattle stations established on their land. It continues apace as corporations supported by states take land and other resources from those whose commons regimes still sustain livelihoods based on farming, hunting, fishing and/or foraging.'[7]

When the European colonial powers crumbled in the 20th century, their underlying foundations remained. Formerly Indigenous nations found themselves being ruled over by small networks of white men, who owned most of the land and used the natural resources. When that was not the case, the imported structure of patriarchy, separationism and need for dominance remained. The European invaders had done the job of wiping out the Indigenous cultures, even if not completely annihilating all the people. Pseudo-culture and religion designed to weaken their courage to unite and resist was left to do the rest. [8i]

From this, the globalised capitalist system we know today arose. It is a world where the same giant companies are present in each nation, while the chain of production and consumption takes place across thousands of miles. A few currencies, each interlinked, underpin the economies of all nations. Schools, colleges and universities the world over follow the same general methodology, defined by a reductionist scientific model, conformity and competition. Even those most defining aspects of variability – music, art, literature and architecture – are lacking in the originality that once existed. Multi-lateral meetings consist of suited men, educated in near identical ways, using the same technological devices, owned by the same companies.

This system may span the Earth and be deeply embedded within every nation but, like everything else, it is still built upon the environment. By destroying the environment, it is gradually paving the way to its own demise. The problem is, in collapsing, it offers no hope for a fresh start afterwards. There are no green pastures people can resettle on; no alternative cultures in lands far away; no second planet teeming with life. Collapse of the system means collapse of everything: ecosystems ravished, multiple kinds of pollution too great to be absorbed further. Without an environment that can nurture us, we will die.

We therefore have a choice: to stop the system before it completely destroys the environment, or to wait for the system to destroy itself.

Signs of the latter may already be present. Unrest and division has opened up within even the wealthiest nations – from Trump's America to Britain's Brexit. The frustration caused by COVID and loss of jobs through automation will only accelerate this process. On an international scale, nations jostle with each other for resources – Turkey and Greece; Russia and the EU; China and the US. Right-wing nationalism and repressive laws are on the rise. All this, and we haven't even reached the level of environmental destabilisation caused by widespread crop failures, inundated cities, and hundreds of millions of people looking desperately to other nations to survive.

Some may argue that the system itself can be reformed. Moreover, how can we hope to survive without it? Cities need global supply chains, just as people need a national government. To accept otherwise is to advocate for starvation and chaos.

Yet, is that really so? In the first place, the very nature of the system is to exploit. It bases 'progress' on 'growth' – and by that term it means the expansion of an economy, as measured by how much is produced and consumed. Environmental destruction is implicit in both things. The drive for profits, or accumulation of wealth, relies upon the exploitation of others.

The world does not have infinite resources, nor is the ecology boundless. Reform of this existing model, therefore, is like tinkering with a square wheel, trying to make the edges a little smoother or adding a bit of oil to help the traction.

No, the whole wheel itself is wrong. It can turn, certainly, but the destruction it causes in the process is unsustainable. What we need is a new kind of wheel – a completely different kind of socio-economic system. And one only has to look into our past, and even some pockets of the world that already exist, to realise that this is possible.

Talking about a revolution

'Society continues to exceed and degrade the Earth's capacities despite clear evidence of the risk that this development path poses to humanity and growing efforts to reduce its environmental impacts. Continuing along this path constitutes an ongoing and increasing risk to current and future prosperity and well-being. [...]Only a system-wide transformation will achieve well-being for all within the Earth's capacity to support life, provide resources and absorb waste. This transformation will involve a fundamental change in the technological, economic and social organization of society, including world views, norms, values and governance.'[18]

What we need is a social transformation that is so radical that it could just as equally be regarded as a revolution. Previous calls to revolution have been national, even international. This one is local. It is about small communities forming and being empowered to act independently from 'the system', restructuring themselves from the bottom up. Far from being a regression, it harbours the potential for great advances. It is not about getting richer, accumulating more status symbols and owning assets. Rather, it is built on creativity, compassion and cooperation. Ultimately, it is a model of better social justice, equality and wellbeing for all – the same ideals on which all previous revolutions have claimed to seek, except this one can be accomplished in a totally different way: from the ground up, rooted in community and reconnection to Earth. Much of the rest of this book provides working examples of how such a transition can happen, together with the challenges and opportunities that it presents.

Not only does localism offer the ability to rapidly transition towards a better socio-economic model, but it also offers a chance to build better adaptation and resilience to climate change. As observed by Rupert Read:

'One of the most recognized aspects of resilient systems is the absence of single points of failure, which means, in other words, that functions are not performed centrally but in a more distributed way. Centralized systems tend to be efficient at the expense of being fragile. For example, a town could get all its water through one pipe, but the supply could stop completely if a bomb should damage the pipe, or it could make everyone sick if it became contaminated. Conversely, if every house stored its own rainwater in an underground tank, the system would cost more to build and maintain but it would be much harder to disrupt, not only because the water tanks are in many places, separate from each other, but also because the water is stored closer to where it is needed.'[19]

We often perceive meaningful structural change to only be initiated through national government, but in actuality a greater amount of change can be implemented on a local level – at a much faster rate. Sometimes it will involve working within, on the borders of, or entirely outside of 'the system'. For example, areas could restore ownership of long-term derelict sites to the community, helping to create sufficient space for each person to grow food. There could be incentives and support to make it easier for people to insulate their homes and access recycling initiatives. Going further, areas could explore circular economic models based on cooperatives and local currencies.

The localism talked about here is not confined to tinkering with reforms relevant to a specific area. It is also about structural and systemic change, for all ages and backgrounds. It could in many respects be regarded as a form of anarchism: a blend between existing models like the Zapatistas in Chiapas and Cooperativa Integral Catalana with the ancient Greek City States, which employed a form of direct democracy where 'the people' and 'the government' were more or less the same thing. As noted by Professor Read, this form of 'radical localism' is an answer to 'a felt malaise, the alienation people feel from their economic participation: a sense of wasted time and money spent on commuting, isolation from their neighbours, despair at what is happening in their high street and, increasingly, concern about societal collapse.'[19]

In place of businesses in pursuit of profit, to benefit rich shareholders, there can be organisations and cooperatives owned by their workers and the community. Collaboration and sharing can replace competition and dominance. All these things are possible, many already exist, and the impacts are well documented. None of us should be reliant upon a mass-produced, export-orientated, intensified agriculture food model that is responsible for significant climate emissions, poisoning of the environment, suffering and outright extinction of other species. Instead, through community allotments and local growing schemes, each person can to some degree feed themselves. It is possible for even dense cities to move towards such a model, as proven by the multifunctional green rooftops of Rotterdam and Copenhagen, or the wastewater reclamation of Singapore. To accomplish this, effective urban planning – with climate adaptation and resilience at its heart – is necessary. Cities are especially relevant considering that 58% of the world's population live in them, increasing to 70% by 2050.[20]

It is not just governance, education, economy and agriculture that need to change but also basic infrastructure. It goes without saying that energy from fossil fuels must end, in place of renewables. Similarly, the era of the car must end. Like the tobacco industry before it, car producers spend huge amounts on adverts and lobbying to convince people how important car ownership is, so much so that to be without one is a real disadvantage, thanks to a half-functioning and poorly invested transport infrastructure. We have cities where roads dominate the landscape, fragmenting communities and creating an array of health problems. It is time to reclaim these polluted, hopeless spaces for people instead. The oft-boasted objective of full vehicle electrification is really a dismal step towards what could be accomplished. We could replace roads and parking places with 'green lanes' of cycle networks, parks, urban farms, recreational areas for young people and affordable homes. An efficient, public transit system, along with 'on-demand' ride shares, could meet all transportation needs.

At the same time, action on a local level is often best brought about by shifting the focus away from 'climate', while still making it relevant. Attempts to tackle climate change by small communities will always seem miniscule, almost pointless, with the problem itself being enough to daunt many from trying. Thus communities can instead to look at restoring their environments and fighting against the 'game' of over-consumption that ultimately does not benefit them. In other words:

> 'One crucial act of resistance is to refuse to enter that game, and to instead create our own. That is what these initiatives and social movements seek to do. In the process they are linking with and learning from enduring ways of improvising and sustaining effective and sustainable social and ecological relations among peoples on the margins of the global economy.' [20]

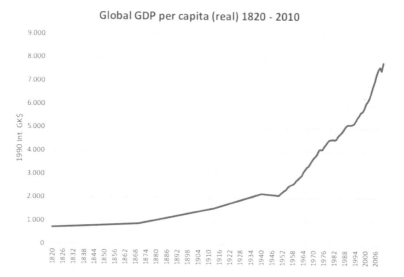

Global GDP per capita (real) 1820 - 2010

Graph of global GDP between 1820-2010. Note the parallel with growing CO_2 emissions on page ____#____

All this requires disconnecting from the lie that 'economic growth' is good; that our lives should be orientated around making 'money'. It is rooted in the same dark irony that frames Western 'development' as beneficial for Indigenous communities and those in the global south – with their land being stolen and resources plundered, all for the 'benefit' of getting poorly paid wage labour in return and 'escaping a life of poverty'. Thanks to such 'development', millions in the Global South continue to suffer forced displacement to make way for dams, transportation systems, plantations and luxury hotels – with an army of banks, government agencies and property developers in the background who measure progress only in terms of private home ownership and sharply increased consumption.[21] Essentially, 'millions of people are being expelled to the margins of fruitful existence in the name of someone else's progress'.[21] By forcing such communities down the Western pathway of high consumption, it also feeds into climate change: if the ultimate goal of a Tanzanian is a lifestyle like the average US citizen, they will emit more carbon in *one day* than they formerly did in eight months.[22] Despite its apparent 'luxury', those in the 'Global North' are entrapped by the same system, with the same form of exploitation played out across huge segments of society: poorly paid work that barely covers the costs of living, unhealthy urban environments, widespread youth unemployment, and ever rising levels of inequality – with 'the top 1%' controlling more wealth and resources than at any other point of history.

What we are looking at is more than a transformation or even a revolution, but instead a fundamental paradigm shift that has not occurred for thousands of years. The last such shift occurred when pockets of settled humans decided that the world belonged to humans, rather than that humans belong to the world. The resulting separation caused people to wage a war upon nature – treating it as an adversary to be suppressed and controlled – while conquering those societies that lived differently. Our present climate emergency is an inheritance of this mind-set; one that has destroyed most of the world's intact natural capital, and will keep on doing so until changed.

Creating strong community participation and leadership, such as through citizen's assemblies, is key to ensure the transition is implemented with understanding and majority consensus. Current levels of apathy, lack of involvement and disconnection from political processes have no place in such a model. All it takes is for people to feel they are being heard, with the power to shape and influence decisions – together with a sense of real belonging and making a difference. This is far easier to achieve on the local level, and there will arise solutions through direct democracy that are unique to each community.

Truly local representation may mean going against policies pushed against the will of residents, including blocking the flow of money that finances climate destruction (directly and indirectly) and refusing to enact or enforce regressive legislation. Practical examples may include taking over derelict sites for community allotments, or establishing local renewable energy systems like the micro-grids in Bangladesh. As the impacts of climate change worsen, such communities will face a struggle against more powerful actors that want to dominate and control. But history has shown that, the more oppression is enacted, the more people are drawn to resist. So far, oppression in most nations is limited to subtle, coercive ways: the manufacturing of consent in the media (itself dominated by a few billionaires), misinformation, upholding pseudo-culture and reinforcing apathy, so that people believe they cannot make a difference. These and other mechanisms have started to be backed by creeping legislation that allows for a tilting of powers against people by government (rather than vice versa), while eroding government transparency. Unfortunately, for all the time it takes governments to implement positive changes, politics can also move extremely fast. Times of disaster are especially conducive to bolstering the appeal of authoritarian regimes – from Nazi Germany, which swept to power from the fringes in a matter of months, to more modern examples like Poland and Hungary, which embraced far-right populism due to disillusionment.

Of course, not all countries are alike and it may be easier to implement structural change in others where there is a 'culture of enabling', which sees people creating initiatives by themselves (i.e. community allotments on derelict land), whereas in others there is a 'culture of impeding', which prevents people from taking the initiative for fear or repercussions (i.e. trying to plant native trees on derelict council owned land, like in UK – which necessitates 'guerrilla planting'). Indeed, fear of power being used to enact penalties or general oppression plays a more potent role than simply lacking encouragement to take positive action. Governments have always had more power than the people and communities below them, and technology has only widened the gap. Independent communities will need to tread carefully. Those in remote, rural locations may be better positioned than their urban counterparts, but the more such communities exist, the greater they can unify and be resilient. Importantly, independent communities will need to find ways to protect themselves, without falling prey to the same divisions, inward-thinking and tendency towards authoritarianism which larger society is experiencing and will worsen in the coming years.

We stand at a juncture. On the one side is societal breakdown and eventual collapse; on the other a radical transformation. Only by shifting power back to people and communities is it possible to achieve a more sustainable, just and resilient society.

Right: Self-started community allotments on unused land beneath a high-rise in Lisbon.

References

1. Ehrlich, P. R. & Ehrlich, A. H. (2013). Can a collapse of global civilization be avoided?. Proc. R. Soc. B, 280.

2. The Climate Reality Project. (2019). *TROUBLE IN PARADISE: HOW DOES CLIMATE CHANGE AFFECT PACIFIC ISLAND NATIONS?*. (https://www.climaterealityproject.org/blog/trouble-paradise-how-does-climate-change-affect-pacific-island-nations)

3. International Organization for Migration. *Migration, Environment and Climate Change (MECC) Division.* (https://www.iom.int/migration-and-climate-change)

4. University of Cumbria (2021). *Over 500 sign #ScholarsWarning on collapse risk.* (http://iflas.blogspot.com/2021/02/over-500-sign-scholarswarning-on.html)

5. Tollefson, J. (2021). *COVID curbed carbon emissions in 2020 — but not by much.* (https://www.nature.com/articles/d41586-021-00090-3)

6. Carrington, D. (2021*). Big banks' trillion-dollar finance for fossil fuels 'shocking', says report. The Guardian*, 24 March.

7. Jolly, J. (2021). *BlackRock holds $85bn in coal despite pledge to sell fossil fuel shares. The Guardian*, 13 January.

8. Peterson-Trujillo, E. and Saggau, H. (2021). *Why insurers must stop fueling climate chaos.* (https://www.citizen.org/news/insurersfuelingclimatechaos/)

9. Human Rights Watch (2021). *G7 Governments: End Fossil Fuel Subsidies.* (https://www.hrw.org/news/2021/06/07/g7-governments-end-fossil-fuel-subsidies)

10. United Nations Environment Programme (2021). *Making Peace with Nature: A Scientific blueprint to tackle the climate, biodiversity and pollution emergencies*, Nairobi. (https://www.unep.org/resources/making-peace-nature)

11. Wildfire, J (2021). *The World's Billionaires Are Going Absolutely Bunkers.* (https://theapeiron.co.uk/the-worlds-billionaires-are-going-absolutely-bunkers-36c9e9c627f8)

12. Newell, P., Daley, F. & Twena, M. (2021). *Changing our ways? Behaviour change and the climate crisis,* Cambridge Sustainability Comissions.

13. Diamond, J. (2011). *Collapse: How societies choose to fail or succeed.* Penguin Books, p.436.

14. Griffin, P. (2017). *CDP Carbon Majors Report 2017,* CDP.

15. United Nations Environment Programme (2021).

16. The World Bank (2019). *Why the Amazon's Biodiversity is Critical for the Globe: An Interview with Thomas Lovejoy.* (https://www.worldbank.org/en/news/feature/2019/05/22/why-the-amazons-biodiversity-is-critical-for-the-globe)

17. Henfrey, T. (2017). *Resilience, Community Action and Societal Transformation: People, Place, Practice, Power, Politics and Possibility in Transition.* Permanent Publications.

18. United Nations Environment Programme (2021).

19. Bendell, J. & Read, R.(2021). *Deep Adaptation: navigating the realities of climate chaos.* John Wiley & Sons.

20. Ritchie, H. & Roser, M. (2018). Urbanization. *Our World in Data.*

21.   Thackara, J. (2015). *How to thrive in the next economy (Vol. 1)*. London: Thames & Hudson.

22.   The World Bank (2021). *CO_2 emissions (metric tons per capita) – Tanzania, United States*. (https://data.worldbank.org/indicator/EN.ATM.CO$_2$E.PC?end=2018&locations=TZ-US&start=1982)

Part 2:
Impacts, Responses
and Solutions

Towards a Transformative Adaptation Strategy in Nepal

Dr Morgan Phillips

Life in Nepal's mountain villages is becoming increasingly hard. Families are at the extreme margins of political decision-making, and economic opportunities are few. Within these families, children, women, and the elderly often find themselves to be disproportionately disadvantaged by healthcare and education provision that is chronically underfunded, and nowhere near universally accessible. Many mountain homes lack reliable sources of electricity and heat, with most still harvesting and burning their own timber to stay warm and fed. Transport infrastructure is incredibly limited – the majority of journeys are still made on foot, with longer ones made by jeep or tractor over very poorly maintained (and frequently blocked or dangerous) unmetalled roads. Income and entrepreneurship opportunities are sparse, forcing many young people to migrate to urban centres or abroad in search of work and prosperity.

The COVID-19 pandemic has multiplied the precariousness of life and livelihoods in the mountains. At the time of writing (late July 2021) the official death toll for Nepal stood at nearly 10,000 people[1], with the impact of the second wave being significantly worse than the first. Sadly, the end is not yet in sight. A chaotic vaccine roll-out system, a chronically under-resourced health system, and the arrival of new COVID-19 variants means that the suffering continues to grow. The wider health, social, and economic impacts will be felt for many years.

Eventually, however, the pandemic will recede. When it does, the looming threat of climate change will come rushing back into view. It is already exacerbating the instability of life in the mountains and has the potential to destroy entire communities and ways of life. Key challenges include:

- The increasingly erratic Monsoon season – rain that was once reliable and consistent is now experienced as periods of deluge and drought. This causes dangerous landslides, intense localised flooding, and disrupts the growing season.
- Higher average temperatures – draw insect pests and parasites to higher altitudes, destroying fruit trees and other crops that were once safe.
- Reduced snowfall and snowmelt – impacts on the volume and flow of water available for households and for agriculture.
- Permafrost thaw in the periglacial environment – increases the likelihood of glacial lake outburst floods and high-altitude landslides.

Nepali people living in the rural Himalayas have very little power to influence the climate change mitigation efforts that are needed to prevent a climate catastrophe. But they can, if well-resourced and properly supported, adapt to the changes they are experiencing. The Glacier Trust charity is working with NGO partners to enable this process of adaptation. Our mission is to do it for as many families as possible, and we prioritise adaptations that are *transformative*.

Transformative adaptation (TrAd)

Transformative adaptation ('TrAd') has its origins in Deep Adaptation, and the vitality of Extinction Rebellion. One of its most prominent advocates, Professor Rupert Read (also featured in this book), emphasises the system-changing agenda at the heart of TrAd, something that distinguishes it from the sometimes-fatalistic Deep Adaptation agenda. Read stresses how TrAd *'requires a willingness to undertake major psychological adjustments away from what has been normal'*[2]. This may sound daunting, yet TrAd is an energising vision of the future, which TrAd proponents see as something to create, rather than merely adapting to. In Read's words: *'TrAd is a win, win, win: We mitigate the effects of dangerous climate change, we work with Nature not against her, and we transform society in the direction it needs to transform anyway.'*

TrAd started life as a vision and philosophy. It is seen as a set of principles to follow by those who can see how fragile Western civilisation now is, but aren't willing to indulge in self-interested retreat. However, as awareness of TrAd – as an idea – has spread, it has also become something of a diagnosis too. It is becoming clear that there are communities who have already started to *do* 'TrAd'. They were doing it before 'TrAD' was even coined as a phrase. They are adapting to climate and ecological breakdown in ways that dovetail with transformations in how their local economies, value systems and democracies are functioning.

In *Great Adaptations*[3], a sister volume to this book, I have argued that the 'Make Rojava Green Again'[4] movement in Kurdish northern Syria is an example of TrAd, something Read and Rathor have also noted[5]. The Rojavan's, inspired in part by the writings of Murray Bookchin[6] and other anarchist thinkers, have developed a model of democratic confederalism that is steeped in feminism, ecological intelligence and deliberative democracy.

Climate change is just one of the ecological challenges Rojavan's face. This is a part of Syria that had aggressive monocultural agriculture forced upon it for decades. Growing crops like wheat and olives in highly intense and pesticide heavy ways had disconnected people from the land, but also depleted soil quality, destroying any remaining natural and 'agro' biodiversity. Reclaiming and re-connecting with the land has given the Make Rojava Green Again movement the opportunity to revitalise the barren fields and adopt an agricultural strategy that is both more resilient to climate change and less of a contributor to it.

Rojavan's also need to create new waste, recycling and composting infrastructure, they need to tackle air pollution and water pollution (a legacy of industrial farming), and they need to move away from reliance on fossil fuels for transport and electricity. The tenacity to solve these problems, their embrace of agro-ecological methods, and their commitment to not just protecting but enhancing their local environment and ecology is inspiring. When coupled with the work done at a societal level to create new political and governance structures that are truly transforming ways of life, the Make Rojava Green Again movement is impressively radical, revolutionary perhaps.

If successful – and there is no guarantee that the movement will survive in what is a very turbulent and fragile part of the world – what is happening in Rojava could one day be looked back on as an early example of TrAd and the creation of a *successor civilisation*. Democratic confederalism, in a land that is adapted to the escalating climate emergency and following strict ecological principles, could be the sort of thing that follows on from a collapsed – or deliberately dismantled – 'Western' civilisation.

Climate change adaptation in rural Nepal

As the impacts of climate change deepen and spread, communities are forced to adapt. Some adapt better than others, and the prospect of *mal*adaptation is always hanging in the air. The geography and geology of Nepal is about as diverse as is possible for a country of its size. The land along its southern border, 'the Terai', is almost pan flat, part of the Indo-Gangetic Plain and of huge agricultural importance. But you don't have to go too far north in Nepal until the foothills of the Himalayas start to rise up. These hills, and the Sivalik range that lies between them and the true mountains, are well populated and characterised by steep wooded valleys, and thousands of rows of ancient agricultural terracing. Then, high up, are the glaciers, followed by the peaks of the iconic Himalayas. Climate change is impacting all of these environments and, as it does, adaptations – good and bad – are springing up too. This chapter focuses on adaptation in the foothills, mid-hills and Sivaliks, with a particular focus on the rural municipality of Thulung Dhudhakoshi in southern Solukhumbu, and Mandan Deupur in Kavrepalanchok.

Deusa Agro Forestry Resource Centre

Solukhumbu is in eastern Nepal and home to Sagarmartha (Mt. Everest), which, for the region, is a blessing and a curse economically and environmentally. In southern Solukhumbu, however, well away from the trekking routes and tourist hotspots, it would be hard to know that, 40 kilometres north, millionaire mountaineers are hurriedly ascending the world's most famous mountain peak. Thulung Dhudhakoshi and the other municipalities that flank the Dhudhakoshi river are off the beaten track, but strongly connected to each other. They are, however, isolated from Nepal's centres of government and business.

The land here is mountainous and difficult to navigate, villages are spread across steep sided valleys, and separated by raging, glacier-fed rivers. The economy is agricultural, and farmers work terraced land at altitudes varying from 300 to 3,000 metres above sea level. Life here is not easy and climate change is making it harder; it is an additional push factor that combines with various pull factors to drive an overall pattern of out-migration. The prospects for farmers in Thulung Dhudhakoshi are, however, improving as they embrace a transformative adaptation strategy of community-led agroforestry.

Agroforestry is the farming of trees and their produce, and is growing in popularity in remote mountain communities around the world. Farmers are diversifying away from reliance on labour intensive cereal crops like rice, maize, millet and wheat, to grow crops that require more technical skill to plant, nurture and harvest, but are more profitable and climate change resilient. In Solukhumbu, in the late 2000s and early 2010s, farmers were beginning to experiment with agroforestry, but with mixed results. At that time, one of The Glacier Trust's key partner organisations, EcoHimal Nepal, were working in Solukhumbu to deliver projects to improve provision of sanitation and education. While there, they observed the nascent attempts farmers were making at agroforestry and listened to their frustrations at not being able to get this way of farming established on their land. The farmers were calling for the technical support, training and tools that would enable them to adopt agroforestry as a climate change adaptation strategy.

It was from listening to these calls and discussing the potential to grow, process and sell high value coffee, nuts and fruits to local, national and international buyers, that the idea to create a community-led Agro Forestry Resource Centre ('AFRC') emerged. EcoHimal and The Glacier Trust consulted for many months with the local community to develop the concept further. The AFRC would be a physical building equipped with training halls, accommodation, kitchen and bathroom facilities, but it would also be surrounded by demonstration plots (an outdoor classroom) that would showcase how agroforestry is done, and how it can complement animal husbandry and the growing of vegetables and pulses.

However, unlike other similar centres, the AFRC would be a not-for-profit organisation, owned and run by the community. That way, decisions could be made democratically and would relate directly to the needs of local farmers. After several years of planning, persuading and fundraising, the first AFRC was built in the village of Deusa on land donated by the community and with cross-party political support. It was formally constituted in 2013 and has since grown in size and scope, becoming a community hub and catalyst for change.

Deusa AFRC was built on land donated to the project by four farmers; they had bought into the concept and joined the committee from the start. It is on what is classed locally as 'marginal' land, which was a deliberate and strategic decision. In this context, marginal land is land that is steep, rocky and lacking in obvious natural sources of water. Situating the AFRC on such land has proven to be of huge benefit because it helps to remove any scepticism lingering in the minds of local farmers who might otherwise have concluded that what is being showcased at Deusa AFRC is only possible because the land it is being demonstrated on is highly favourable. The marginal nature of the AFRC's land means that the opposite is true; it is more likely that farmers have more favourable land, so if agroforestry and the other climate change adaptation strategies are possible at Deusa AFRC, they almost certainly must be possible elsewhere.

Volunteers from right across the village, who are now Deusa AFRC members, worked together to construct the main building and the terraced land that flanks it. One thousand people spent a total of three thousand hours doing this work in 2012. It was a true community effort and there are now 250 hectares of agricultural land on a ten-step terrace. The terraces were built to grow plant seedlings, tree saplings and organic vegetables. These are all now thriving, with a huge diversity of crops growing in the open and under polytunnels. Most of what is grown is for sale in the local community, which has increased the amount and variety of produce available in Deusa, improving diets and bolstering agrobiodiversity. Other parts of the AFRC's land are used to grow crops that the agricultural specialists employed by the centre want to test in a controlled environment. They want to establish what grows well in the changing conditions. By doing this, they put themselves in a position to recommend appropriate, climate smart crops to AFRC members.

The AFRC's main purpose, however, is educational. By 2013, the AFRC's expert staff were delivering regular training workshops for local farmers on various agroforestry and agroecology techniques and methods. Farmers come from near and far, with some staying overnight to benefit from two or three days' worth of training events. Working with EcoHimal, the AFRC has developed an outreach programme through a family of seven *satellite* mini-AFRCs. These satellite AFRC's are dotted around the local environment, at different altitudes, and are managed by *lead* farmers who are AFRC members. Deusa AFRC is therefore a hub and the satellites are its spokes.

The advantage of creating the satellites is three-fold. Firstly, the farmers who run them are happy to host workshops on their land so that AFRC staff and members can come together to learn agro forestry and adaptation strategies that are appropriate at Deusa's different levels of altitude. Regular workshops are therefore held, on location, covering water harvesting, layer farming, ecologically mindful insect pest control and how to grow altitude specific crops.

Secondly, the satellite AFRCs are small-scale plant nurseries where local farmers can come to buy seeds, seedlings and saplings at a more convenient location, saving them what can be a long and tiring journey to the main AFRC hub. Thirdly, the farmers who host the satellites have a wealth of knowledge and experience. They take on an informal *lead* farmer role, acting as coaches who pass on advice and wisdom to less experienced neighbours.

Deusa AFRC has also become a central meeting place for a newly established farmers cooperative. By organising into a cooperative, farmers have been able to work together to source buyers for the high value crops the AFRC has taught them to grow. The cooperative at Deusa is now 48 members strong, 25 of whom are women. They receive regular training from EcoHimal Nepal on how to effectively run and govern their cooperative. They are selling fruits, vegetables, nuts and coffee locally, nationally and, in the case of coffee, internationally[7].

It is clear in Deusa and Thulung Dhudhakoshi more broadly that climate change adaptation isn't a siloed activity. It is part of a wider effort to transform the area socially, economically and ecologically. The influence EcoHimal Nepal and its partners are having is difficult to fully quantify, but the effort being made to address climate change, while also tackling gender inequality, economic inequality, ecological breakdown, and the lack of health and education provision is profound. Civilisation was slowly migrating away from these hill communities; it was collapsing. Now we have witnessed a TrAd process, with the emergence of a *successor* civilisation. Neighbouring municipalities are paying attention and starting to replicate the community-led, not for profit, AFRC model, as they too being to adapt to climate change transformative ways.

Avoiding maladaptation in Kavrepalanchok

The success of Deusa AFRC led to a replication in the central Nepal district of Kavrepalanchok, an area very badly affected by the catastrophic earthquakes in 2015. In January 2019, EcoHimal Nepal opened their second AFRC in the village of Mandan Deupur. The soil across the Mandan Deupur area is poor and overworked, as well as standing at a lower altitude to Deusa, so is more susceptible to temperature extremes.

Like in Deusa, marginal land was selected as the location for the main building and plant nursery. Mandan Deupur AFRC is on the site of an abandoned mini reservoir and had been left by the local community to go untended. The arrival of EcoHimal and the AFRC has breathed new life into the land and community and is changing the way farmers grow crops, together with how the village adapts to climate change. The first priority has been to tackle the climate *mal*adaptive strategy of increased use of toxic chemical pesticide and fertiliser use.

The use of chemical pesticides and fertilisers is rampant in this part of Nepal and the impacts of climate change are leading to stronger doses being applied. The greatest driver of this is the influx of insects, spreading due to higher temperatures, that swarm onto agricultural land, destroying entire crops of fruits and vegetables before they are harvested.

Farmers are turning to organophosphates to protect crops like cauliflower, bottle gourd, coffee and cabbages. This is a far from benign adaptation strategy, since organophosphates applied at these levels are creating very serious health risks for people and planet. It is not just the use of these chemicals that is dangerous – it is the misuse of them too. Farmers are, for example, spraying crops with pesticides right up until one or two days before they are harvested – they are not supposed to spray them at all for the week before harvest. Vegetables are therefore arriving at the market laced in toxic chemicals that can't just be washed off under a tap. This means that organophosphates are finding their way into the bodies of unsuspecting customers, as well as pickers, handlers, shop staff and chefs. Consumption of vegetables high in organophosphates can cause nausea, diarrhoea, stomach cramps, anxiety, and there are serious risks for foetus development in pregnant women. If chemically laced vegetables are a regular part of diets over the long term, the dangers increase to include kidney failure, lung disease, mental health problems and cancer[8].

At Mandan Deupur AFRC, agricultural specialists are doing two things to tackle this problem. Firstly, they are demonstrating that it is possible to grow healthy, organic fruit and vegetable without resorting to chemical use. Secondly, they are running regular workshops at the AFRC to teach farmers how to make bio-pesticides and fertilisers that work just as well and make organic farming possible. This upskills local farmers, improves their health, and encourages them to switch to organic methods and away from heavy chemical use. It is not easy to change the mind-set of farmers who have been seduced by fast acting chemicals, immediate results and initially higher production, but many farmers have subsequently been impressed with the alternative organic soil fertility and pest control measures.

Mandan Deupur AFRC are also developing a new project – the development of three 'model organic villages' that will be community-wide chemical free zones. This is transformative adaptation at the village level. The local farmers of the three villages (totalling 75 households) are being provided with training, orientations, seeds, seedlings, and tools as basic support for starting organic farming. In addition, farmers are being made aware of the importance of organic farming, the benefits of consuming organic produce and the beneficial effects for humans and the environment.

Farmers in all three villages have been provided with capacity building, focusing on the preparation of organic manure, bio-pesticides, Bordeaux paste preparation and its application, together with other innovative and organic production techniques. There is a further plan to establish small outlet centres in all three villages to assist them in selling vegetables, fruit and seedlings. The first priority is to encourage farmers to cultivate organically and consume the products themselves, which will assist in convincing them to adopt organic farming procedures. Lead farmers from the organic villages will eventually be used to spread the concepts and technologies in the surrounding villages.

Final word

This chapter has explored the need for, potential and emerging practice of transformative climate change adaptation in Nepal. Societal transformation is impossible without personal transformation, so the final word must go to someone whose life has been transformed. We thus conclude by turning to the words of Mr. Hari Prasad Bajgain, a farmer who returned to Nepal from the Middle East with the dream of working the land in his home village. Here is Hari's story in his own words, translated from the original Nepali:

> 'From an early age, I went abroad in search of better earnings and a better standard of living for my family. I have invested 10 young energetic years of my life in the Middle East, but it was not worth mentioning in terms of the income I could generate or save. I was not satisfied with my progress there and returned back to my motherland in 2018 with a strong determination to work for my own nation and not to invest further energy overseas.

I wanted to seek an opportunity to improve my living standard through improved agriculture in my own motherland so I could stay together with my beloved family members. However, in my own country of Nepal, the situation never seemed preferable to start a new livelihood, and I was always in confusion. Finding no choice, I continued the traditional farming methods but I was never able to gain benefits that satisfied my requirement or expectations.

So yet again, two more unproductive years went past – in those two years, I consulted the agriculture section of local government many times, hoping to receive technical guidance and resource support to initiate an improved agricultural system, but never found any solutions that suited me.

However, on one visit I was told about the newly opened Mandan Deupur Agroforestry Resource Centre (MD-AFRC), which I immediately visited and where I had a wonderful opportunity to observe climate resilient improved agriculture and new tree crop practices, and to discuss with the personnel there about all their improved farming technologies. Following a guided tour of all the MD-AFRC demonstration sites, I was impressed with the improved techniques and learnt a lot about the benefits of agroforestry and sustainable farming.

I requested for an opportunity to enhance my knowledge and skills by any means, and, just a few days later, I was called to participate in a training on bio-intensive and climate resilient farming techniques. In line with my interest, MD-AFRC provided me with the pathway that I had long looked for, and I have been able to move ahead utilising the limited resources that I have.

Right after the training and strong motivation, I invested my money, labour and time to follow this new and improved farming system, using all the knowledge and skills provided to me by the MD-AFRC staff. I started cultivation of fruits, nuts, and other high value tree crops in my farm, using bio-intensive techniques. I have definitely made progress, and in a relatively short space of time, I can see that the survival status and growth of the planted fruit and nut seedlings, is very satisfactory compared to the traditional techniques I was using before. Together with five of my neighbours, I have also started organic vegetable farming through a system of sharing our land.

My connection to MD-AFRC changed my perception of farming and showed me the right way to improve my livelihood. I acknowledge that though it takes some time to reap real benefits from the new agriculture techniques that I have learnt and adopted, it definitely facilitates in the optimal utilisation of resources for the maximisation of crop, fruit and nut production. I have now successfully utilised the barren areas on my farm, deemed useless before, for tree crops and vegetables.

As I consider myself a progressive farmer, I am now optimistic towards a better livelihood from agriculture in the near future. I see that my family is on a path toward prosperity from the farming activities I have initiated, and I am hopeful for the future and want to flourish to my fullest potential.'

References

1. The Kathmandu Post (2021) *Covid 19 Updates*, Available online at: https://vimeo.com/580246933/08256124c7 [Accessed 28th July 2021]

2. Read, R. (2021) *Transformative Adaptation*, Permaculture Magazine, Vol. 10, Spring 2021

3. Phillips, M. (2021) *Great Adaptations* – in the shadow of a climate crisis, Arkbound, UK

4. Internationalist Commune of Rojava (2018) *Make Rojava Green Again*, Dog Section Press

5. Read, R. and Rathor, S. (2021) *How we will free ourselves* – Together, Permaculture Magazine, Vol. 11, Summer 2021

6. Bookchin, M. (2015) *The Next Revolution: Popular Assemblies and the Promise of Direct Democracy*, Verso

7. Moore, M., Phillips, M. (2019) *Coffee. Climate. Community.* The Glacier Trust. Available online at: www.theglaciertrust.org/coffee [Accessed 28th July 2021]

8. Prasain, K. (2021) *Pesticides use on vegetables continues but more is being used to fight climate change impact*, The Kathmandu Post, Available online at: https://kathmandupost.com/national/2021/01/27/pesticides-use-on-vegetables-continues-but-more-is-being-used-to-fight-climate-change-impact [Accessed 28th July 2021]

Stories from the Blue Continent

Women activists, allies and radical difference

Janis Steele

When I was young I was taught that there are only three kinds of stories: man against nature; man against man; and man against himself.

Now *that's* a tragedy! If there is any takeaway from this misbegotten lesson about conflict and the structure of narrative, however, it is the element of relationality, and that is fundamentally what this chapter is about.

A number of years ago, I came across a statement formulated by an Australian Aboriginal collective and often attributed to Lilla Watson, a Murri visual artist, activist and academic working in the field of Women's issues and Aboriginal epistemology. It goes like this:

> 'If you have come here to help me you are wasting your time,
> but if you have come because your liberation is bound up
> with mine, then let us work together.'[1]

This quote has both guided and unsettled me in my pursuit of allyship[i] and solidarity and it helps contextualise the stories that feature in the following pages. 'Stories' is perhaps too substantive a word; these are, instead, wispy narrative threads that I knot together to introduce several Pacific Islander women – just a few among many – who are theorising, acting on, and engaging the climate emergency and environmental degradation.

One of my intents is to make readers somewhat uncomfortable as consumers of these narratives, just as I must necessarily be in representing them. Such discomfort, and any critical reflections that may flow from it, are vital to condition our mutual efforts to pursue reciprocity amidst our global crises. This chapter entreats that whether you are a representative and activist at COP climate change meetings, a member of a climate movement seeking to scale up, or active in local communities, we must all 'attend to solidarity in edgy ways.'[2] To move forward we must challenge ourselves to dwell within the discomforting yet electrifying modes of relationality, or intimacy, that hinge on radical differences and incommensurable interdependency. While a fair accounting of the extensive literature on postcoloniality/decoloniality is beyond the scope of this chapter, I hope that by situating it with respect to those aesthetic and political considerations and contestations, it may stir readers to reshape the terrain of the global in more robust reciprocal terms.

As a NGO actor in Vanuatu, an archipelago in the Southwest Pacific, since 2014, I've partnered with a volunteer network of environmental stewards known as the Vanua'tai (of Land and Sea) Resource Monitors (under the umbrella of Wan Smolbag[ii], men and women committed to action on behalf of their local communities. I have engaged directly with local communities across the island chain on a variety of climate adaptation and resilience projects, working in consultation with government departments and others

---

i   The concept of allyship employed here refers to 'an active, consistent, and arduous practice of unlearning and re-evaluating, in which a person in a position of privilege and power seeks to operate in solidarity with a marginalized group.[3]

ii   https://www.wansmolbag.org

in the nonprofit sector. These activities have led me to meet climate activists throughout the region, including participants in the 350 movement, Pacific Climate Action Network and Pacific Islands Students Fighting Climate Change. I've also had the opportunity to speak with women across Vanuatu as part of producing two short documentaries about women's climate and environmental leadership.[4,5]

These experiences position me to write this chapter, yet when viewed through a decolonising lens, my authorship warrants disruption. As an ally and storyteller, shadows loom at the edge of the frame, luring me to occupy positions of protagonist for the Indigenous women in this story.[6] Pacific scholar Katerina Teaiwa, impatient with tropic representations of Pacific Islanders, calls out those who stake a claim to representation that all too often has the effect of sidelining people in their own place – in this case, the very women we seek to centre.[7]

So, I urge you, reader, to take these stories as partial, interpretive and contingent. Recognise that it is precisely such struggles of relationality that must be illuminated as we envision a collective future on the planet. Achille Mbembe alerts us to how, 'In our world of hierarchical division, the idea of common humanity is the object of many pious declarations'.[8] In their book, *On Decoloniality*, Mignolo and Walsh assert that a focus on relationalities concerns 'the ways that different local histories and embodied conceptions and practices of decoloniality, including our own, can enter into conversations and build understandings that both cross geopolitical locations and colonial differences, and contest the totalizing claims and political epistemic violence of modernity.'[9]

First stories

Nigerian writer Chimamanda Adichi, drawing upon the work of Palestinian poet Mourid Barghouti, considers how if you want to dispossess a people, neglect all that happened 'first' and start your story with 'secondly':

> 'Start the story with the arrows of the Native Americans, and not with the arrival of the British, and you have an entirely different story. Start the story with the failure of the African state, and not with the colonial creation of the African state, and you have an entirely different story.'[10]

Begin with the story of climate emergency and sinking islands in the Pacific, and you are starting 'secondly.' Yet these are the stories that dominate media in an era of climate crisis. Drowning islands feature prominently, and Pacific Islanders too often appear as voiceless, hapless victims, poster children of the *Anthropogenic Climate Emergency*. The roots of the current crisis, located in the frameworks of modernity/coloniality, of invasion, predation and dislocation, are obscured.[11]

Katerina Teaiwa is an anthropologist, artist and activist of Banaban, I-Kiribati and African American heritage, born and raised in Fiji and currently based at the Australian National University. She is the author of the ethnography, Consuming Ocean Island (2014) which tells an intimate and geopolitically powerful story of the Kiribati island known to its residents as Banaba.12 For 80 years, between 1900 and 1980, the island was slowly consumed by the phosphate mining industry in order to produce fertiliser for the global market. Eventually, Banaba became uninhabitable and its residents were relocated to a Fijian island. Teaiwa asserts that Banaba's history is not separate or different from climate change; rather, the climate crisis can be understood as 'the culmination of all the effects of resource extraction.' Indigenous theorists like Teaiwa argue that the apocalypse on our horizon, portended by global warming and biodiversity loss, is only seen as 'new' to Global North/Euro-centric societies.13 For indigenous peoples caught up in centuries of resource extraction, slavery, dislocation, missionism, introduced diseases, ecosystem loss, nuclear testing, pipelines, and neoliberal development agendas, the crisis has been ongoing for hundreds of years.14,15 Climate grief, in this way, is nothing new to the colonised.16

Tammy Tabe, raised in Solomon Islands and of I-Kiribati and Tuvalu descent, is also a cultural anthropologist currently lecturing at the University of South Pacific in Suva, Fiji. She has worked widely in the Pacific Islands and her areas of study include historical relocations of Pacific Islands people, and climate change induced migration and displacement. Like Teaiwa, Tabe writes about the effects of forced migration in the colonial history of the Gilbertese relocation to Solomon Islands in the early 1960s. According to British colonial accounts the resettlement was considered a necessary solution to degrading environmental conditions of the land; however, many of the Gilbertese settlers considered that their relocation was forced upon them as a result of nuclear testing conducted on Christmas Island, a fact that was silenced in the Gilbertese relocation history and in the colonial archives.17,18

According to Tabe, while much has been written about migration in relation to climate change, very little has been written from the Pacific islands' standpoint. She stresses that Pacific Islanders must reflect on dominant narratives of migration and displacement and who is giving these voice.[19] For example, she draws distinction between a heritage of movement among Pacific Islanders across seascapes and dynamics of imposed migration and displacement. As part of this reclaiming of narrative, Tabe emphasizes that Pacific Islanders' stories and perspectives must be acknowledged and privileged in climate change discourses and policymaking (Tabe, T. personal communication, May 2021).[20]

Both Tabe and Teaiwa's work points to the vital importance of including Pacific Island voices in climate stories. Teaiwa is particularly adamant that stories of Pacific Islanders in the climate narratives 'center empowered Pacific people first and foremost.' An example of this ethic can be found in the message of 350 Pacific Climate Warriors: 'We're not Drowning, We are Fighting'. Additionally, both Pacific scholars point to the need to give prominence to connections between people and place, or as Teaiwa puts it, 'values, stories and relations grounded in kinships, landscapes, seascapes and skyscapes'.[21]

The blue continent and ontological difference

This emphasis on people and place is reflected in a vital reframing that has emerged in recent years as Pacific Island states seek to change how they are perceived and engaged with upon the world stage. Rather than being viewed as small island states, Pacific Island countries position themselves as 'large ocean states' and their people as custodians of this vast region's rich marine life and ocean health. This framework was laid out in a speech by Samoan Prime Minister Tuilaepa Sailele at the 2017 UN Oceans Conference in New York titled 'Our Values and Identity as Stewards of the World's Largest Oceanic Continent.' The Prime Minister emphasized the 'inseparable link between our ocean, seas, and Pacific Island peoples', and stressed that the notion of a Blue continent underscored how the Pacific Ocean is core in shaping peoples' values, traditional practices, and spiritual connections. Accordingly, this position asserts that all policymaking and decisions should be subject to an understanding of the region's ocean identity, ocean geography, and ocean resources.[22,23,24*]

Uprisings of Indigenous demands for sovereignty, self-determination and self-direction are widespread across the globe. Intrinsic to many of these movements is a rejection of the nature-culture divide, a core feature of the Eurocentric or North Atlantic ontological worldview.[25,26,27] At the same time, it is increasingly evident that areas of the Earth under Indigenous stewardship feature far more robust biodiversity.[28] It is no wonder there is growing eagerness for an alternative model of relating to nature as we stare down the rapidly constricting tunnel of catastrophic effects induced by the inextricably linked paradigms of colonialism, capitalism, and patriarchy. Yet possibilities for building coalitions and pursuing alternative models for a liveable future often remain mired in these very paradigms. Indigenous peoples may be recognised as stewards of nature, yet discounted for failing to conform to a modern norm; allies can thus operate with narratives that 'privilege themselves as the protagonists who will save Indigenous peoples from colonial violence and the climate crisis'.[29,30] Others have characterised this as a 'benevolent decolonising agenda' in which well-meaning allies appropriate ontological forms as political models, without accounting for how they themselves are not subject to the local 'eco-biomes' or ecological worlds that actually give form to those worldviews.[31,iii]

To illustrate this better, let's pivot for a moment to another region of the globe. In her study of how such ontological differences played out in a battle to stop mountain mining in the Andes, Peruvian anthropologist Marisol de la Cadena exposes how the goal to protect the mountain on the part of local community activists and environmental NGO activists did not arise from the same ontological interest:

---

iii How questions of 'difference' are theorised is part of the 'ontological turn' that has taken place recent decades in anthropology and other disciplines. This turn shifted away from the premise that epistemologies (forms of knowing or understanding) vary, but that there is only one ontology (form of being or existing), in other words, many worldviews, only one world. The ontological turn rejects the universalising of nature, and instead proposes that worlds, as well as worldviews, may vary.[33,34]

'The fact that the mountain was also an earth-being was carefully hidden from the contest as it unfolded publicly. The reason: in the field of modern politics, tirakuna [earth-being relations] are cultural beliefs and, as such, weak matters of political concern when confronted with the facts offered by science, the economy and nature.' [32]

By attending to radical difference and profound incommensurability, de la Cadena proposes that new possibilities of allyship emerge:

'An oxymoronic condition, this alliance would also house hope for a commons constantly emerging from the uncommons as grounds for political negotiation of what the interest in common – and thus the commons- would be. Instead of the expression of shared relations, and stewardship of nature, this commons would be the expression of a worlding of many worlds ecologically-related across their constitutive divergence.' [35]

Another way of capturing this idea of a worlding of many worlds is through the idea of the pluriverse as explored in *Pluriverse: A Post-Development Dictionary* (2019).[36] The authors describe the pluriverse as 'a broad trans-cultural compilation of concepts, worldviews and practices from around the world, challenging the modernist ontology of universalism in favor of a multiplicity of possible worlds'.

'Gender, a white man's word'

Gender is a cross-cutting issue in addressing the climate emergency and environmental collapse. Not only do women disproportionately experience the impacts of these states of emergency, but the source of the crises themselves can be seen to lie in the hierarchies and violence of the colonialist/capitalist/capitalist/patriarchal paradigms. Climate change, as Majandra Rodgriquez Acha contends, is not a problem, it is a symptom.[37,38,39]

While focused here on empowered leadership, this is not to dismiss the reality that in the Pacific region, climate impacts such as extreme weather events, drought, flooding and coastal erosion, as well as impacts from extractive industries, present life and death challenges, particularly for rural women as they go about their work providing food, water, fuels and shelter to their families. In Vanuatu, for example, the vast majority of the population are subsistence harvesters, with small to moderate cash crops. When food and water sovereignty are threatened, when their homes are destroyed by intensified cyclones or coastal erosion, women often bear the brunt of stress and labour, including increased risk of violence from destabilised men as stress levels increase.

I met Jocelyn Usua through a common acquaintance. I was looking for a place to stay on the island of Tanna where my associate and I were meeting with a Vanua'tai monitor and members of his community who were developing a locally managed marine protected area. Jocelyn offered to put me up and we shared her small bedroom for the next few days.

In our early conversations, I learned that Jocelyn is a fierce advocate on behalf of Ni-Vanuatu women. She was already actively engaged in advocating for women's reproductive health on the island and assumed many roles of leadership among women. After learning about the Vanua'tai during our initial visit, Jocelyn went on to join the network and eventually became the first chairperson of the Tanna Usiusi Environment Network.

Jocelyn had experienced domestic violence and great losses as a younger woman. Now, married to a Paramount Chief, she can be outspoken among women on an island where women are expected to have their husbands speak for them in the *Nakamal* (a traditional meeting place where important community discussions occur). Jocelyn attended school up until year 10, at which point family funds were depleted. Determined that her education would not end, she made it her concern to pursue learning at every opportunity. As she explained to me, she read every book she could get her hands on, and when she'd hear about a workshop taking place, she'd find a way to attend in order to build her knowledge and advance her activism (Usua, J. personal commuication, April 2017).

Before going further, I pause to alert readers to some questions that are occurring to me at this point in writing, some of which can be captured in a struggle about names. Previously, I referred to Katerina Teaiwa and Tammy Tabe using their surnames, as is standard in academic writing. Here, I have felt compelled to shift to using Jocelyn's first name, not only because I consider her a friend, but because of an authoritative tension that exists between representations of the academy and the grassroots that imposes itself in this narrative. We see this often in anthropological texts, where references to scholarly theorists employ surnames, but references to local actors – our grassroots interlocutors – are most often made using first names, as if this somehow lends weight to the writer's authority, authenticity, and access: 'I was on the ground; I know these people and therefore I have the intimate authority to translate their story'. By this point, dynamics of sidelining people may be well in hand for readers. If, as feminist critic and literary theorist Gayatri Chakravorty Spivak argues, ethics is a problem of relationality rather than a problem of knowledge, such ethics are made manifest in this struggle.[40] So, I will make a deliberated choice here and shift entirely to surnames. This does not release me in these representations from what Spivak refers to as a double-bind, nor should it. To emerge on the other side of a double bind 'comforted and confident is impossible and unproductive' explains Huddleston, engaging with Spivak's work. Instead, he suggests, 'we must wrestle with it clumsily'.[41]

So, clumsily, I now move forward with this name-frame, returning to my narrative thread about Usua (oh, that feels awkward!) and a short discussion about gender.

As part of examining the positioning of 'Other Women' Spivak considers that while both men and women of the Global South may be engaged in attending to the past and its relationship to a contemporaneity 'not forever marked by the West', they do not do so equally. Across classes, she notes, it is women who are expected to maintain or 'hold the marks' of traditional culture.[42] Yet, Spivak does not see the efforts of globalising feminism and 'hasty gender training' as a solution. It is clear from the evidence, she observes, 'that individual rights or universalist feminists infiltrate the gendering of the rural South to recast it hastily into the individual rights model'.

Such intrinsic tensions were evoked by Usua when she led a workshop for her fellow Vanua'tai monitors – male and female – on gender roles. Presumably, her presentation was shaped in part through her own exposures with civil society organisations active in the region. It was the way she introduced the topic that struck me, with the opening line: 'Gender, what is this white man's word? What has it got to do with us?'

Usua's leadership roles place her squarely in an entangled process in which she is simultaneously engaged in the (re)vitalization of local traditions and knowledge and the interrogation of those local contexts, as well as the navigation of introduced framings such as gender. The following story which she shared with me in an on-camera interview helps illustrate this point (Usua, J. (2018) Interview conducted with Janis Steele).

One day, seeking to actualize things she was learning, Usua and her husband invited the president of the Council of Chiefs to dine with them. She announced to the party that the topic of conversation would be custom and she began by asking the chief if custom ever changes. When he replied no, custom is a constant, she challenged him. She asked: 'Chief, why are you wearing trousers and a shirt? This cotton clothing, is that our custom or is that the way of the white man?' Through continued dialogue, Usua reported to me that they were able to find agreement that indeed customs do change. 'It's one thing to protect our language,' Jocelyn emphasised to me. 'That is an example of a custom we must protect. But in any society, there are always things that need changing.' Whether or not Usua and the chief went into detail about women and men's roles in that conversation, she chose not to discuss with me then. Her story, however, points to the imperative that in the pursuit of climate adaptation and justice, Indigenous and local women must have a say in determining which activities fairly express local customary values and practices that need protection, and what needs to change, or requires innovation, to help ensure a robust response to the crises that are besetting them.

Tools for change

At a recent gathering, or *Talanoa*[iv], organised by the Pacific Islands Climate Action Network in Fiji on the occasion of the 5th anniversary of the Paris Agreement, the topic of tools for change was an important theme among the participants. One of these participants was **Noelene Nabulivou**, political advisor to DIVA for Equality, a radical feminist collective located in Fiji. In company with their focus on gender justice, DIVA supports all women and their communities to highlight their role and capacity to build their own responses to environmental and climate problems.[43] Nabulivou introduced to the discussion the work of American writer, feminist and civil rights activist, Audrey Lorde, specifically her well-known 1984 essay, 'The Master's Tools Will Never Dismantle the Master's House'.[44] In that essay, Lorde goes on to say that those tools 'may allow us temporarily to beat him at his own game, but they will never enable us to bring about genuine change'. Nabulivou's reference to Lorde helped frame an arena of tension and possibility for Pacific Islander activists.

Also in attendance at this *Talanoa* was **Kathy Jetñil-Kijiner**, a poet and climate change activist from the Marshall Islands who received international acclaim for her powerful poetry performance at the opening of the 2014 United Nations Climate Summit in New York.[45] Like other speakers at the *Talanoa*, Jetñil-Kijiner was concerned about the question of access to tools for Pacific Islander activists and the experience of many youth negotiators who have had to learn on the fly without adequate preparation.[46] After the event, I turned to a speech to a speech she gave at the 2020 Pacific Ocean Pacific Climate Change Conference for some more context.

When she thinks back to attending COP25, Jetñil-Kijiner describes the experience the following way:

---

iv   In Fiji, 'Talanoa' means to hold a conversation in an inclusive, receptive space. It is a traditional method of solving differences in the Pacific.

'COP is an abusive space for Pacific Islanders.

It's an abusive space for people of color, the Global South, any disenfranchised so-called "minority group." It is a battlefield that requires strategy, an inordinate amount of funding in the case of first world countries, and for our countries in particular, grit. I honestly don't love how often militaristic language gets co-opted to discuss the climate movement, and yet the cruelty of the COP negotiations space brings these similarities to mind. Emotions get shelved, and though you may be fighting for the survival of your country, you must deliver your interventions calmly or you lose the floor.'[47]

As part of reflecting on the question of the tools required for this battlefield, Jetñil-Kijiner draws upon an analogy she owes to a friend. As a youth activist, the friend had long wanted a seat at the table, but was frustrated to realise when she got there that she didn't know how to use the forks and knives. For Jetñil-Kijiner, this metaphor spotlights the paradox of working in these spaces. She emphasises the imperative of helping prepare Pacific Islander activists to join the table, better equipped with tools – such as greater fluency with concepts related to mitigation and adaptation – and bolstered with what she refers to as holistic support.

The Pacific Climate movement is one that is largely youth-led. Reflecting this reality, Jetñil-Kijiner was part of introducing the Kwon Gesh pledge at a Climate Summit in September 2019. The Republic of the Marshall Islands and Ireland serve as co-leads of this Youth Engagement and Public Mobilization coalition. The pledge asks governments to commit to including youth in a meaningful way in national and sub-national climate action policymaking. There are currently over 50 states that are signatories (Kabua, A.E. and Nason, G.B. (2019). Letter to United Nations).

Taking a seat at the table is also a concern for **Belyndar Rikimani** and **Atina Schutz**. These two young Pacific Islanders are part of a pilot project for PICAN called the Pacific Youth in Climate Diplomacy program. Both are students of law at the University of the South Pacific campus in Port Vila, Vanuatu, and are also members of Pacific Islands Students Fighting Climate Change (PISFC), a young organisation whose core campaign is focused on convincing governments to seek an advisory opinion from the International Court of Justice concerning legal obligations related to environmental treaties and human rights.[48]

Rikimani is from the Solomon Islands, where she grew up with an interest in advocacy for women experiencing domestic violence. She came to understand ways violence can intersect with climate change and more broadly, how the changing climate is impacting her homeland. When she began at USP, she joined up with PISFC and currently is the organisation's vice president.

Rikimani had the opportunity to attend COP25, but it was an experience that she found depressing for reasons similar to those expressed by Jetñil-Kijiner (Rikimani, B. personal communication, June 2021).

Schutz is from the Marshall Islands and currently serves as the awareness chair of PISFC. What drew Schutz to join the cause is the inequity experienced by climate vulnerable regions, like her home islands, who contribute almost nothing to global emissions, yet who are faced with the devastating effects of the climate crisis (Schutz, A. personal communication, June 2021).

The Pacific Youth in Climate Diplomacy project that they are helping coordinate through PICAN is intended to build the skills and capacity of youth interested in international climate diplomacy. Inviting applications from youth from Fiji, Vanuatu, Solomon Islands, Kiribati and Tuvalu, the project will run throughout the preparations leading up to and during COP26 and will pair youth with experienced climate negotiators from the region in order to help prepare them to meaningfully participate in UNFCCC processes and COP meetings.

In the midst of strong feelings of frustration and anger at the way international negotiations unfold, Pacific climate activists such as Rikimani, Schutz and Jetñil-Kijiner continue to pursue climate justice through mechanisms such as COP and the International Court of Justice with great determination. As Jetñil-Kijiner states, despite the problematic nature of the UNFCCC process, it is still a critical means to deal with this global issue. Yet they are not insensitive to the paradoxes here. The 'table' at which they take a seat remains ensconced in business-as-usual and the processes are hindered by what is aptly described as 'the inability of global politics to imagine a response that does not take as a point of departure the same modus operandi that caused the crisis in the first place'.[49]

Rather than simply picking up the master's tools, Jetñil-Kijiner, Navulivou, Rikimani, Schutz and Pacific climate activists across the region may be considered to be both pushing boundaries and deploying alternative approaches. These efforts may include using those tools in strategic or refashioned ways, as well as devising new ones. The challenge is great. Mignolo and Walsh (2018) consider that an alternative new world will be made by those using both old and new tools to 'build houses of their own on more or less generous soil.'[50] They elaborate:

> 'It is our view that the proper response is to follow their lead, transcending rather than dismantling Western ideas through building our own houses of thought. When enough houses are built, the hegemony of the master's house – in fact, mastery itself – will cease to maintain its imperial status.'

Knowledge broker

This theme of tools brings me to a final narrative thread in the knot. My interest here stems from the hands-on activities that rural women engage as part of their adaptive strategies. Having earned my livelihood these past two decades as a forest farmer in North America and voyaged across two oceans, there are certain elements of land and sea that I share in common with Ni-Vanuatu with whom I strive to work in alliance. Here, I think back to De la Cadena's idea of 'alternative alliance' in which 'the commons would be the expression of a worlding of many worlds ecologically-related across their constitutive divergence'.[51] Though the meanings of our landscapes are thus constitutively divergent, perhaps some of that common ground of many worlds ecologically-related may come from a non-verbal world of working the land and working the sea.

I think of Leisavi Joel here. Joel lives on the island of Moso, in the Vanuatu province of Efate. She is a long-standing member of the Vanua'tai network and current chairperson of the Havannah & TasiVanua Environment and Climate Network. Joel is also a mother, a farmer, an entrepreneur, a planter of corals and mangroves, and an advocate for fish and turtles. In nearly every instant, she is hands-on and hands-in. I emphasise this here because ontological differences find expression in forms of participation of the physical body that are exactly not abstracted from mind and spirit but fully entangled. When Joel plants a mangrove stem on the shoreline, when she ropes a coral fragment into a coral nursery, when she leads community youth in building a conservation ethic with games, when she swims over the reef, she is not (or not only) exercising and implementing introduced adaptation strategies. She is also simultaneously revitalising and innovating what it means to be a Ni-Vanautu woman confronting a crisis.

Joel describes her journey as circular. She reflects on how, previously, she only worked with women in her community. Then she began to go out and participate in more workshops and trainings, and she met many different women. "This is a really good experience", she explains. 'For those of us who are able to step outside of our communities, we can learn about new ideas that we can bring back to share with women in our communities and raise awareness' (Joel, L. personal communication, July 2017). As an activist and mentor, Joel's skill and challenge lie in her distinctive and creative manner of brokering local knowledge and Western science across a spectrum of relationships. Through her actions, I experience her robustness as both ally and Other.

The ethical space

In this brief chapter, I set out to do two things. First, in following Teaiwa, I have attempted 'to center empowered Pacific people first and foremost' through presenting readers with what can only be spare narrative threads that I have knotted together to build a story. These are not principally stories of loss; rather, they point to what some have referred to as, '[c]reating new practices, activity, concepts and projects from the ashes that we sit in.'[52] Secondly, I have tried to illuminate some of the challenges and pathways to building solidarity across difference. I have tried to 'stay with the trouble' where I can in an effort to think carefully and critically about ways we seek to enable change and work in alliance.[53] At stake is the capacity to confront the climate emergency and environmental collapse and help our young ones – both the human and more-than-human – survive and thrive.[54]

Previously I raised Spivak's notion that ethics is a problem of relationality and I began the chapter with an Aboriginal quote inviting liberation through working together. In both utterances, it may be seen that the object of ethical action is not an object of benevolence but rather one in which responses intersect from both sides, a solidarity that stems from an active orientation towards others.[55] For Achilles Mbembe, this is expressed through the concept of reciprocity:

> '...The difficulty with a politics of recognition is that I might recognize you, but I don't really believe that we owe anything to each other. ...I have no obligation to speak to you or to listen when you address me... [there needs to be] an investment that is premised on some concept of mutuality or reciprocity... the mutual and the reciprocal go beyond the individual. The in-common is not about communalism. It's a third-space between communalism and individualism.[56]

Here, Mbembe raises the notion of third-space as the realm of such engagements. Postcolonial theorist Homi Bhabha's influential writings on third-space locate it as a liminal, hybrid space of uneven forces of representation that can give rise to something different and unrecognisable.[57] Similarly, Willie J Ermine, Sturgeon Lake First Nation scholar, addressing negotiations between settler colonialism and First Nations, employs the concept of Ethical Space. Pointing to the 'unwavering construction of difference and diversity between human communities' Ermine directs our attention to interstices between colliding cultures and urges us to reflect 'on the electrifying nature of that area between entities that we thought was empty'.[58] An essentialist reading of cultures as fixed, bounded entities is not an interest in either approach; rather the entire process is much more porous and fluid. As Injairu Kulundu-Bolus, Dylan McGarry and Heila Lotz-Sisitka offer in their essay, *Learning, Living and Leading into Transgression – A reflection on decolonial praxis in a neoliberal world*: 'This is an injunction to remember to joyously perform the creative release that can be found by placing oneself between troubling contradictions'.[59]

In closing, I like to think, as Spivak suggested, that to be born human is to be born angled toward others.[60] In these pages, reader, I have attempted to angle you towards Pacific Island women leaders. Perhaps a measure of success is whether you experience discomfort and trouble, as I do, yet feel electrified to move forward in action, together.

References

1. Watson, L. *Lilla: International Women's Network.* (https://lillanetwork.wordpress.com/about/)

2. Gaztambide-Fernandez, R. (2012). *Decolonization and the Pegagogy of Solidarity. Decolonization: Indigeneity, Education & Society, 1*(1), pp. 41-67.

3. The Anti-Oppression Network (2015). Allyship. (https://theantioppressionnetwork.com/allyship/)

4. *Women's Leadership and Climate Change in Vanuatu: Yumi Redi* (2017). Produced by: J. Steele. YouTube. (https://www.youtube.com/watch?v=lhsiZrvV53o&t=10s)

5. *Women Vanua'tai Resource Monitors of Land & Sea* **(2018)**. Produced by: J. Steele. YouTube. (https://www.youtube.com/watch?v=UdwS7n9iSps&t=893s)

6. Whyte, K.P. (2018). *Indigenous Science (Fiction) for the Anthropocene: Ancestral Dystopias and Fantasies of Climate Change Crises. Environment and Planning E: Nature and Space, 1*(1-2), pp. 224-242.

7. Chandler, J. (2021). *Not Drowning, Fighting. Insdiestory.org.* (https://insidestory.org.au/not-drowning-fighting)

8. Mbembe, A. (2017). *Critique of Black Reason,* (Translated by L. Dubois) Durham, NC. Duke University Press, p. 161.

9. Mignolo, W.D. and Walsh, C.E. (2018). *On Decoloniality: Concepts, Analytics, Praxis,* Durham, NC. Duke University Press, p. 1.

10. Adichie, C.N. (2009). *The Danger of a Single Story. Ted Global.* (https://www.ted.com/talks/chimamanda_ngozi_adichie_the_danger_of_a_single_story?language=en)

11. Mignolo, W.D. and Walsh, C.E. (2018).

12. Teaiwa, K. (2014). *Consuming Ocean Island: Stories of People and Phosphate from Banaba,* Bloomington. Indiana University Press.

13. Chandler, J. (2021).

14. Hoelle, J. and Kawa, N.C. (2021). *Placing the Anthropos in Anthropocene. Annals of the American Association of Geographers, 111*(3), pp. 655-662.

15. Teaiwa, K. (2014).

16. Chandler, J. (2021).

17. Tabe, T. (2019). *Colonial Archives and the Politics of Migration Memories. Transregional Academies* (https://academies.hypotheses.org/5527)

18. Tabe, T. (2019a). *Climate Change Migration and Displacement: Learning from Past Relocations in the Pacific. Social Sciences, MDPI Open Access Journal, 8*(7), pp. 1-18.

19. PICAN (2020). *Still FIghting for our Survival: PICAN Talanoa on the 5th Anniversary of the Paris Agreement,* Suva, Fiji. *Facebook.* (https://www.facebook.com/CANPacificIslands/videos/375814490370549)

20. PICAN (2020).

21. Teaiwa, K. (2020). *On decoloniality: a view from Oceania. Postcolonial Studies, 23*(4), pp. 601-603. (https://theantioppressionnetwork.com/allyship)

22. Pacific Islands Forum (2020). *forumsec.org*. (https://www.forumsec.org)

23. Wyeth, G. (2018). *Paying Attention to the Blue Pacific. The Diplomat*, 30 October. (https://thediplomat.com/2018/10/paying-attention-to-the-blue-pacific)

24. Teaiwa, K. (2020), p. 4.

25. Mignolo, W.D. and Walsh, C.E. (2018).

26. Wyeth, G. (2018).

27. Hoelle, J. and Kawa, N.C. (2021).

28. ICCA Consortium (2021). *Territories of Life: 2021 Report*, Worldwide. (https://report.territoriesoflife.org/)

29. Ferrari, E. (2020). *Infinite Possibilities in a Finite World: Ontological Politics and Climate Emergency. Irish Studies in International Affairs, 31*, p. 93.

30. Whyte, K.P. (2018), p. 224.

31. Butt, D. (2015). Double-Bound: Gatyatri Chakravorty Spivak's An Aestehtic Education in the Era of Globalization, Melbourne, Australia. Research Unit in Public Cultures, School of Culture and Communication, The University of Melbourne, p. 12. (https://arts.unimelb.edu.au/__data/assets/pdf_file/0005/1867847/rupc-working-paper-butt.pdf)

32. De la Cadena, M. (2020). Protesting from the Uncommons. Indigenous Women and Climate Change, Copenhagen. International Work Group for Indigenous Affairs, pp. 33-42.

33. Viveiros de Castro, E. (1998). Cosmological deixis and Amerindian perspectivism. Journal of the Royal Anthropological Institute, 4, pp. 469-88.

34. Heywood, P. (2017). The Ontological Turn. University of Cambridge. (http://doi.org/10.29164/17ontology)

35. De la Cadena, M. (2020), p. 41.

36. Kothari, A. et al. (2019). *Pluriverse: A Post-Development Dictionary*, New Delhi. Tulika Books.

37. Acha, M.R. (2020). *Climate Justice Must Be Anti-Patriarchal Or It Will Not Be Systemic*, Copenhagen. *Indigenous Women and Climate Change.* International Work Group for Indigenous Affairs, pp. 105-112.

38. Santisteban, R.S. (2020). Indigenous Women & Climate Change: An Introduction. *Indigenous Women and Climate Change*, Copenhagen. *International Work Group for Indigenous Affairs*, pp. 7-14.

39. Hoelle, J. and Kawa, N.C. (2021).

40. Spivak, G.C. (2012). *An Aesthetic Education in the Era of Globalization*, Massachusetts. Harvard University Press, p.104.

41. Huddleston, G. (2015). *An Awkward Stance: On Gayatri Spivak and Double Binds. Critical Literacy: Theories and Practices, 9*(1), pp. 17-28.

42. Spivak, G.C. (2012), pp. 108-109.

43. DIVA for Equality. *The Pacific Community.* (https://www.spc.int/diva-equality)

44. Lorde, A. (2018). *The Master's Tools Will Never Dismantle the Master's House*, London. Penguin Classics.

45. *Statement and poem by Kathy Jetnil-Kijiner, Climate Summit 2014 - Opening Ceremony* (2014). Produced by: United Nations. YouTube. (https://www.youtube.com/watch?v=mc_lgE7TBSY)

46. PICAN (2020).

47. Jetnil-Kijiner, K. (2021). *Remarks for 2020 Pacific Ocean Pacific Climate Change Conference.* (https://www.kathyjetnilkijiner.com/remarks-for-2020-pacific-ocean-pacific-climate-change-conference/)

48. Pacific Islands Students Fighting Climate Change. (https://www.pisfcc.org/)

49. Ferrari, E. (2020).

50. Mignolo, W.D. and Walsh, C.E. (2018).

51. De la Cadena, M. (2020), p. 41.

52. Kulundu-Bolus, I., McGarry, D., and Lotz-Sisitka, H. (2020). *Learning, Living and Leading Into Transgression -- A Reflection On Decolonial Praxis in a Neoliberal World. Southern African Journal of Environmental Education, 36,* pp. 111-130.

53. Haraway, D. (2016). *Staying with the Trouble: Making Kind in the Chthulucene,* Durham. Duke University Press.

54. Tsing, A. (2005). *Friction: An Ethnography of Global Connection,* Princeton, NJ. Princeton University Press.

55. Gaztambide-Fernandez, R. (2012).

56. Mbembe, A. and Goldberg, D.T. (2018). *In Conversation; Achille Mbembe & David Theo Goldberg on 'Critique of Black Reason'.* (https://www.theoryculturesociety.org/: https://www.theoryculturesociety.org/blog/interviews-achille-mbembe-david-theo-goldberg-critique-black-reason)

57. Bhabha, H. (1994). *The Location of Culture,* Oxfordshire, UK. Routledge.

58. Ermine, W. (2007). *The Ethical Space of Engagement. Indigenous Law Journal, 6,* pp. 193-203.

59. Kulundu-Bolus, I., McGarry, D., and Lotz-Sisitka, H. (2020), p. 120.

60. Spivak, G.C. (2012), p. 98.

Droughts in Lamu County

Fazeela Mubarak

Lamu county, located on Kenya's north coast and bordering Somalia, is made up of about 65 islands and mainland areas. As Kenya is situated on the equator, our seasons are divided into the long and short dry seasons and the long and short rains. Farmers, villagers and even fishermen rely on these cycles to plan their crops, planting cycles and even their water collection points around the areas they live. The knowledge passed on from one generation to another ensures that they did not settle along migration routes of wildlife, which greatly reduced incidences of conflict. This knowledge was revered so much that community members were able to predict the droughts or flooding that rarely occurred, and when they did occur, they were prepared for it. Sadly, as the climate breaks down, the weather patterns are not only unpredictable, but the community members are unprepared for this, and therefore losses are more.

In September 2016, as a regular volunteer in the Tsavo Conservation Area, I had noticed that the waterholes in the wildlife habitats started drying out faster than anticipated. If the water holes were not quickly attended to, we would risk wildlife, as well as causing elephants to go in search of water in nearby villages, damaging properties and posing a threat to humans. With my friend Tiju Aziz, we set out to ensure water was delivered to the animals, and we sought to restore boreholes in the area that would see a sustainable water source for the park. Unknown to us at that time, this was actually a preparation for the upcoming humongous task we'd have in a few months.

Fast forward to mid-March 2017, and the much anticipated long rains after a prolonged dry season failed to appear. On 16th March, a video was circulating on social media, taken on the mainland of Lamu in a town called Chomo. It showed hippos in a shallow water pond, clinging on to the little bits of moisture, their young ones in the middle, mothers trying to keep them safe from getting burnt by the harsh sun. Around them lay carcasses of other hippos – probably relatives that didn't make it, plus buffalo that had become stuck in the mud and couldn't make it out. The post included a passionate plea for help from one of the residents stating how the wildlife in the area was suffering, how the lack of water had led to wildlife going into nearby villages and inadvertently destroying crops on small farms and at times causing injuries to children. Since the rains had failed, the little the villagers had was destroyed.

Due to its location and remoteness, it was difficult to get help to this area. I was at work in Nairobi. But when I saw this, especially after my previous experience in Tsavo dealing with the water issues, I called Tiju, who is based near that area, and we quickly discussed what we could do as quickly as possible. With advice from the rangers on the ground, we began our task to urgently source hay to supplement the diet of the hippos and buffalos.

I made enquiries and luckily was able to find a supplier of hay and a transporter. After work, I visited the hay depot in Thika and waited for the driver, although it was getting dark. The hay promptly arrived; I had managed to procure over 300 bails. The hippos will be happy, I thought to myself. Half my work was done, I just had to ensure that it was transported a little more than 800 km to its destination. Time was of the essence, and it was quickly ticking away.

The driver who would transport the hay kept making promises that he was getting closer, from a distance of 200 km. After a four-hour wait, it dawned on me that the driver was not going to come, I had a whole lorry full of hay that needed to go, the lorry driver was getting impatient. I was frantically making calls. It was almost 10 pm. My best bet, according to the supplier of the hay, was to get to the highway leading to Mombasa. There, he told me, I wouldn't miss an empty lorry heading toward the coast. Demand for these trucks was low, he said, so I'd get a good price, and the hay would be halfway to its destination by dawn. Knowing I had nothing to lose, we headed to the site with the hay loaded with a trusted friend by my side. We parked by the highway, which was close to a few roadside motels, and waited for empty lorries to pass by. By midnight, we had managed to get only one, but he was charging too much and would not relent. We couldn't take his services. We waited. Tense moments as it was in the middle of the night, and the traffic had started to ease. Would the hay make it on time?

Finally, a lorry parked nearby and was willing to take it at a reasonable cost. With the help of a few volunteers, the task of transferring hay in the middle of the night started. After two hours, it was finally done, a I breathed a sigh of relief as I saw the back lights of the lorry disappear along the highway, headed toward the hippos. My adrenaline levels started to drop as I headed home, tired and looking for a few hours' sleep. Little did I know that this was just a small taste of what was to come in the next 45 days, and that it would take me to the heart of it all and change everything I had ever known about nature.

Devastation

The next day quickly dawned, and I rushed to make travel arrangements to get to Lamu and meet with the rangers I would be working with over the next six weeks. In the meantime, I kept up with the movements of the hay, which finally reached Lamu in the late evening.

I got a flight for around midday the next day that would take me to Manda Island, and from there I would connect to the Lamu mainland where we would carry out the relief projects. The view from the plane before we landed was of mangroves, channels of the ocean, greens and blues – nothing compared to the chaos on the mainland. I was welcomed by the rangers of the area and, after visiting their office, we took a boat to the mainland, from where we then took a vehicle, loaded it with the hay and went on our way to one of the worst hit areas: Chomo Dam.

The roads at that time were not tarmacked, so it took us at least an hour to get to the dam. After meandering through bush and narrow paths, we finally reached it. What I saw still haunts me today. As we neared the spot, we were hit with a putrid smell of decaying wildlife carcasses; bones were littered all around; the bodies of dead hippos rotted at the side of the water; a huge buffalo was stuck in the middle of the reservoir as he had tried to get a few drops from the drying mud. A whole family of hippos – luckily all of them alive – huddled in a small section of the mud, which was quickly drying up from the fierce heat. A tiny hippo calf was in the middle of the hippo pod, in a small puddle of mud to safeguard him from the heat and from predators such as the hyena who frequented the area. A baboon with her young clinging to her belly paced up and down, looking for water. The massive reservoir was nothing but a dried-up bank with cracks.

We set out the hay as it was now nearing dusk and the predators would arrive soon. We were dangerously close to the infamous Boni Forest that is known to harbour militants from neighbouring Somalia. They regularly raid the nearby farms, at times causing casualties. That's why we were always escorted by armed rangers.

Each day, our work started at the crack of dawn to make the best use of the daylight, and we left just as it was about to get dark, resolving to come back the next day and work out what we could do.

On the second day, I waited for Tiju to arrive. She had experience with drought situations in the park. I believed that, with her expertise, we would lead a more efficient project that would have a long-term impact. She arrived early in the morning and, after a briefing from the rangers, we decided to visit Chomo and the other areas that were experiencing difficulties: Mpeketoni, Mkunumbi and Lake Kenyatta.

We started out by going by boat from Lamu Island to the mainland, where we went on to the main offices of the wildlife service. There we loaded up on hay for distribution to other places that had not yet received any. The plan was to go ahead with the rangers' vehicle and to deliver water to Chomo Dam for the hippos, while Tiju and the other rangers went on to the other sites in Mpeketoni and Kibokoni.

It was another hot day with the sun's heat scorching; we had to act fast. I met the ranger, Adan, but there was a problem: the lorry with the water bowser had broken down. Nothing from jump starts to pushes worked. Time was ticking. We had to act. I went on to the main road with another friend, Huzeima, who was accompanying me. We had to get another truck with a water bowser as soon as possible. As luck would have it, we saw a large tanker with water heading for delivery to a nearby town. We waved at the driver to stop. He did and we spoke to him. He was making a delivery that had already been paid for, and the customer was waiting. I pleaded with the driver, explaining to him what the issue was and that if we didn't help the wildlife, they would all die. He listened to me and told me that he was willing to take it to Chomo Dam if his boss would allow it. He quickly dialled the number and spoke to his boss. After a little bit of convincing, he agreed. The hippos of Chomo Dam would get some relief from the sun.

With my guide, Huzeima, we boarded the truck and headed toward the site. The homesteads we passed were spaced out, at times kilometres apart, and it was common to see small forests between neighbours. It was easy to see why this area was frequented by wildlife and, now that the rains were delayed, the animals in their desperation for water would come into the homesteads, destroying precious water reserves that had been collected by women who had trekked for several miles.

The sand path we took was dotted with palm trees, so the driver had to be extra careful as he took the sandy corners, beeping in advance when nearing blind spots. Though it was only about 30 km from the point where we'd found the truck, it took us more than an hour to reach the dam. No sooner had we reached it when the hippos sadly looking at us the day before, got up. It looked like they had gotten a new bout of energy as soon as they had heard the engine from a distance.

Credit: Tiju Aziz and Fazeela Mubarak

The alpha male stood and approached the truck. He was calm. They knew water was there. From a safe distance, we got out, and the driver revved up the water pump. The hippos wallowed in the little bit that had poured into the dam. The calf surfaced and wiggled his tiny pink bottom at the joy of just having water after a long time. The mother baboon with her baby from the previous day rushed to the dam and gulped down water and then gave some to her baby. The buffalo stuck in the middle of the dam was relieved; there was finally some water for drinking.

As the water slowly entered the dried dam, there appeared a small puddle. In the distance, in the dried grass, we spotted an upright tail running fast toward the dam. It was a warthog coming through! He came, rested on his forelegs, and gulped at water. Cattle egrets glided through, followed by doves; a small kingfisher bird perched in one of the acacia trees, patiently waiting for the big birds to finish so it could also have a dip. Just a few minutes after we had started pumping the water, the area had gone from a quiet, desperate and almost lifeless place to a dynamic oasis full of life. After pumping 30,000 litres, we had exhausted all the water.

I had hoped that the mud softening would help the buffalo become unstuck, but he still seemed unable to move. Leaving him there would mean he would either die of dehydration or starvation, condemning him to a slow painful death. We had to act quickly. I called Tiju and asked her how things were on her side. It turned out that she had come across the same issue and was heading out to get ropes from the nearest hardware store. I asked the truck driver if there was any hardware store around. We headed back to the main road and got the toughest ropes we could find and headed back to the dam. One of the rangers from the wildlife service tied the rope to the horn of the buffalo, (which was incredibly dangerous in normal situations and only possible because the buffalo was weak, exhausted and dehydrated) in the mud and fastened the other end to the water truck. Then began the task of hauling the buffalo out. The tyres screeched against the dry mud and, after a lot of pulling, the buffalo slowly edged out of the mud. After a few minutes, he was out! But no sooner had he scratched the mud off when he ran toward us. We rushed to the truck and got inside. The buffalo came close, looked at us in the eye and walked away. This would become our routine for the next 45 days as we did our best to keep the wildlife alive.

Short-term solutions

About 80 km away, in Mpeketoni village, Tiju was met by the village elder, Ahmed. The situation was dire: the nearby dam had completely dried out, with carcasses of hippo strewn all over. Some had already decayed to bone, and an overbearing stench of death and despair hung over everyone. There were constant raids on the community's farms from hippo and buffalo. The nights were worse as they were cooler and more wildlife came in search of food and water, going into people's homesteads and causing damage and injuries. We had a gigantic task ahead of us. We had to act fast to stop the wildlife from going into people's farms. The wildlife needed water.

However, it wasn't just a case of pouring water into the dam as this would mean that the water would be contaminated by the rotting carcasses. Tiju and Ahmed came up with a brilliant short-term plan that would help the immediate situation. They went to the town and bought empty 200 litre barrels. They could cut them vertically to make troughs, which they could fill with water and put around the dam with hay. At night, buffalo, hippo and hyena came around these barrels to feed. The rangers volunteered to keep an eye on them to protect them from poachers. During the day, the local herders brought their livestock to feed there too. Over the next few days, the wildlife conflicts and incidences of the raids in the area reduced drastically.

After organising the logistics for Mpeketoni and Chomo Dam, the next big task was Lake Kenyatta. As we came near the lake, we could see the devastation caused by the drought. Most of it had dried out; what had been an expansive water pan was now just cracked and dry mud, leaving casualties of hippo and the community living nearby. We met two women, Khadija and Fatma, from the community, who owned fishponds from which they earned a living.

I returned to Nairobi as our funds were running low, and I had to do my best to raise the attention of the country and the world at large. What was happening was of catastrophic proportions, made only more difficult by the fact that North Kenya's rural coast had such limited access. Luckily, a reporter from a tabloid had picked up our story and wanted to publish it. Africa Geographic allowed us to use their blog page to tell of our work. This gave us a much needed boost, and we received small donations of US$10 to US$25. This helped us continue for a couple more days and covered transport of the water, fuel costs and liaising with the community.

Sadly, this was the only publicity we got as we tried our best to draw attention to the crisis. I called and emailed several local and international publications, to which I got absolutely no response, except for a few system-generated emails. Several "animal welfare" organisations with a massive social media reach were even on this list, but it was to no avail. We had to rely on our own social media posts, with a combined reach of less than 3,000. We resorted to posting on Facebook wildlife groups, which was received well at first, but then we were subjected to cyber-bullying and comments related to our religion. It was only the Kenyan media outlet, The Star, that published a small article at the bottom of page 5. The group had come in and filmed the situation, but it only aired almost a month after the rains finally started.

By this time, at the beginning of April, the rains were still nowhere to be seen, and we had thousands of wildlife and livestock that depended on our water delivery to stay alive. Almost every day we had incidences of wildlife that were dehydrated or stuck in the dried up waterholes and needed to be rescued. This meant increased costs to mobilise rangers.

One of the most heart-breaking incidents we had was of a baby buffalo that had been abandoned by its mother due to the lack of water. The rangers came across this baby, gave him water and took him to the nearest livestock shed. It was almost dark. The baby was severely dehydrated and in need of medical attention. The ranger who had found him, Adan, made frantic calls for a vet, and the only one that could make it would take at least a day to get there, given the remoteness of the area. All we could do was wait. Each second felt like an hour. In the wee hours of the next day, his breathing declined rapidly. We saw him take his final breaths of his short-lived life. Another victim of climate change – so young, gone forever.

A look to the future

With funds running low, we had to make the best use of the limited resources we had. The water levels in Chomo Dam had been stabilised, so we reduced the amount of water we poured to 20,000 litres per day. One of the wildlife service vehicles was repaired, which saved us costs of hiring a car. Next was Mkunumbi. Tiju and the village elders spoke to the community, explaining how vital it was that we all worked together to reduce conflicts, save wildlife and protect the individuals' property from damage. The immediate task was to clear the massive dried reservoir that still had dozens of hippo and buffalo carcasses. Once the dam was clear, we could look into filling it with water or, if the rains came, so that the water would be fit for livestock consumption.

About 20 people from the community came forward and cleared the carcasses, silt and bones from the area. This took about four days to complete. It was heartening to see a community that had suffered so much from wildlife injuries and destruction of their property, come together to look out for their fellow creatures who were suffering in this drought.

Credit: Tiju Aziz and Fazeela Mubarak

As we worked to solve the immediate crisis, we explored lasting solutions as one thing was clear: climate change meant that we would experience this again in the near future. The next task was to rebuild a collapsed wall nearby that had been vital to storing the water and prevent it from running into the ocean. With a small purchase of stone, cement and our supply of labour, the men got to work. After another week, our wall was ready. When the rains came, our dam would be full of water and sustain the community for about nine months.

Limited resources

At Lake Kenyatta, with the situation getting desperate, Tiju worked out a brilliant way with the community to get water flowing. Since it was a lake bed, they figured that the water pan wouldn't be far from the surface, so they dug through some rocky patches that had been wet and found a small stream of water. They continued to dig in several places, and these formed several tiny streams that made a puddle of water. After a few days, there were several small ponds with fresh water that would sustain the wildlife in the area for the next few weeks.

As the rangers delivered water trucks to the dam, they often came across girls and women who had to trek long miles to access water for their homes and livestock. This meant girls had to skip out on school, be in danger of being attacked by wildlife or, even worse, militants. They were some of the other casualties of climate change. Whenever rangers came across them, they would fill up their water containers and give them transport so they could safely return to their homesteads.

Finally, after weeks of making rounds to the various sites in the scorching heat, we were making progress with limited resources. The work had fallen into a seamless routine of water and hay deliveries, wildlife rescue efforts and working with the community on any issues that came up.

We could concentrate on sustainable water solutions, starting with Mkunumbi, one of the areas hardest hit by the drought. The biggest challenge we had was the lack of funding again. We had to make use of what we had in the most effective way. For a continuous source of water, a borehole had to be constructed. This would ensure that water would be available for the community and the livestock throughout the year. We sought quotations from reputable companies. Sadly, however, the amounts were more than 10 times the remaining funds in our kitty. We had to look for another way to go about this.

Tiju, on the recommendation of community elders, located a traditional driller, Faiswal, who used the indigenous methods of the Giriama people – knowledge that had been handed down from generations – to locate the depth of the water. The best part was that it would cost us about US$1,500, just about the maximum our budget would allow. Faiswal identified the freshwater spot within two days. It was a couple of metres down in the earth, and work started immediately. After tending their farms and livestock, the community members came to the borehole site and helped with labour, making the work move faster. After two weeks, the borehole was ready! Once they had installed the last parts of the hand pump, it was ready to be used. The borehole was commissioned by the village elder, Mzee Ahmed, followed by community members who came with their plastic jerry cans to fill with water for their homes and livestock. In the evening, water was pumped and filled the dam, so wildlife visiting in the night could drink and avoid going into people's farms.

We visited the next site, Chomo Dam. The good news was that there was water, again a few hundred metres in the ground. It would cost about the same amount of money to do. And, sadly, our funds had dwindled, and all we had was a few days' supplies of hay and fuel to take us through. We longed to hear the croaking of the frogs as the elders said the noise heralded rain. Not even that happened. All we could do was pray... and pray we did, with rangers, with farmers, with children, with mosque and church elders.

Work continues

It was nearing the middle of May. It had been over 40 gruelling days of continuous logistics planning, fund raising, animal rescues and working on sustainable water solutions that would see the communities through another situation like this, if it ever came around again. We were visiting the site at Mkunumbi to assess the borehole and see if we could have a solar powered pump installed so that water would flow directly back into the dam. After a long day of meeting with the community members and talking about what more we could do, we retired to our hostels nearby. As we neared the vehicles in the early evening, a miracle happened: there were raindrops, tiny glistening glitters of hope, followed by the scent of wet mud. The wind had changed. The skies turned to grey with clouds heavy with rain. Small drops graduated into drizzles, and finally there was thunder, sweet thunder. In the distance, we could hear hippos grunting in relief. There was gurgling and the splashing of water – they were swimming in the dam that had filled up instantly. It was a luxury they hadn't experienced for almost two months. The buffalos let out moos. For the first time in 45 days, we slept in peace, knowing we wouldn't have to look for rain clouds the next day.

The next morning, we went to check out the dam where the wall had been built at Mkunumbi, and were delighted to see that it had started filling up. There were heavy rains predicted for the next few days, which meant that, for the meantime, we could return to our homes, take a much needed break and strategise for long-term solutions for the remaining two sites. Our funds were exhausted, as was our limited audience from our continuous calls for donations.

We were constantly in touch with the community elders and rangers from the different areas as, finally, the places started to regenerate. Our borehole at Mkunumbi was still serving the community and saved women trekking to get water.

In June, I met a wonderful woman, Brandy from Taiwan, who had come to Kenya to learn about grassroots conservation. We formed a small online Facebook page – Wild Heart Kenya – where we documented conservation projects to reduce human-wildlife conflicts and to raise awareness about how climate change was affecting communities living close to wildlife. This helped us build a base of supporters for our work.

In January 2018, we visited the sites to see how the reservoirs were doing. Sadly, again, the waterholes had started to dry up. This time though, we had experience with this, and we did another crowdfunding effort where we got support from Taiwan through Brandy. We had built a close community through our Facebook page, and we used this to gather support for a new borehole for Chomo Dam. A week later, we got the funds and the work started. After a month, our borehole was ready for community members to draw water and to fill the reservoir for the wildlife.

A month later, we had another sponsor. The Young Muslim Association installed solar panels to power the pumping of water from the borehole. Community members came in and helped to look after the panels. Water was pumped every day and, bit by bit, the area transformed into an oasis for wildlife and livestock. School-going girls from the surrounding area could concentrate on their studies as their trekking time in search of water was drastically reduced. Poachers coming to hunt wildlife were chased away and reported to the authorities. It was quite a sight to see this area bounce back as the same community that had been affected by those conflicts from wildlife had now become the guardians of it.

Today, we visit the area as much as we can when the conditions allow as these places are under constant threat to attacks from militants. The hippo pod at Chomo Dam has now grown bigger, and the bird life is thriving. We hope we will be prepared for the next crisis, which – with how the climate currently continues to change – every year is different with new challenges posed. We keep our hopes up and continue lobbying for better climate mitigation practises and policies.

Local Agro-ecological Transition in Brazil

Concepts for a bottom-up perspective towards a sustainable and inclusive food system

Rodrigo Machado Moreira

Introduction

The current agricultural model is unsustainable, especially with global warming, growing social inequality and accelerated biodiversity loss. Farming today systematically contaminates drinking water and aquatic ecosystems, the people who work in pesticide factories, those who apply the chemicals to crops and consumers too. This leads to a food system incompatible with an agro-ecosystem´s resilience.

The main goal of this chapter is to describe a local agro-ecological transition. I suggest actions, guidelines and indicators, especially in these turbulent socio-political times when Brazil´s democracy and natural resources are under growing attack.

Brazil´s current dilemma regarding the shaping of a sustainable food system

Brazil is an example of a critical situation being shaped by a globalised and unsustainable food system, worsened by ultra-neoliberal economic policies pushed by international capital and local rentier elites, along with the dismantling of participatory citizenship. The process reached new pace with the election of president Jair Bolsonaro in 2018.

Politically, Bolsonaro´s government has demolished various civil society participation spaces, starting with the National Council of Food Security (CONSEA). CONSEA was one of the main props sustaining the intersection of family farming, agro-ecology, solidarity economy, nutritional and healthy food demands.

The rise of such a ´leader` came about after six years of political and economic turmoil, due to political disputes after former President Dilma Roussef's re-election in 2014. The instability increased poverty and social inequality between 2014 and 2018.

Bolsonaro´s government has led to several setbacks in agrarian, social and environmental policies, directly affecting the Indigenous and quilombola people, plus small family farmers and land reform settlements. These setbacks resulted in huge properties being sold to foreign buyers without congressional approvals and water privatisation attempts.

The Amazon was central to the new government agenda, attacking people who preserve forests, fields and waters. By promoting the Amazon as a space populated by resources to be explored, Bolsonaro's government has caused a new wave of deforestation and attacked Indigenous rights to land demarcation.

Together with all these national policy setbacks, it is important to realise that this destruction presents a significant obstacle to agro-ecological transition. More on this in a moment.

As a result of the green revolution's institutional, technical and political legacy, especially in intensive agriculture areas, such barriers are preventing the emergence of a technological innovation system compatible with agro-ecological transitions.

Nonetheless, efforts are being made to remodel food systems through agro-ecology and it is urgent that we integrate and stimulate key actions in the areas of knowledge building, social innovation and public and intersectoral policies, all connected to networks and territories.

Despite the demolition of national public policies, it is relevant to point out that 10 Brazilian states discuss and/or implement regional policies on agro-ecology and organic production (PEAPOs). In addition, municipalities are beginning to organise local agro-ecology policies.

Local agro-ecological transition: conceptual evolution from *praxis* in Botucatu, São Paulo

The main conceptual and methodological basis of the transition we are referring to is agro-ecology, which is a trans-disciplinary field born in the 1980s as a convergence of social and natural science and popular epistemology. It covers the principles and guidelines to implement real sustainable rural development.

Agro-ecology is based on participatory action research and extension agendas, and it questions the research and technology transfer/diffusion system paradigm. Agro-ecology also demands working on a new food pedagogy. It can help us to recognise the locally needed social relation transformations, especially in gender inequality and feminist claims.

As a social movement within territories, agro-ecology involves knowledge building, socialisation and territorial articulation of agro-ecological practices, technologies and experiences, adjusted to local specificities. It is, indeed, becoming a broad field of thought and action that integrates sciences, practices and movements to induce changes in all parts of the food system.

It is clear that an 'agro-ecological transition' is a multi-dimensional process, not only because of food system complexity but also because paths and arrival points are permeated by social, environmental, cultural, ethical and political needs for sustainable development.

An agro-ecological transition for farmers means expanding production spaces and increasing the capacity for social and economic reproduction through agriculture. Cooperation and agricultural greening acquires a positive synergy[13] and farmers are pushed to develop a coherence between how they manage, organise and relate to their agro-ecosystem.[14]

A local agro-ecological transition involves creating a sustainable local culture that brings food production and consumption closer together and necessitates policies to do that.[15] It transforms local food systems based on equity, participation, democracy and social justice and to restore and protect local life support systems.[16]

Local development should be based on social change towards a broad/extensive sustainability framework to re-direct society and nature´s co-evolution at a local level. If based on cooperation and strong bottom-up processes within all components of the food systems, socio-political changes can nourish an agro-ecological transition within and outside agro-ecosystems.[17] The ideal sustainable agriculture 'locus' is family farming[18] and peasant agriculture, which have an intrinsic ecological rationale. [19] This indicates that the priority is to build the necessary conditions for the production and reproduction of small-scale agriculture so it can be viable based on the strategic

alliances between movements for agro-ecology and food sovereignty.[20]

Local agro-ecological transition does not mean, however, that entrepreneurial and corporate farms do not need their socio-technological transitions'. On the contrary, a transition landmark for sustainability considering all agrarian styles is needed to mitigate, adapt and prevent the negative socio-environmental impacts of the current agricultural models.

Finally, it is about developing a broad set of disincentives for unsustainable industrial agriculture and strong incentives for agro-ecological transitions. Some incentives can be seen at a recent study that mapped 1,500 local laws in all five Brazilian regions that can support this change process, carried out by the National Agro-ecology Network.[21]

Local agro-ecological transition concept, dimensions, guidelines and indicators

Local agro-ecological transition can be defined as a set of endogenous and participatory social processes reflecting gradual transitions from the current local food system to one governed by ecological principles.

As agro-ecological transition develops at a farm level, support and guidance are needed via market formation and public policy building, implementation, development and monitoring. These policies have to invest and govern necessary changes for local food production and consumption, considering agro-ecological rural extension, participatory research, permanent educational and communicative processes and social and organisational networks recognition, formation and promotion.

Practical experiences in the territories serves as 'agro-ecological lighthouses', anchored by local networks around a system of values, thought and action compatible with the processes that farmers and consumers go through. Social forces contained in a local movement, articulated through forms of collective social action, therefore, increases popular organisation for a healthy, sustainable, nutrition-sensitive and inclusive local food system.

Advancing local agro-ecological transition requires guaranteeing networks of vertical and horizontal social cooperation within the scope of three dimensions: eco-structural (compatible management systems and technologies); socio- political (private and public support institutions); and micro-sociocultural (individual and collective cooperation dynamics).

These concepts were developed by analysing the municipality of Botucatu, in the state of São Paulo in Brazil, based on a variety of participatory action research processes, semi structured interviews, workshops and local advocacy experience.[22] The research involved farmers, technicians and researchers from public and non-governmental private sectors. It designed the following action lines, guidelines and monitoring indicators (Table 1).[23]

Table 1: Dimensions, lines of action and analysis and indicators for monitoring the local agro-ecological transition

ECO-STRUCTURAL DIMENSION From production to local marketing		
Action and Analysis lines and programmes	Guidelines	Indicators
Diagnosis, design and redesign of sustainable agroecosystems	Participatory diagnoses of the territory	External inputs; Local inputs; subsystems and mediators in between; agroecosystem analysed; sustainability indicators in terms of impact assessment and set of ecological practices; number of farmers registered as organic farmers or in the agro-ecological transition programme.
	Perform Agroecosystem Analysis[24]	
	Encourage agro-ecological innovations in agroecosystems	
	Qualify production and exchange of ecologically based inputs	
Agro-ecological seeds and breeds	Perform agrobiodiversity participatory diagnoses[25]	Local agrobiodiversity; number and diversity of farmers and institutions involved; seeds and breeds rescued and/or multiplied locally; tests performed and seeds exchanged.
	Promote participatory improvement of Creole seeds and seed banks	
	Encourage local and regional 'in situ' conservation programmes with seeds and breeds adapted to local conditions	
Recycling in rural areas and composting of urban waste	Structuring systems for collecting recyclable materials in rural areas.	Number of farmers recycling; tonnage of compost produced distributed or sold annually; composting urban waste coverage locally.
	Produce and distribute compost made with domestic organic waste from urban areas	
Environmental recovery,[26] conservation and protection	Recover rural roads and landscapes and recover and protect natural areas	Deficit of forests; landscape connectivity; farmers engagement in contingency plans against environmental disasters; rural infrastructure resilience and stability.
	Connect landscapes through ecologic corridors	
	Municipal contingency plans for environmental disasters in rural areas	

Direct and indirect marketing	Support and structure public and private spaces for local sale by local ecology-based product[27]	Accessibility to local marketing spaces; number of CSA and other initiatives; number of farmers involved in local and regional circuits; local network density between consumers and farmers; farmers income.
	Encourage C.S.A projects, baskets and other forms of association between networks of local producers and consumers	
	Build expedition centres, intelligence and communication for local and regional sales circuits	
Adding value to small-scale agricultural production	Enable artisanal agro-industrialisation	Functional and legalised artisanal agro-industries; farmers engaged into organic quality protocols and processes; existence and functioning of SIM (municipal inspection system).
	Guarantee small and medium scale agriculture access to quality seals based on participatory approaches	
Income diversification in rural areas	Carry out activities to qualify local production of other local, cultural and environmental products	Agricultural and non-agricultural activities providing income to rural areas
	Create opportunities for local and regional market growth for local, cultural and environmental products	
	Qualify non-agricultural entrepreneurial activities in family farming and medium producers	

Table 2: Dimensions, lines of action and analysis and indicators for monitoring the local agro-ecological transition (continued)

SOCIO-POLITICAL DIMENSION Examples of social institutions and public policies for local agro-ecological transition		
Action and Analysis lines and programmes	**Guidelines**	**Indicators**
Education and training in agro-ecology	Innovate in pedagogical plans (methods and content) of all educational levels[28]	Number and diversity of courses that incorporated agro-ecology in a transversal way; students access to topics related to agro-ecology; courses and training activities in agro-ecology; teaching materials produced.
	Train farmers, technicians and researchers	
	Promote exchanges between conventional farmers and those at different levels of agro-ecological transition	
	Prepare and reproduce teaching materials on topics related to agro-ecology	

Table 2 (cont.) Dimensions, lines of action and analysis and indicators for monitoring the Local Agro-ecological Transition

SOCIO-POLITICAL DIMENSION Science & technology social institutions and public policies for local agroecological transition		
Action and Analysis lines and programmes	**Guidelines**	**Indicators**
Food sovereignty and security	Value and increase productive yards.	Food sovereignty biophysical indicators (mileage of local consumed food and energy); quality and quantity of available food produced locally based on agro-ecological principles in private and institutional markets; tonnage and diversity of pesticides applied annually; level of use of ecological pest and disease management practices; intersectoral presence in SISAN (national food security system) governance; council representation level; municipal food security plan and indicators; diversity of participation in plan monitoring;
	Encourage the agricultural use of urban space[29]	
	Ensure legislative and administrative conditions for institutional purchases by family farmers.	
	Ensure local surveillance of food and natural resources contaminated by pesticides and reducing pesticide use.	
	Ensure the functioning of the SISAN (national food security system) components in the municipality	

Table 2 (cont.): Dimensions, lines of action and analysis and indicators for monitoring the Local Agro-ecological Transition

SOCIOCULTURAL DIMENSION Mobilisation, cooperation and communication for local agro-ecological transition		
Action and analysis lines and programmes	**Guidelines**	**Indicators**
Collective social action[30]	Qualify existing organisations for its self-management	Number of qualified organisations and groups; levels of participation within organised groups; number and diversity of groups and local networks engaged in the local agro-ecological transition; projects developed towards local agro-ecological transition.
	Expand famers and socio-technical organisational capacity	
	Strengthen the capacity of these organisations to raise funds and develop projects	
	Empower informal and formal groups	
	Support new groups and networks formation	
Social cooperation and popular and solidarity economy	Carry out practices of mutual support/ reciprocity and cooperation at different levels	Number and diversity of self-management organisations; number of microcredit projects; number of cooperative and associative credit projects; number of joint efforts carried out; other mutual support practices.
	Promote access to individual microcredit and subsidised agricultural credit	
Rural women[31] and youth	Perform participatory diagnoses of gender and youth	Level of awareness for gender equality; women involvement in local agro-ecological network; women's collectives or groups; youth groups or collectives involved; projects managed by women or young people; women and young peoples' level of participation in agricultural and non-agricultural work; credit projects accessed by women and youth; number of young people, women or neo-rural families involved with the local agro-ecological transition.
	Create local development projects with rural women and young people	
	Promote training activities specifically developed for rural youth and women.	

Conclusions

Brazil has shown that a 'top-down' (national level) perspective has its limitations under governments that can shift rapidly every four years from a progressive and democratic tendency to an authoritarian and conservative one. The national perspective should be considered when it is possible. However, it is also prudent to avoid creating a false sense that agro-ecology is advancing when it might not be.

Therefore, we advocate for 'municipality' development level as one that can create legislative and executive governmental and non-governmental measures based on social control instruments capable of conferring space for building agro-ecological territories and changing local food systems. Local councils and social movements are key factors to implement local agro-ecological transition. A local agro-ecological transition is show below.

Figure 1: Schematic view of the dimensions and lines of analysis and action for local agro-ecological transition. Source: End Note 25 – Moreira (2012).

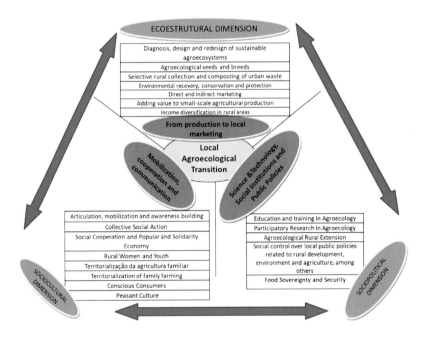

This scheme has been discussed and developed to some extent in Botucatu since 2003, which led to a recognition of the need for an agro-ecology policy at the city master plan in 2017. In 2019, this proposal was debated and included, partly, into the municipal food and nutritional security policy, through the Botucatu municipal food and nutrition security council).

If the local agro-ecological transition is applied, the result will be a future with:

- a higher number of farmers engaged in designing and managing sustainable agroecosystems resilient to climate change
- better seeds and animal breeds adapted to local small farmer's conditions
- better use of solid waste and local nutrient cycling from local food consumption
- increase in the availability of organic fertilisers
- closer relations between producers and consumers of local food
- increases in the local supply of agro-ecological food at a fair price
- greater 'added value' to locally produced food
- reduction of the local ecological footprint related to food consumption
- better conditions for reproducing family-farming methods
- greater number of conscious and engaged local consumers
- stronger collective social action related to changes in the local food system
- greater public resources investments towards healthy, sustainable and inclusive food systems
- higher appreciation of women and young people's role in agriculture
- more and better access to land for family farmers and other small-scale food producers
- stronger local countryside culture
- more access to health, telecommunication, culture and opportunities to generate income from high quality local food production
- more participatory education, research and rural extension to boost local agro-ecological transition
- decreasing levels of pesticide residues in the municipality's soil and drinking water
- increase in soil biological quality and conservation conditions in the municipality
- greater social participation, social control and intersectoral tools for fomenting public support towards local food system redesign
- greater high quality local food production autonomy in
- less poverty and more opportunities for local economic development based on social inclusion and solidarity economy
- and greater sovereignty and food and nutritional security towards ensuring human right to adequate food

In 2021, our local agro-ecological transition proposal is a reference to build Botucatu agro-ecology policy as a la, based on a participatory approach involving local councils of food and nutrition security, environment and rural development and a great variety on local stakeholders. This makes local development level an arena for political agro-ecology to minimise the negative effects of national policy dismantling and industrial agriculture advances and to give, effectively, some chance of sustainability.

References

1. Niederle, P. et al. (2019). Narrative disputes over family-farming public policies in Brazil: conservative attacks and restricted countermovements. Latin American Research Review, 54(3), pp. 707–720.

2. Cepal (Comissão Econômica para a América Latina e o Caribe) (2019). Panorama social da América Latina. (https://repositorio.cepal.org/bitstream/handle/11362/45090/S1900909_pt.pdf?sequence=1&isAllowed=y)

3. Brasil (2019a). Lei Nº 13.844, de 18 de Junho de 2019. Dispõe sobre a conversão da medida provisória nº 870 de 01/01/2019. Presidência da República-Secretaria-Geral – subchefia para Assuntos Jurídicos. (http://www.planalto.gov.br/ccivil_03/_ato2019-2022/2019/ Lei/L13844.htm); Brasil (2019b). Medida provisória Nº 910, de 10 de Dezembro de 2019. Altera a Lei nº 11.952, de 25 de junho de 2009, que dispõe sobre a regularização fundiária das ocupações incidentes em terras situadas em áreas da União e da outras providencias. Presidência da República-Secretaria-Geral – subchefia para Assuntos Jurídicos. (http://www.planalto.gov.br/ccivil_03/_ato2019-2022/2019/Mpv/mpv910.html); Brasil (2019c). Projeto de Lei 3.261/2019 do Senado Federal. Atualiza o marco regulatório do saneamento básico no Brasil. (https://www.camara.leg.br/proposicoesWeb/fichadetramitacao?idProposicao=2207613); Brasil (2019d). Projeto de Lei nº 2963, de 2019. Senado Federal. Regulamenta a aquisição, posse e o cadastro de propriedade rural por pessoa física ou jurídica estrangeira. (https://www25.senado.leg.br/web/atividade/materias/-/materia/136853); Brasil (2019e). Lei Nº 13.870, de 17 de setembro de 2019 amplia posse de arma no meio rural. (https://www2.camara.leg.br/legin/fed/lei/2019/lei- 13870-17-setembro-2019-789117-norma-pl.html)

4. Pereira, E.J.A.L. et al. (2020). Brazilian policy and agribusiness damage the Amazon rainforest. Land Use Policy, 92. (https://ideas.repec.org/a/eee/lauspo/v92y2020ics0264837719314899.html)

5. Schiller, K.J.F. et al. (2020). Exploring barriers to the agro-ecological transition in Nicaragua: A technological innovation systems approach. Agro-ecology and Sustainable Food Systems, 44(1), pp. 88–132.

6. FAO (2018). Scaling up agro-ecology initiative: transforming food and agricultural systems in support of the SDGs (A proposal prepared for the International Symposium on Agro-ecology, 3–5 April 2018). (http://www.fao.org/3/ca3666en/ca3666en.pdf)

7. Sabourin, E. et al. (org) (2019). Construção de políticas estaduais de agroecologia e produção orgânica no Brasil: avanços, obstáculos e efeitos das dinâmicas subnacionais, Curitiba. CRV, p. 272.

8. Altieri, M. (2002). Agroecologia: bases científicas para uma agricultura sustentável, Rio de Janeir. ASPTA; Guaíba. Agropecuária, p. 592.; Sevilla-Guzman, E. (2006.) De la Sociologia Rural a la Agroecologia: bases ecológicas de la producción, Barcelona. Icaria Editorial.

9. Hatt, S. et al. (2016). Towards sustainable food systems: the concept of agro-ecology and how it questions current research practices. A review Biotechnol. Agron. Soc. Environ. 20(S1), pp. 215-224.

10. Stamato, B. (2012). Pedagogía del hambre versus pedagogía del alimento: contribuciones hacia un nuevo proyecto pedagógico para las ciencias agrarias en Brasil a partir del programa de formación de técnicos de ATER en Botucatu/SP y de los cursos de grado en Agroecología. Tese Doutoral da Faculdade de Ciencias de la Educación da Universidade de Córdoba – Espanha.

11. Siliprandi, E. (2015). Mulheres e agroecologia: transformando o campo, as florestas e as

pessoas,1 edição, Rio de Janeiro. Universidade Federal Rural do Rio de Janeiro.

12. Petersen, P., Mussoi, E. M., and Dal Soglio, F. (2013). Institutionalization of the agro-ecological approach in Brazil: advances and challenges. Agro-ecology and Sustainable Food Systems, 37(1), pp. 103–14.

13. Costabeber, J.A. (1998). Acción colectiva y procesos de transición agroecológica en Rio Grande do Sul, Brasil. Tese de Doutorado (Programa de Doctorado en Agroecología, Campesinado e Historia) – ISEC-ETSIAN. Universidad de Córdoba, p. 422.

14. Moreira, R.M. (2003). Transição Agroecológica: conceitos, bases sociais e a localidade de Botucatu/SP, Brasil. Dissertação de Mestrado. Unicamp, p.153.

15. Gliessman, S. R. (2007). Agro-ecology: the ecology of sustainable food system, Boca Raton. Taylor and Francis Group.

16. Gliessman, S. R. (2016). Transforming food systems with agro-ecology. Agro-ecology and Sustainable Food Systems, 40(3), pp. 187-189.

17. Calle Collado, A. and Gallar, D. (2010). Agroecologia política: transición social y Campesinado, Porto de Galinhas (PE). Trabajo presentado en el VII Congresso Latiinoamericano de Sociologia Rural. ALASRU.

18. Carmo, M.S. (1998). A produção familiar como lócus ideal da agricultura sustentável, Curitiba. Para Pensar Outra Agricultura, p. 218.

19. Toledo, V.M. (2010). Ecologia, espiritualidade, conocimiento: de la sociedad del riesgo a la sociedad sustentable, Edicion corregida y aumentada, Morelia. Red Utopía A.C.

20. Holt-Giménez, E. and Altieri, M.A. (2013). Agro-ecology, food sovereignty, and the new green revolution. Agroecology and Sustainable Food Systems, 37(1), pp. 90–102.

21. ANA – Articulação Nacional de Agroecologia (2020). Agroecologia nos municípios: dados da pesquisa, Rio de Janeiro. (https://agroecologia.org.br/2020/10/22/municipios-agroecologicos/)

22. Moreira, R. M. (2012). Da hegemonia do agronegocio à heterogeneidad restauradoura da agroecología: estratégias de fortalecimento da transição agroecológica na agricultura familiar camponesa do Programa de Extensão Rural Agroecológica de Botucatu e Região, São Paulo. PROGERA. Tese de doutorado do Instituto de Sociologia y Estudios Campesinos da Universidade de Córdoba.

23. This policy is already part of the Municipal Master/Director Plan since 2017. Botucatu (2017). Plano diretor municipal. (https://leismunicipais.com.br/plano-diretor- botucatu-sp)

24. Articulação Nacional de Agroecologia (2017). Método de análise econômico-ecológica de Agroecossistemas , Rio de Janeiro. AS-PTA, p. 246.; Rickerl, D. et al. (2004). Agroecosystems analysis, Wisconsin. Series Agronomy, 43. American Society of Agronomy, Inc.; Crop Science Society of America, Inc.; and Soil Science Society of America, Inc.

25. Mazé, A., Domenech, A., and Goldringer, I. (2020). Restoring cultivated agrobiodiversity: the political ecology of knowledge networks between local peasant seed groups in France. Ecological Economics,179(202).

26. Siqueira L.P. et al. (2021). Engaging people for large-scale forest restoration: governance lessons from the Atlantic forest of Brazil. The Atlantic Forest, pp.389-402.

27. Muñoz, E.F.P. et al. (2021). Agri-food markets towards agro-ecology: tensions and compromises faced by small-scale farmers in Brazil and Chile. Sustainability 2021, 13(6).

28. Moreno, C. et al. (2021). Transforming higher education in Bolivia by linking two contra-hegemonic movements: agro-ecology and the decolonial turn. International Journal of Qualitative Studies in Education, pp. 1-18.

29. Tornaghi, C., And Dehaene, M. (Eds.). (2021). Resourcing an agro-ecological urbanism: political, transformational and territorial dimensions (1st ed.). Routledge.

30. Holt-Gimenez, E. (Ed.) (2012). Food movements unite!: strategies to transform our food system, San Francisco. Food First.

31. Mestmacher, J. And Braun, A. (2020). Women, agro-ecology and the state: new perspectives on scaling-up agro-ecology based on a field research in Chile. Francis and Taylor. Agro-ecology and Sustainable Food Systems, 45(7), pp. 981-1006.

Climate Migration

Isobel Thomas-Horton

Old stories, new meanings

The *cyfarwydd* (storyteller) got to his feet and tried to sense the mood of his expectant audience so as to know which type of tale they might best enjoy. He began with the story of Brân, the king who – long before the cities of Cantre'r Gwaelod existed – walked back and forth across what is now sea between Wales and Ireland. At a time when it was not covered with water, when it was dry land. Then the ocean rose, slowly flooding the land connection, until it was no longer passable on foot. The people who once lived there fled to its margins and built their cities along the coastline, hoping to defy the rising waters. Among those great cities were Cantre'r Gwaelod, now beneath the waters of Cardigan Bay. Lost to history and geography... but not to memory.

Half a world away, in the northwest Pacific Ocean during a firelit evening on the island of Pohnpei, an elderly matriarch had gathered her extended family to tell stories of the lost island of Nahlapenlohd: where it once stood, its conspicuous and pristine beauty, and how it came to disappear. For it became the site of a pitched battle between rival polities, she explained, and so much warrior blood was shed on the sandy ground that this became washed away. When she was young, the stumps of coconut palms stuck out through the ocean at the low tide, showing where Nahlapenlohd once stood, but now they were all gone. An island vanished from the map ... yet remembered still.

What recently happened to small sand islands across the northwest Pacific is exactly what is happening today along much of the coast of Cardigan Bay. The ocean surface is rising, cutting into the land where it is weakest, surging across its low-lying parts, ineluctably altering familiar geographies. Like people living along the coast of Cardigan Bay 9,000 years ago (when the ocean surface was some 10 metres lower than at present), we today live in a time when the ocean is rising. And there is not much to be done about it.

Of course, that does not mean we must passively accept what is happening. We will continue to erect sea walls and raise dwellings. Recent research looking into how people 7,000 years and more ago responded to rising sea levels suggest that they also actively resisted its encroachment onto the land. People along the Nullarbor coast of southern Australia built sea defences, palisades of wooden 'spears' and perhaps rock walls. People at Dwaraka on the coast of northwest India also built sea defences, maybe even relocating an ancient city slightly further inland. And the people of Cantre'r Gwaelod built a succession of sea walls and dykes with floodgates, of increasing height and complexity, to try and keep the ocean at bay. But in the end, the ocean triumphed, as it did at Dwaraka and the Nullarbor.

Many Welsh people know the story of Cantre'r Gwaelod and how one night, King Gwyddno's intemperate steward, the hapless Seithennin, left open a floodgate at high tide, allowing the water to flood the city and forcing its abandonment. That story, of course, is likely a metaphor for what actually happened. It is far easier to blame the actions of a tangible being for disaster than it is to admit that humans cannot control Nature – and that sea level rises and falls of its own accord.

* * *

Dotted with islands which are often hundreds, sometimes thousands, of kilometres apart, the Pacific Ocean occupies around one-third of the Earth's surface. Long before people in Europe knew the Pacific existed, almost every island had been settled by people who originated from its western continental rim, the coasts of what today we call East Asia, starting around 5,000 years ago. It is probable that rising sea levels along these coasts caused what we today label 'coastal squeeze', the crowding of people along the fringes of the land, competing for livelihoods, caused by landwards movement of the shoreline. In this case, as in many throughout history in every part of the world, the growing conflict unavoidable in such situations eventually led to people getting into boats, setting sail for the eastern horizon, hoping to find land. This is how we believe the first people reached island groups in the western Pacific, the earliest involving a journey between the Philippines and Guam around 3,500 years ago that required an unbroken ocean crossing of more than 2,000 kilometres.

People have lived on western Pacific islands ever since this time. When, typically within the last 200 years, they started to be colonised by people from far away, Pacific Island people were living mostly inland, away from the coast. Realising the disadvantages of this to the management of the islands' population, colonial officials and missionaries moved most people to the coast. Reflecting on this situation, a Fijian elder in a remote coastal village told me in 2019 that:

> 'My grandfather told me that his grandfather was forever saying it was a mistake for our people to leave the hills and move to the coast. In the hills we were safe from the waves, our land was not eaten from under us like it is today. But we had no choice – you people, you Europeans, you came along and forced us all to move to the water's edge. The old ones, they knew it was dangerous, and they told us not to go. But we did, here we are and dina saraga – too true – we now discover it is a dangerous place! We need to listen to the past.'

How ironic for so many Pacific Islanders that their ancestors spend thousands of years learning the safest places to live on islands only to have this traditional knowledge displaced by invaders who believed they knew better. But did not. Most coastal communities in the Pacific are today threatened by sea level rise. Their beaches are disappearing, trees toppling into the ocean, graveyards submerged; even coastal villages often go underwater every time the tide is high, their gum-booted occupants sloshing along raised paths between elevated or barricaded buildings to visit one another. Many coastal villages know they will have to relocate upslope – in some cases offshore – over the next few decades if sea level continues to rise as it has been recently.

Patrick Nunn (www.patricknunn.org)

Adaptation to migration

I first discovered Professor Patrick Nunn's work through a piece he wrote in 2003. He suggested that the first 'true' Pacific Islanders may have been environmental refugees from the coasts of East Asia. They had been displaced during the sea level rise following the glacial melt at the end of the last ice age. This period of rising sea levels had impacts across the world, including, as you have read, in the area we now call Wales.

This idea arrested me. Sonia Shah has suggested that 'from the earliest years of childhood, we are taught that plants, animals and people belong in certain places'. The focus on where a thing is 'from' suggests that there was an original placement, that we're all slowly dispersing from, finding and intermingling with each other, like different coloured felt-tips pressed to wet paper. According to her, we've 'constructed a story about our past, our bodies, and the natural world in which migration is the anomaly'. The truth, as always, is more complicated.

Recognising that sea levels and average global temperatures have risen and fallen throughout history places the current 'migrant crisis' in context. Climate migration is not new. Climate fluctuates, and humans have always moved. For most of our history we had no choice. Today anthropologists agree that early human tribes were likely nomadic, whether based in the Siberian Tundra or Great Plains. It is the technologies and lifestyle that would have seemed godlike to these ancestors that make us weaker than them in the face of rising sea levels.

Our nomadic ancestors walked on earth anchored by roots, a living nexus which could generally survive changing conditions by virtue of having done it before. Their larders were the same plants that held the soil together. Possessions were what could be carried with the group, generally tools which served some important function and took too much energy to recraft at every encampment.

Today the typical home in the United Kingdom cannot adapt to its environment, nor be moved when the rains fall too heavily or disease moves in. Indeed, the materials we build our cities from increase the risk of flooding; tarmac doesn't drain the way soil does, and you cannot plant thirsty crops in it.

Even for the poorest nations on Earth, families tend to accumulate too many possessions to be truly mobile. In 1994, photographer Peter Menzel published his book *Material World: A Global Family Portrait*. It contained a portrait of a 'statistically average' family from 30 different countries, all sat outside their homes with all of their possessions. For our ancient ancestors, even the poorest among them would have been more secure than most. The Getu family of Ethiopia, for example, owned their own crops and house, as well as a breeding pair of oxen. It is these possessions though, both the land and the home they have built and crops they have grown, which root them to their location. This is the same for each of the 30 families Menzel photographed. Even the Regzen family of Mongolia who live in the same kind of portable tent used for centuries by their nomadic ancestors now pitch it on a small section of owned land. Their possessions, including a china cabinet and large bed, showcase this permanency.

That the average family unit even in the poorest parts of the world own so much is a testament to modern civilisation. Yet it has also turned what was once one of humanity's greatest survival instincts into something we fear.

We are rooted now, not only by physical possessions, like the land we own, but by the intangible. Invisible lines criss-cross the globe. Passports are needed for migratory routes that have been used by humanity for thousands of years. Take the Darien Gap example. For tens of thousands of years this small wedge of land was the sole land bridge between two vast continents, a thoroughfare for nature and humans alike. The National Geographic Magazine has lamented the lack of archaeological digs in the area, considering that its unique location was likely witness to the interplay of cultures otherwise disconnected. Today it contains the border between Panama and Colombia, and is widely considered to be one of the most dangerous places on Earth. Migrants still pass through there. Many are fleeing the same kinds of disasters that displaced their ancestors; for example, many of the migrants were victims of the Haitian Earthquake of 2010.

The dense jungle and tropical diseases have always made the journey from South to North America not for the faint of heart, but modern travellers face an additional challenge. Between many migrants and the promised land they hope to reach is not just jungles and gangs of traffickers and narcotics dealers but policed borders and the wrath of the United States immigration police.

Who are the climate refugees?

Like many, the first time the words 'migrant crisis' entered my world was the summer of 2015. Images of capsizing boats, drowned bodies and the shell-shocked, petrol burnt survivors suddenly appeared on the cover of every newspaper. Millions, we were told, were fleeing their homes, hoping to rebuild them in Europe.

It was difficult to match the faces of those on the television screens with the stories they told. Could these really be home-owners who had until recently worked 9 to 5 then come home to eat dinner before a TV screen? I would experience this more directly several years later during a placement at the Johannes Gutenberg University in Mainz, Germany. The placement introduced us to a number of refugees now settled in the area. Back in their home countries, many of those we spoke to had well-paying jobs. One man I spoke to showed me images of his home, his mother and his cars, all still waiting for him in Syria. Another man I spoke to was in the final year of his architecture degree. These people were not anomalies. Male asylum seekers from Iraq, Cote d'Ivoire and Gambia actually average higher levels of education among men than the general population at home. It has been suggested that the earlier waves of the migration crisis consisted of those who have a good education and transferable skills, along with good health and the money available to pay the traffickers. The findings of various studies have led Professor Robert McLeman to dub the demographics making up migrants the 'bedrock of successful communities'.

Even armed with this knowledge, when embarking on the research for this project, I expected large amounts of my time to be taken up speaking to people on the other side of the world, whose life experiences were vastly different from my own. By far the most well-known potential 'climate refugees' are from the islands of Kiribati, from where in 2012 Ioane Teitiota made history being the first to apply for asylum explicitly on climate change grounds. This chapter will dip in occasionally to mention statistics and interviews with people from the atolls, who perhaps most keenly represent the public image of who a climate refugee is, but it will spend an equal amount of time documenting my conversations with the residents of the Welsh village of Fairbourne.

After all, why not? We may be used to thinking of climate migration as something far-flung, which happens to people in other places, but the impact of climate change does not respect the invisible lines we have painted across the Earth.

Fairbourne has a golf course, school and church, and is very reliant on the tourists who appear in the summer months to populate their second homes and summer lets and vanish in the winter months, leaving the town quiet and ghostly. Fairbourne is also sinking into the sea.

It is not the first time parts of this coast have been surrendered to the waves. At Ynyslas at low tide you can still see the trunks of ancient trees, inspiring the myth of Cantre'r Gwaelod, the legendary sunken city. It is however the first time a town of this magnitude has essentially been abandoned to the sea in this country. The BBC branded the residents of Fairbourne the UK's 'first climate refugees', but this isn't quite true. The residents are still there, running businesses, collecting mail and living their lives.

This was the first important lesson for me. In Mainz, I had spoken to people who had given up everything, walking away from their lives to start again. This is the image we often have of the victims of climate change. Once humans moved in nomadic tribes, ebbing and flowing over the centuries, using land when it was available and leaving when it wasn't. Today, while the young may leave (and indeed this is happening in Fairbourne), those who own homes and businesses are likely to stay. Not able to carry what they have collected with them, they have little choice. For the vast majority of people, a home represents years or even decades of labour and may even function as their retirement savings. This was the case for a retiree I spoke to in Fairbourne who told me, 'I own my land. I own my house. That would be theft if they took over it.' Nine thousand miles away, literally the other side of the globe, an I-Kiribati grandmother told reporter Mike Ives something similar, 'This is where I belong... I would rather stay'. The sentiment of these women was far from unusual. Over the course of my research I would find that the people I spoke to often did not consider themselves to be potential refugees, climate or otherwise, because they often had simply no intention of leaving. The image of a 'refugee' – the bedraggled, salt-water drenched victims of wars in Syria and

Afghanistan – were simply not applicable, nor a source of identity for people still, though increasingly precariously, entrenched in their homes.

How the term 'climate refugee' has become attached to these disparate groups and their relationship to the term is complicated. For many years campaigners have aimed to create the protected class of 'climate refugee' for migrants of places such as Kiribati, but it has always been a term more used by the press than by the people themselves. The then president of Kiribati Anote Tong explicitly told ABC in 2014 that, 'I have never encouraged the status of our people being refugees', while acknowledging that residents will have to leave the islands. Broadly, the image we have of refugees is not an inviting one, for all the drama it may bring to a press story, so perhaps it is not surprising so many are uncomfortable with the term. A resident of Fairbourne referred to the term as, 'it's new, and it's a new sexy phrase, everybody was interested in it'. She went on to add that Member of Parliament Liz Saville-Roberts suggested in the House of Commons the residents may become the 'UK's first climate refugees', but then 'she didn't follow it up with anything like 'but we are going to be doing this and this to help fix it'. The residents I speak to agree that the term brought public interest to the town, but they're broadly unsure if it has helped the situation. 'We've had everybody from Germany to Sweden coming over to talk to us, and ITV, and this and that and all the rest of it, but where's it getting us?' one resident asked me.

In 2019, the BBC ran an article claiming that Fairbourne has only 10 years left. Perhaps this was due to a misreading of the shoreline management plan, or perhaps in a more deliberate attempt to create an eye-catching headline. But this article has left the townspeople in a difficult situation and feeling abandoned, perhaps more than any of the bureaucratic failures they have dealt with. Such an idea first put out by the BBC and then picked up by other news outlets had decimated house prices in the area, making it economically impossible for many of the residents to leave. Since 83% of Fairbourne residents own the property they live in, this is an issue close to many. Angela Thomas, a resident of the town, told me that, 'Houses overnight lost over 40% of their value, and it became impossible to sell unless it was a cash sale. You cannot get a mortgage in Fairbourne'. Another resident, who asked not to be named, has been trying for years now to get an equity release on her property. She explained her difficulties simply, 'He'd gone onto the internet, googled Fairbourne, and he'd found the 10 years... Once you are labelled, you are labelled'.

The money problem

Of course, there would have been economic impacts with or without the BBC article, though the residents might be right in concluding that it sped things up. The first thing to tank in a community facing an exodus is always going to be the economy. When more people want to leave a place than stay, house prices fall drastically. People don't start businesses, so there are no jobs. The young people leave first, either for work or because they are not willing to invest their earnings in a home with a value which is continually declining. Fewer young people means the population skews towards the elderly, and indeed 62% of the residents of the Arthog Community Council Area (where the town is located) are older than 55.

Fairbourne faces a drain of its youth to cities like Cardiff and London only because they are allowed to travel there. Of course, the opportunity to leave is not present for all victims of the waves. For the I-Kiribati, on the other side of the globe, leaving for work is more complicated. The whole of the island is threatened, so international investment is unlikely to be long-term, even in the cities. This, combined with coastal flooding pushing formerly rural agricultural or fishing workers to the cities, has resulted in unemployment rising.

In 2015 the I-Kiribati government adopted the National Labour Migration Policy, which aimed to make it easier for residents to work abroad, which would both alleviate unemployment and bring much needed cash flow into the local economy. While migrant labour adds billions to the economies the labourers travel to worldwide, they also send more than US$500 billion home every year. For countries like Lebanon, Nepal and Moldovia, these 'remittances' account for around 20% of the GDP.

For the I-Kiribati it is even more important. Earlier, we discussed the education level of migrants, but their access to liquid assets is equally vital. Land or home ownership can make a person less likely to leave, since abandoning a home means giving up all of the capital that has been sunk into it. Having sunk all their money into a home or land can therefore keep someone from leaving, even if they wanted to, as is the case with some of the retirees in Fairbourne. Liquid assets, on the other hand, could enable the people of the atolls to move to new homes in countries less at risk. Working abroad may also increase their desire to do so. As mentioned earlier, leaving the islands is very unattractive to many I-Kiribati, who fear losing their culture and do not want to be so far from family. Young people who have worked abroad, however, will find it easier to adjust and build lives elsewhere as the cost of living on the island becomes untenable economically.

The dark truth of the matter is that, behind the plans to decommission Fairbourne and move the residents of Kiribati, there is an economic calculation. Solutions exist for the protection of the land, but the cost is prohibitive. In other words, the experts behind the shoreline management plan have judged Fairbourne not economically productive enough to save, and as a global community we have decided that Kiribati is not 'worth' the resources it would take to maintain it in a livable condition.

Yet, as we will see, there seems to be little desire to provide the funds to resettle these populations either – leaving them all in limbo.

What is likely to occur?

'It's not about the place going underwater,' Professor Simon Donner told reporter Mike Ives, 'It's about it becoming prohibitively expensive to live in. That's the real challenge for Kiribati'. According to the World Bank, key elements raising the cost of living will include the need to import more food, since current food supplies are heavily dependent on the reefs which are being damaged by the warmer water. Other issues include the washing away of roads and bridges vital to the island economy, and workers becoming sick more often due to the changing disease profile of the country. Another key problem is fresh water. Water on Kiribati has come from a phenomenon called freshwater lenses. These resources are finite, however, and can become contaminated easily. Already half of the residents rely on rainwater for their fresh water, and much of their food is imported. As the cost of living rises, more and more residents will be forced to make homes elsewhere.

Here in the United Kingdom, utility suppliers are obliged by law to continue to supply an area as long as it is needed, but in practise it is unclear how this will turn out. Public services there will be shut off when the town is deemed no longer safe to live in. This process, called 'decommissioning', will essentially shut down Fairbourne's services one by one, like a body on life support. Eventually the flood defences, no longer maintained, will fail.

It's difficult to say exactly when this will happen. The 10 years till submersion so publicly given by the BBC and then taken up by other outlets is only for a small section of the area called Friog Corner, which has no residents. The shoreline management plan divides the town and coast into segments, giving different estimates for each, but in 2005, the UK's Department for Environment, Food and Rural Affairs (DEFRA) set the date for the town at large at between 2055 to 2065. Evidence of sea level rise measured at the nearby town of Barmouth suggests that Fairbourne will 'no longer be safe nor sustainable' before this date.

Like many of the places affected by rising sea levels, the death of Fairbourne and the island atolls of Kiribati will be quiet and protracted rather than dramatic and cinematic. For all the images of rising water may be sexy, the real fear for many 'climate migrants' is economic. Indeed the line between economic and environmental migrants is likely to blur significantly in the coming years. Lawyer Michael Kidd, who represented Kiribatian Ioane Teitiota in his petition to become the first official climate refugee, has said that the distinction is arbitrary: 'You're either a refugee or you're not'.

Displacement

Kidd and Teitiota were unsuccessful. Currently no one has been granted asylum as a climate refugee, though his work resulted in a 2020 ruling by the UN Human Rights Committee that nations must take into account human rights violations caused by climate change when considering deportation for asylum seekers. This decision was badly needed. The 1951 Refugee Convention was created with the dark years of World War Two and the holocaust in mind, rather than the kind of migrations climate change causes. Even those fitting the definition of a refugee according to the convention are not necessarily safe. 'Safe third-country' agreements allow wealthier nations to return migrants to poorer countries they have encountered on the way, if they are considered 'safe'. Perhaps the most famous is the EU's Dublin Regulation, which allowed countries to return migrants to the first EU country they had entered. Greece, already in the midst of a financial disaster, was unable to cope with the number of incoming migrants and treat them humanely, indeed in 2011 the European Court of Human Rights ruled that Greece's migrant camps constituted torture. In the Americas, people fleeing natural disasters are able to enter the United States under a 'temporary protective status' programme, but this is only for a limited amount of time, regardless of the permanency of the damage to their homes and communities.

In short, the global community is failing asylum seekers of all kinds. While this is the case, the victory of recognition for the status of environmental migrants is hollow. With Norman Myers estimating that there may be as many as 200 million environmental refugees by the middle of the century, agreeing upon a robust and sustainable migration system is perhaps the single most important task facing the United Nations after upholding climate change mitigation accords like the Paris Agreement. Sub-organisations like the United Nations Global Compact for Safe, Orderly and Regular Migration have been working to create guidelines and suggestions to make the asylum seeking process easier. Ideas include a network which allows the digital storage and transfer of identification for migrants, as well as a system which would make it easier for migrants to access funds and educational qualifications from their home country. The United Nations Refugee Agency also directly assists with resettlements and naturalisations, resettling 107,800 people in 2019. For all countries, but particularly those with an aging population or dealing with 'brain drain' to neighbouring countries, refugees can be an incredible resource, but there needs to be a system capable of dealing with enormous numbers of them.

For whole countries like Kiribati, the process is always going to be different. The Kiribati government purchased land in Fiji recently, but it is mainly so they can use the soil for sea walls. It is thought that perhaps 500 citizens will be able to relocate there, so the question of where the rest of the population will go is still unanswered. Some particularly science-fictionesque answers like floating cities have been cooked up, and if you are in need of some entertainment, feel free to look up the Green Float or Ocean Spiral floating city concepts. The main phase that is being suggested in serious circles is that of 'migration with dignity'. No sub-aquatic, hydro-electric metropolis, but perhaps relocation in groups, so that communities are not scattered across the world. It is not yet clear where the citizens of the atolls will be located to, or even if this vision of communities moved together will be borne out. Thus far no concrete plan appears to have been sketched out. With around 1% of the world's population already displaced, there seems to be no version of 'migration with dignity' possible in the current system.

Closer to home, the government is aware of the predicament the people of Fairbourne face. In one document, they list the exact fears the population have, acknowledging that property in Fairbourne 'has significantly reduced in value', that employment prospects have lessened and that residents cannot get mortgages. It acknowledges that while utility providers have a 'duty of care' to supply homes where there is demand, it is unlikely that maintenance and improvements will be priorities for the companies providing them. In one particularly grim section it discusses plans 'to deal with abandoned assets'. These 'assets' are the residents' homes and businesses. One resident was concerned that she would be charged for the demolition of her family home.

Despite recognition of the issues, solution funding seem to be scarce. Funding is still required for the resettlement of the townspeople and as of yet there seems no clear plan as to whether they'll be moved to a purpose-built town or separated and fed into the welfare system. This is especially important as so much of the community is older, and may not have the community of partners or siblings. For Angela Thomas, the decision to stop maintaining the sea wall is a foolish one, even when ignoring the emotional toll. 'Maintaining the sea wall would be the cheaper option anyway because if 400 plus homes are decommissioned that will make 700 or more people reliant on the state. Nobody in Fairbourne has a spare £180,000 or 200,000 in the bank to buy a replacement home', she noted. The overwhelming sentiment of people I've spoken to is one of frustration and fear. They feel abandoned. 'With Covid and everything it's all gone very quiet', the resident continued.

Migration with dignity in practice

Our modern lifestyle may tie us down to locations with the weight of our possessions and national and cultural identity, but it is also well suited to serve a more mobile society if only we let it. Money, qualifications and even the company of loved ones can be transmitted across the world, albeit in a digital form. Simultaneously, it is the same material which renders our homes immovable in the face of sea level rise that also allows us to build skyscrapers which provide ample living space for hundreds.

Today, three-quarters of the world's asylum seekers live in urban areas, but our aid and refugee processing facilities are still designed to serve large-scale refugee camps. For 'migration with dignity' to exist for anyone, the global paths to resettlement as well as the support we provide migrants needs to be revamped. There are hundreds of thousands of empty homes in the United Kingdom, and millions of them in the United States. Right now 85% of refugees are hosted in developing countries. True dignity will never be possible for migrants until they are trusted enough to be hosted by wealthier states. Just as with Fairbourne's sea wall, we have the resources to support migrants, but have made an economic decision to allocate them elsewhere.

A better worldwide resettlement programme is an important facet of global adaptation, but there is perhaps a better solution for whole communities which are being displaced, such as those of Fairbourne or the I-Kiribati city of Tuvalu, and it's a remarkably simple one. We need to build them new communities.

The construction of a new town sounds absurd given my previous assessment that empty homes could be opened up to current asylum seekers, but the situation in Fairbourne and on the atolls of Tuvalu is different. Prior to this point, it has been individuals and family units displaced. As larger groups of people begin to be affected, the precedent of preserving community culture needs to be set. People are happier and healthier the closer the relationships they have, and communities which are bonded are more self-reliant. Fracturing communities is therefore a bad decision socially as well as culturally.

It would also send out an important message, that we acknowledge as a global community that the damage was done by a few key groups and that these key groups are happy to pay their part in supporting the victims of the consequences.

Purpose-built towns also allow countries to showcase their adoption of not only a greener way of living but also a more socially conscious one. The towns could contain solar panels and cycle paths, and simultaneously be built with biodiversity in mind, parks and gardens considered as essential as water pipes and roads. Greenery is shown not just to improve the biodiversity of an area but also to improve resident's health, both physical and mental. It will never make up for the loss of a home, but the provision of a safe place to live out their days or raise their children is really the least we can offer anyone, particularly victims of our own sustained refusal to do better.

Before you continue on your journey through this book I'd like to leave you with some final words from Professor Nunn who we encountered at the beginning of this chapter.

Old stories, new meanings continued

All the science says that sea levels will continue rising, not just for this century (for there is nothing special about the year 2100) but for several thereafter. We could save ourselves a lot of trouble, a lot of expense and heartache, to act now in anticipation of this. Building a seawall, and seeing how it repels the waves may make us feel good, but that feeling does not always last long. In the Pacific islands, most seawalls last no more than a couple of years before they collapse, once again exposing coastal settlements and farms and infrastructure to the rising seas. Much better to 'listen to the past' and relocate upslope now.

You might think the barriers to relocation in the Pacific islands are less than they are in places like Cardigan Bay. But they are not. In the Pacific, people often privilege spiritual understandings of climate change and sea level rise over scientific ones, favour prayer over practical action. It is deceptively easy to ridicule such beliefs, but they are not too different from what happens in places like Cardigan Bay. No one wants to move or to be moved. It is natural to feel aggrieved, understandable to angrily deny the necessity, to condemn the science behind it.

Climate change may seem like a global problem, not least because it is no respecter of political borders and therefore requires concerted international responses to mitigate its causes. Mitigation is one thing, but the more immediate concern is adaptation. We have inadvertently set in train a pattern of warming and ocean rise that will last far longer than effective mitigation of its causes. We have no choice but to adapt. And this is something best rationalised, best designed, implemented and sustained locally. By working together, by drawing on their long experience of particular places, local residents – be they on remote Pacific islands or the Welsh coast – people are often best placed to do this. Ancient memories often help immensely.

Earth Rejuvenation

Restoring the Earth through Cooperatives

Carol Manetta

In the days gone by, all of Earth was quiet. Standing on a hilltop, the only sound you heard was that of the wind, birds, and the scurrying of small animals in the undergrowth. If you were near a water source, you could hear the peaceful gurgling of a brook or the roar of a waterfall. Today, let's compare this to the cacophony of trains, cars and the screeching of brakes.

The purpose of this chapter is to look at these contrasts. Soon, all must merge into a peaceful coexistence among humans and nature; otherwise, doom will prevail in short order. This much we know from collective scientific opinion.

Let's explore a new alternative. Human ingenuity needs to foster new forms of agriculture that emphasise protecting natural life, not just the outcomes of farm production. To those who see modern industrialised agriculture as a wasteland in the making, it is clear we need to forge alliances to go back to nature and embrace it with both arms.

By looking at cooperative ventures in many countries, we can learn that there are duties involved that mimic nature's resilience. For instance, it is the premise of all cooperatives to support the community around them. This happens in nature quite regularly. As the tree provides seeds or nuts to the birds and small animals under its boughs, they take these forms of nourishment and deposit them back to the soil. This allows for a vibrant, living ecosystem that has no waste, and which replenishes itself.

Adjustment from that tendency is not needed. It has worked for eons to build nature as we understand it. Willingness to remain heartily alive is the spirit of nature. Thus, humans can imitate nature with their cooperative stance in assisting each other. By thoughtfully taking another step forward with this observation, we have the ability to combine cooperatives to enhance nature and humanity even further. While cooperatives do work with each other as a matter of chosen form, this is an arrangement to supply goods to one another and exchange them. As we learn more about trees, we understand that they cooperate with each other through communications under the ground. If there is a negative impact happening by certain elements or animals, the trees communicate with each other for lifesaving strategies. Peter Wohlleben wrote in his book, *The Hidden Life of Trees*, 'we can describe this as the 'wood-wide web'. All the trees are connected to each other through underground fungal networks, and also use them to communicate. They send distress signals about drought and disease, for example, or insect attacks, and other trees alter their behavior when they receive these messages'.[1] In cooperatives, there is the same kind of mutual agreement to assist each other, in good times and bad.

Thus, cooperatives can benefit each other and the return is justified by the ripple effect of kindness throughout the community surrounding them. What they share is sometimes the decision-making as to where one cooperative's 'territory' ends and another's begins. This is also true of tree roots, for entanglement and competition among the roots for food and nourishment would starve both sets of trees and do harm in the long run. So instead Instead, they cooperate by sharing resources such as tools, other equipment, together with knowledge based on experience and labour.

As humans evolved, they rose in self-importance due to abilities to hunt and collect materials for building, considering themselves superior to animals that could not. Therefore, they took over ever larger tracts of land for their own usage. It was nature and the animal kingdom that allowed for plants, including trees, to proliferate. This is still the case. As we humans have banished animals to small confines within patches of land, the world has suffered greatly. Going forward, we must renew the landscapes that harmonise with Earth below them. The more we understand about the Earth's biosphere, the more we understand about the entanglement process that is both beneficial and sometimes detrimental. In the case of dying landscapes, there is much to be learned about the survival process of tree roots, tiny animals and the microbes that support all complex life forms. It takes generations for forests to grow and prosper, while in a moment those forests can be decimated with logging, burning and acids from plant-killing chemicals. These attacks against nature are evident around the world, and yet humans have ignored such processes for multiple generations.

It is with hope we continue to dwell on this topic. We must face squarely the processes that cause harm and why they are generated in the first place. Unmitigated increase in material production, or 'growth', causes increasing destruction to Earth's resources. As we trace the history of this movement of destruction, we also see the germination of an idea to right the wrongs and rectify the behaviours of the present and past.

In the Amazonian jungle, there is hope in replanting species that are native to the land, while forging new livelihoods. For instance, a new project was announced by Conservation International in 2017 to plant 73 million trees by 2023 – covering 30,000 hectares of land and involving local communities.[2] These livelihoods of rainforest locals include selling a variety of fruits, nuts and small herbs for immediate gain by the farmers who plant them. As observed by the Rainforest Alliance:

> 'When forests are managed responsibly, communities that live in and around them can cultivate thriving businesses out of a rich assortment of non-timber forest products: from honey to flowers and fruit. The Rainforest Alliance offers training in business planning to help forest communities build sustainable enterprises.'[3]

Wishing for the degradation to stop does not make it so. Instead, concerted efforts by regions and small villages are the future answer to deforestation and its disharmony with nature and all life. It is this same model that has inspired my organisation, Reap Goodness, to transform a barren North American landscape.

Reap Goodness partnered with Tolani Lake Enterprises (a nonprofit business incubator of the Navajo Nation) who had need for food security by encouraging agriculture in the semi-arid high desert of Arizona at an elevation of ~1500 metres. After having completed the agreed-upon work with the Navajo people in developing hydroponics and greenhouse year-round agriculture production, the nonprofit's focus changed to the degraded land and scarce water in many places around the world. Now Reap Goodness has aligned with Arizona State University to test the formation of a *'trio of worker-owned cooperatives'*, a model which could be potentially applicable anywhere on Earth.

Situation analysis	Solution concept	Proof of concept	Training production	Translations begin	Worldwide usage
❯	❯	❯	❯	❯	❯
Earth, species in trouble	*Training* for trios of cooperatives	Heartland Trial with students	3 ebooks, VR overview, video series in English	Training products in 5 languages	30 languages total

The nonprofit and university have established a trial, *the Heartland Trial*, in an area of southern Arizona that has been decimated by animal agriculture. In the trial, one cooperative will store water on land via water catchment ditches, pond formation and rooftop rain capture from a roof as a set of rainwater harvesting systems.[4] A second cooperative will plant and harvest from a food forest near the captured water sources.[5] A third cooperative will focus on area water cleansing, while planting high-nutrient foods for local wildlife sanctuaries.[6]

In preparation for the Heartland Trial, a wide variety of students with different sets of knowledge are being invited to test a process that follows a typical formation of worker cooperatives around the world. This means that as one participant has knowledge in one area of Earth reclamation, such as rain capture, another participant has knowledge in an adjoining area, such as permaculture for food forestry, and so on. With each relevant participant contributing their knowledge, it harmonises the overall practices of the group, and allows for agreements to be made, just as they would be with any set of worker cooperatives. For example, each participant can contribute a certain area of knowledge that aids discussions during the planning stage. It is the recording of these discussions that is being collected throughout the trial, starting with pre-trial discussions online until each student is satisfied their participation is worth it.

As participants begin to plan, they must consider the territory in place. It exists in the semi-arid Sonoran Desert in the southern part of the state of Arizona, USA, at around 4700 feet (just over 1430 metres) in elevation. Cattle ranching there has been the norm for generations, even though there has been extensive drought for 20 years in the western US. As the cattle have roamed freely through this cowboy land, they have eaten all the natural grassland and tree foliage, to the extent that there are no large trees in sight. At the same time, they have deposited seeds from elsewhere for new trees to grow that are native to the area - the mesquite tree. This nitrogen fixing tree has numerous uses, including providing food in the form of beans within their pods, all edible by humans and animals. The trees on this property and in all the land around it are no more than 1 ½ feet (half a metre) high. Even though they contain numerous thorns, the cattle have eaten their leaves and soft twigs to keep them very short.

Credit: HaritMakwana

To address this issue, the plan's first consideration is fencing off the entire property, which is 40 acres, to prevent the cattle from obtaining access. This is an important part of the discussion process, since cattle are responsible for a large amount of land decimation. Once fenced off, the plans then turn to regulating water flow from nearby mountains. Close to the land is the only surviving river in the entire state of Arizona, the San Pedro River. Many nearby species rely on its water supply, including the cattle themselves. It is also precious to the wild animals that call this area home, either permanently or during migration.

The water flow can be partially redirected from its usual route to create a pond on-site, while leaving the rest of the water for the river. By creating a pond, it can enable support for the beginnings of the planned food forest on-site, as well as provide water for the wildlife who will visit to quench their thirst. It is the participants' shared expertise that will help the entire group make a decision as to which methods can be used. This way they will all make the agreement together as to which will be the most viable source for water flow and retention, and how they will do this together.

Another consideration will be what foods to grow in the food forest. The participants have been granted approximately five acres upon which to grow a food forest by their own design. Knowing they have only one year in which to combine their efforts for this completed trial, the entire set of participants must agree on how to move forward. After their efforts in design and erecting the food forest are complete, they must decide on how the foods will be used within the community.

A key aim of the cooperatives is to implement adjunct decisions in agreement with the local people of these communities. In some places, these cooperatives will be members of the community who stay on after their initial work of reclamation and growth is in its mature stages. So the decisions made by this kind of cooperative trio will be somewhat different than by those who intend to stay, only to see the work of the cooperatives flourish and then be taken over by others. There is room for both kinds of trios around the world, those of people who remain a long-standing part of the community, or those who establish the physical improvements and then hand over the benefits, while the trio moves on to another community in need.

Jointly, the food forestry during the trial will be determined by those who understand harmony among plants in the format of a natural forest. The agricultural norm today focuses squarely upon monoculture, whether the food source is an annual crop or a single perennial crop such as orchards.

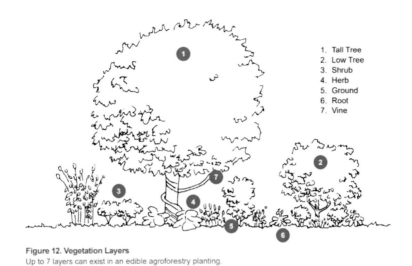

1. Tall Tree
2. Low Tree
3. Shrub
4. Herb
5. Ground
6. Root
7. Vine

Figure 12. Vegetation Layers
Up to 7 layers can exist in an edible agroforestry planting.
Drawing by Fred Meyer

Credit: Backyard Abundance, Edible Agroforestry Design Templates, BackyardAbundance.org

Instead, food forestry depends on numerous levels of perennial crops, which, once established, requires only a few hours of maintenance per month to produce on-going crops for nearby residents. The beauty in this format of agriculture is the harmony given to the Earth's soil, its reduced use of water and its ability to produce for many years without the need for regular hard labour.

The third cooperative has before it a daunting task: the reclamation of polluted waters due to animal agriculture, crop agricultural runoff, golf course runoff, manufacturing wastage and roadways runoff. Joining forces with the other two cooperatives, they will select and plant local water reclamation plants for the pond, and begin a new process that can be replicated worldwide. This process is related to roadways around the world, which are a source of vast pollution of streams, rivers and eventually the ocean. It is caused by the worn, microscopic parts of vehicle tyres that, while initially found in roadside ditches, inevitably find their way into rivers and then oceans.[7]

Since roadside ditches can be planted with plants well known for their water cleansing properties, the local cooperatives will have great effect on pollution reduction. As part of the reclamation process, a variety of plants - including water hyacinth, calendula officinalis and *Salvia splendens* - can remove pollution from stationary water. Other useful species can be cultivated to attract local small pollinators and beneficial insects for keeping in balance the needs of the food forest.

To reach agreements prior to the Heartland Trial the test participants will be imitating planning within a community, but from disparate sources, made necessary due to the need for distance during the COVID-19 pandemic. All of the planning meetings will be recorded. That way, as the plans begin to unfold, the community will have a record of what the plan was, so that they may adjust them as they go through their work together. That is also why the trial will be recorded on video and used as a teaching tool for subsequent cooperative trios. As we consider recordings, we have a plan to record them in a number of formats, starting with e-books.

The second format will look into the potential to access the trial via virtual reality (VR) content. This VR overview is being done specifically because it is highly portable on cell phones and does not require Wi-Fi anywhere in the world. Instead, all that's required is a functioning cell phone and the installed virtual reality conversion app, plus the information file that explains the work. It will be developed so that people in rural areas in developing countries will understand what they see, mostly by visuals and audio translations. Highly visual posters can accompany this VR overview with trained facilitators interacting with the people of the land in their own language.

The third format will be a documentary set of videos disbursed via YouTube. These shorter length videos will describe the process from beginning to end, with our trial participants taking part. YouTube provides the ability to have subtitles in many different languages.

So, from the very beginning of our Heartland Trial, the decisions made by a trio of cooperatives can be of comprehensive benefit in local communities anywhere in the world. It is hoped the new model is learned and understood by many people as quickly as possible, as there is no time to waste. Action taken now can be replicated with the decisions of small groups of people in harmony for the immediate and beneficial future of land in their own community, nearby communities through teachings, and for children.

It is the children who are important to talk about next. They are the future. The children are the crux and focus of all Reap Goodness' work. With species disappearing every day, future generations are being robbed of the opportunity to reach out to and study all these beautiful creatures. In restoring the land and waters, these children of today and in the future will have what is their right within a lifetime.

With this cooperative model being observed by schoolchildren of all ages, they will know what to do - not only to survive, but have a rich life for themselves and the other beings who create a robust experience for all during their lifetime. It is the intention to create curriculum insertions regarding cooperative trios and how Earth can be made rich once again for the next generation. Furthermore, they may one day choose to become a member of one of these trios. If so, they will know exactly what to do to continue the process.

Those who choose to pursue this line of work will understand localised decision-making for the Earth's survival and bringing back species that are on the brink of extinction. Furthermore, everyone outside of these cooperatives will be additionally grateful for their existence, for the goodness that is extended to everyone will be shared by all of life.

References

1   Wohlleben, P. (2016) *The Hidden Life of Trees: What They Feel, How they Communicate---Discoveries from a Secret World.* Vancouver: Greystone Books.

2   Vander Velde, B. (2017) *Conservation International.*
    Available at: https://www.conservation.org/blog/massive-reforestation-effort-puts-down-roots-in-brazilian-amazon (Accessed: 19 May 2021).

3   The Rainforest Alliance (2019) *Our Mission to Protect the World's Forests.*
    Available at: https://www.rainforest-alliance.org/articles/our-mission-to-protect-the-worlds-forests (Accessed: 19 June 2021).

4   Pacey, A. and Cullis, A. (1986) *Rainwater Harvesting: The Collection of Rainfall and Runoff in Rural Areas.* London: Intermediate Technology Publications.

5   Crawford, M. (2010) *Creating a Forest Garden: Working with Nature to Grow Edible Crops.* Cambridge: Green Books, Ltd.

6   Sharma, S., Singh, B. and Manchanda, V.K. (2015) *Phytoremediation: Role of Terrestrial Plants and Aquatic Macrophytes in the Remediation of Radionuclides and Heavy Metal Contaminated Soil and Water, Environmental Science and Pollution Research, 22,* pp. 946-962.

7   Boucher, J. and Friot, D. (2017) *Primary Microplastics in the Oceans: A Global Evaluation of Sources.* Gland: International Union for Conservation of Nature and Natural Resources.

Wayfinding in a time of Covid

Jane Riddiford

The Covid-19 pandemic provided glimpses of how we might live in a more local, sustainable, life-giving way in the midst of a climate-changed world. During this often fearful and confusing period, as the air cleared and birds flocked back into the city, the natural world was appreciated more than ever. The doors of many institutions closed and, as a result, we drew upon the power of local green spaces and local communities.

Global Generation, an environmental education charity, connects people of all ages who live in the city to nature. Through a wide range of nature oriented activities, we unlock the imaginations of children and young people, and we support them to become catalysts for positive social and environmental change. Our two home bases, the Story Garden and the Paper Garden, north and south of the River Thames in London, became sanctuaries for the young and the not so young. When meeting our participants indoors was no longer a safe option, we appreciated our gardens all the more. We grew food, we lit fires and people came and shared their stories. Children and young people learned to appreciate the wonders of the universe hidden beyond the expanse of our skies, and they explored the healing power of the plants that grow in tiny hidden spaces mere moments from their doorsteps. During this time, with many of our plans turned upside down, we asked ourselves big questions and began to imagine what a kinder future might be. Our preparations for this challenging period actually began several years before when we consciously adopted a way of being that then helped us navigate our way through unknown waters.

Wayfinding

Back in 2016, a group of colleagues and friends of Global Generation gathered in one of our community gardens, which at the time was called the Skip Garden – so named because many of the garden beds were constructed out of builders' skips (also known as dumpsters). Around us, the sun shone on the concrete and the glass of the new high-rise buildings in King's Cross. Despite the air feeling hot and stifling, there was a special feeling there where vegetables and flowers tumbled out of skips converted into garden beds. Newly built structures created out of reclaimed materials by architecture students caught the attention of one of our visitors that day. Her name was Chellie Spiller. She brought us a gift that would stand us in good stead in the months and years to come. In retrospect, one could say soul and survival work was about to begin.

We were there for a workshop afternoon with Chellie, a Māori leadership scholar and co-author of a book called Wayfinding Leadership, and her mother Monica.[1] As we settled into our portable cabin classroom, our guides welcomed us with a karakiai[i] as part of a traditional Māori greeting. The atmosphere was captivating and powerful. During the afternoon we were introduced to practices handed down from early Pacific explorers who had braved treacherous waters to

---

i   A Karakia is a ritualised Māori way of chanting a prayer

unknown destinations. Deeply attuned to the interconnection between all things, these wayfinders paid attention to the subtle changes within themselves and their team. They learned to read the ripples of the seas beneath them and the movement of the clouds and the birds in the skies above them, adapting and adjusting as they journeyed forward. Chellie described how one must step beyond the knowledge of one's own horizon to be a wayfinder. This way of being, fully aware of the clues that arise in the present, runs counter to the ideas of a pre-ordained world that many leadership approaches are based on. Wayfinding as a fluid way of being is well suited to the unknown realities that now lie ahead of us in the face of climatechange.

On that hot summer afternoon with Chellie, we explored our ancestral roots that spread around the planet. We were called upon to identify and find strength in these roots. As we told stories of forebears from long ago and of places in the lands that hold meaning for us now, we were reminded that there is a deeply intuitive and infinitely more creative way of being than the lockstep of a master planned process. Since then, viewing Global Generation as a wayfinding organisation has brought a sense of trust and patience to a journey in which we have become more aware than ever that the end is not yet written. It is very much a relational journey that depends upon the interconnection between all things.

Like the double-hulled wooden canoes of the original wayfinders, our metal garden-bed skips have often marked the beginning of new journeys and new possibilities for Global Generation.

Fast forward four years to 2020, and, glancing upwards, I received a thumbs up from the window of the passing 390 bus. "That's great", "Thank you", or "What a good idea" was the response of nearly every person that walked by. It was somewhat surreal to feel so uplifted in this extreme circumstance. As I explain this later, was no ordinary Saturday. We were just a few days into more intensified measures set out by the UK government in response to Covid-19. While we were not in complete lockdown, all of us were doing our best to keep two metres apart. It was like one of those awareness-building activities where you are asked to move around a room without touching. People who stopped to talk to us stood a good distance away. We were clambering in and out of skips, drilling, sawing, moving soil and planting; taking care not to spread the virus. In those early days of the pandemic, none of us really knew what it was to socially distance, and we had never heard the expression "stay home to save lives". I was with my neighbours who are all part of Greening Leighton, a hands-on campaign to make Leighton Road and the surrounding Kentish Town streets a greener place to live.[2]

How the skips came to leighton road

The reason we all came together on that special Saturday is because one of the neighbours, who is a strong community activist, invited me to an evening meeting in February 2020, about greening our local neighbourhood. As the proceedings drew to a close, my neighbour spoke up and said, "I like the idea of the Skip Garden in King's Cross. Might we use the same idea of using skips to create street-side pocket gardens or parklets on the side of Leighton Road. This would bring the neighbours together and perhaps it would slow the traffic down."

"Well as it happens," I said, "we're just about to move the Skip Garden to a new location near the British Library. It'll be called the Story Garden. We have a couple of skips going spare."

Fortunately for us, the head of the local borough council was at the meeting and miraculously she managed to by-pass the layers of red tape involved in getting approval from the transport authority for such a move. Within days the idea was approved and the skips, replete with soil and plants, were loaded onto a skip lorry and delivered to Leighton Road.

Credit: John Sturrock

By the next Saturday, we were filling the open space with soil in the middle of the flowering garden beds that sat around the edges of each skip. The central opening was surrounded by shallow wooden growing beds that were now blooming with tulips and daffodils. Having been involved with Global Generation's mobile skip gardens for the last ten years, I wasn't so keen on this new design initially. 'How long will the skips be here for? How will we move them with all that heavy soil inside?' I asked. A few words conveyed the vision and commitment behind what was happening: 'We want them here for ten years or more...maybe forever!' came the response. 'What an ideal destination for the Skip Garden,' I thought. 'This is community-based regeneration at its best; bottom up, collaborative and spontaneous.'

What's more, it was being done for next to nothing. Nearly everything was found or donated, with people sharing tools and bringing cuttings from their gardens. A growing arch out of found piping had been installed in one of the skips. A wire had been cunningly stretched across the pavement to a nearby garden; in time, this would support a perfumed jasmine walkway. During the three hours that we worked together, there was talk of how we might green the remainder of the street-side parking spaces that had been allocated to our efforts. A pallet garden, a community composter, water butts from the downpipes of the nearby houses...these were just some of the ideas. Then, with the restrictions on movement, many of us were working from home. 'Perhaps we could all come out and garden at the same time each day?' were our parting words.

During the afternoon, I picked up several emails from my colleagues in Global Generation. A few miles down the road in King's Cross, there was more collaboration, more wayfinding and thinking on the spot. Local organisations were coming together and evolving a shared response to the challenges that COVID was presenting us with. This included setting up foodbanks and collectively applying for emergency funding provided by the government and grant making trusts and foundations.

In Rebecca Solnit's book, *A Paradise Built in Hell,* she tells the stories of some of the small, localised utopias that developed in response to major disasters, from the 1906 San Francisco earthquake and fire to Hurricane Katrina in New Orleans.[3] In San Fransico the parks became inhabited by people in tents, who had lost their homes; food was grown, cooked and shared and people came together at night to play cards, tell stories and provide support for each other. Solnit describes how embedded in the word 'emergency''is the *emergence* of new ways of being and living together, possibilities that even a week previously I would have found hard to imagine. Amidst a sea of uncertainty, local organisations pulled together, and new ways of working came into being.

The synchronicity of the right people being in the right place at the right time meant our first two street-side parklets were delivered quickly, avoiding the many bureaucratic obstacles we were to encounter in trying to deliver two more parklets in the street. A sign of success for us was that unexpected things emerged as different people got involved. As with many of Global Generation's projects, the encouragement to experiment was accompanied with permission for people to proudly say some things worked and others didn't. This 'can-do' citizen-led approach runs counter to the way a risk-averse local authority works. Gaining permission and permits can be painstakingly slow, withering the life blood out of many a good idea. Our aim was to influence public policy to the degree that the parklets could be easily created across the borough, and so we decided to pursue a by the book, above-the-parapet, route. This needed the agreement and co-ordination of different council interests: highways, sustainability, parks and community. We found ourselves on a merry go round of layers of procedure that seemed to lead nowhere, and I soon realised this was no small task. Despite an ambitious climate change policy in the London Borough of Camden – which seemed to bode well for our plans – but sadly, at the time of writing this, more than a year later, approval for two more parklets has still not been achieved.

Credit: Brendon Bell

Foodbank

For many weeks during the first Covid lockdown, food was one of the few things we were allowed to leave our homes for. It made sense that food and growing more of it was the first step the Global Generation team focused on in our response to the pandemic. Food was thrust back upon its pedestal as we realised once again how it is central to our survival. In the early spring, the Global Generation garden team and several local volunteers created more growing beds in the Story Garden and sowed thousands of seeds.

Like all of Global Generation's gardens to date, the Story Garden is on a "meanwhile site", which will eventually be built on to create the Alan Turing Research Centre for the British Library. In a temporary context, a few years or even a few months can seem like large and fruitful parcels of time. By April, we were delivering our harvests of fresh, leafy vegetables next door to the mobile food bank operated by Urban Community Projects. This was based in the Living Centre run by our neighbours at the Somers Town Community Association. Whilst the foodbank was able to get hold of dried goods and non-perishables from the many restaurants which had ceased to operate, sourcing fresh vegetables was a challenge, and the Story Garden vegetable harvest was well received.

Enthusiasm spread to the Paper Garden, another community garden which Global Generation operates across the river in Canada Water, which is on the Rotherhithe Peninsula. This almost island-like part of London is formed by a huge bend in the River Thames, an area where the docks used to be and where many of the original docker families still live. It is also an area that is undergoing huge changes. Like many parts of London, large-scale regeneration is underway, bringing with it multi-storey buildings and an influx of people with a diversity of cultural backgrounds, experiences and expectations. The Paper Garden is based in an old tool store and the largely abandoned carpark of a 1980s metal-clad industrial building. This was formerly a newspaper print-works which employed many people who lived locally.

The Paper Garden is surrounded by communities divided over changes to the area. The process of enabling a diversity of people to come together to achieve something special using waste materials has been incremental. Designing a genuinely collaborative community process is a delicate and sometimes excruciating balance of how much to define in advance and how much to leave open for what will come out through the workshop process.[4] The work has been both fast and slow. In 2020, almost overnight, schools and businesses closed and the carpark became empty once more. Before long, the garden and a range of portable food growing beds had spread further across the concrete terrain of the carpark. As in King's Cross, the Global Generation team worked with community organisations and primary schools. We provided salad leaves, radishes, beetroot and chard, along with edible flowers and fragrant herbs, for distribution to local families. In turn, during the lockdown and afterwards, families along with workers from the NHS were welcomed in safe numbers into the garden, as a place of sanctuary and refuge.

Credit: Brendon Bell

Voices of the Earth

The disruption caused by the pandemic encouraged self-organising amongst the Global Generation team, revealing previously hidden talents. In the early stages of lockdown, storytelling, cooking and craft sessions went online, and we created downloadable Stay at Home Garden packs which included stories and downloadable nature oriented activities for children to do at home with their parents.[5] Young people became accustomed to meeting each other on screen.

Discussion and creative writing provided an opportunity to find words for unfamiliar experiences and to share fears about the lived realities of each day.

> "Our life has changed, waking up to something new that has never happened before. Numbers to read every day on cases and deaths, and I am scared".
>
> Ana, 15 years

From the constraints of their bedrooms, teenagers explored big and challenging questions and asked themselves what the future might be. As Emma, our Paper Garden manager, explained of her youth work sessions:

> "We dived into race, migration and privilege ... how might we spark change. We cooked healthy food separately but together and we investigated activists that fight powerfully for all living things."
>
> Emma, Paper Garden Manager

Whilst new possibilities were opening, thanks to technology, it soon became obvious that Global Generation's role was to help people come outdoors, away from their computers and screens, into the wide green spaces beneath the trees and the tiny mysterious spaces in the cracks upon the pavements, where the dandelion, the nettle and the fireweed find their way through.

> "Something small like a daisy or big like an oak tree can have a much a greater impact on us than I realised. The plants, stories and songs that I encountered over the last year will be with me forever."

Credit: Sarah Ainslie

These are the words of 18-year-old Tsion, one of the young participants in Global Generation's Voices of the Earth project, in which we encouraged young people to discover the healing power of plants. The project had been planned with the British Library, the Royal College of Physicians and local people. Our hope was a marriage of scientific and mythic dimensions. As we had the opportunity to work with a range of people – physicians, herbalists, storytellers and historians, parents and children – we hoped to draw upon different ways of seeing the world which are sometimes oppositional. In a time when the institutions were forced to close their doors, we drew more deeply on the often hidden resources within local neighbourhoods. Invitations for young people to stop, look and appreciate the plants that grew on their balconies and around their back-doorsteps brought forth unexpected moments of connection.

> "The project gave me a reason to leave my bedroom and go outside. Feeling the sun on my face, being in nature, made me feel connected even if I was physically distanced from others."
>
> Cassie, 17 years old

Through all of the repeated lockdowns during 2020 and 2021, we managed to keep our gardens open. We designed activities for small numbers of people to work in safely distanced ways. Some of these were families who came with health workers, some were referred by schools, and others lived in the housing estates along the edges of our gardens. In this more intimate setting, we heard from mothers about the healing practices of their childhood. We lit fires amongst circles of logs and trees. We learned about the hand warming fires that constantly burn in the villages of Bangladesh and the use of wild yarrow in the forests of Bosnia to heal wounds. For some of our participants, plants like the ash tree in our local cemetery, which is known as the Hardy Tree, inspired interest in myths and legends. We adapted the story of Yggdrasil, the tree of unification in Norse mythology whose roots stretch the whole way around the planet. The ash trees are now suffering from chalara, a form of die-back. In the Norse legend, when Yggdrasil died, it was a sign that life on earth was under threat. For other young people, the Voices of the Earth project was an opportunity to highlight the darker history of sugarcane and slavery.

> "The project sparked an opportunity to carefully and precisely express my culture, my history and whatever shadows may loom around them. To continue shedding light on Black history and connect it to something that will make people think, appreciate and remember that Black lives do matter."
>
> Eben, 17 years old

As one of our Voices of the Earth collaborators were the well-known theatre company, Complicité, we had planned for there to be a public performance of the young people's work. However, due to social distancing, this plan needed to morph into the production of audio pieces that could be listened to individually. Thanks to the wizardry of sound designer Daniel Balfour from Theatre Complicité, personal reflections, songs and traditional stories about seven different plants – oak, sugar cane, marigold, thyme, daisy, ash and yarrow –were woven together into seven different soundscapes; each represented one plant and linked to a particular location in and around the King's Cross Story Garden.

Story walks

For many people the constraints brought on by Covid-19 meant that parks were a natural place to be and green spaces like the well-known public park, Hampstead Heath, thronged with people. For others, the idea of going outdoors was met with fear and trepidation. The message of staying home to save lives was adopted to the extreme. Jane Myat, my local doctor, and I decided to invite some of her patients to join us for a story, a poem or two and some gentle qigong as we walked through the green spaces that lie between the Listening Space, an organic garden in the middle of her Caversham GP practice in Kentish Town, and Global Generation's Story Garden in King's Cross, which is a mile or so away. We began during the first lockdown in London and, in one form or another, we continued. Over the months that followed, I got to know the sweet chestnut in Camden Square and the avenue of plane trees in St Pancras Gardens, but most of all I got to know my neighbours and myself in ways that I never had before. Together we lived our way into a practice we began to call story walking.

We walked in small groups and, as the pandemic intensified, we found our way on our own to the safety of the Story Garden, where we sat in widely spaced circles watching the flames of a fire grow. We saw individuals who had previously considered themselves unwell, initiating activities, meeting up outdoors to walk and volunteer in their local park. As trust between us developed, different people started to write about their experience.

> "At 81, through the first lockdown, I wondered how I was going to take pleasure in my remaining time on earth. These walks opened up a new lease of life and the start of a new community which I could embrace. We share poems and stories that have beauty and relevance for us – enjoy the green spaces and let our imaginations soar. We do qigong exercises, watch our breathing and feel open to the skies above us and more aware of the ground beneath us."
>
> Pamela

Together we reflected on what we were kindling, and we wondered what role our story walks might have to play in the wider story of health. As we wove our way into the green cloak that still covers parts of Camden, we realised that the story walks brought to the surface ingredients that most of us need for living a healthy life: connection, meaning, movement, art, time for reflection and inspiration ... and, importantly, time to pause. No longer were the sometimes disempowering dynamics of expert knowledge at play. We were no longer patients relying on our doctor, as important as that may be. All of us were discovering and helping each other as we shared wise and creative parts of ourselves. However, if it were not for the relationship we had with our GP, none of us would have met each other and our story walking community would never have had a chance to grow. We began to think of it as doing doctoring differently.

This was how our GP, Jane Myat, described her experience:

> "I'm feeling grateful for being on this journey of encouragement and wisdom to trust instinct, intuition, to slow down, to notice and respect other ways of knowing. Such a different approach from the scientific empiricism inherent in modern medicine. I think through all the wonderful and varied folk who have walked with us, some every week, some coming and going, the flow and the energy this has provided. Would I have got through this time of pandemic without this rhythm to my week, the regularity of these encounters, the hope, possibility, solidarity, kindness and humour? And what of walking with people, who are patients of mine? I feel bonded and connected, in the right place I'd say for someone gifted the role of healer. A responsibility and a privilege."

Towards the end of the first year of the Covid-19 pandemic, we moved into a tier 5 lockdown, which meant meeting in person was no longer an option. Our story walks went online, and the group stayed together and found new ways for silence, creativity and connection to run between us. One of the participants, Chrissie Nicholls, an artist, introduced the idea of creating weathergrams out of brown paper in the shape of leaves, that held small messages. The WhatsApp group buzzed over the following days, providing clues about the trees on the walks people had taken, where they had been hung. Posts came in about the people, including the postman, who had found the weathergrams with their simple messages in the branches of trees around the neighbourhood.

Go into the wild

Learn to dance on a shifting carpet

Look up at the stars and wonder why the universe exists

Amidst the uncertainty of the times we were living through, it felt like a way of "singing-up" the steady and healing energies of the ground that lies between us.

Voices of the universe

Much of what I have brought to Global Generation's work has roots in the group of islands 18,300 km across the seas from London that form Aotearoa New Zealand, the land where I was born and where I now call home. The Covid-19 pandemic meant that what might have been a brief trip for me and my husband to visit my 95-year-old mother turned into a five-month stay. This time in New Zealand was a chance to immerse ourselves more deeply in the renaissance throughout the country in Te Ao Māori, the relational world view of the Indigenous people of New Zealand. During our visit we reconnected with Chellie Spiller and her wayfinding leadership work. As I left her house, Chellie gave me Nga Kete Matauranga, a large treasure of a book holding stories of Māori scholars working at the interface of Western and Indigenous knowledge.[6]

Slowly I made my way through different chapters as we travelled around the country. Chellie's chapter, "Wayfinding Odyssey: Into the Interspace", calls forth an eternal inner space of strength. Quoting Mau Piailug, Chellie describes how, in these stormy times, rather than praying for fair weather, we should pray for courage. Not for the first time, I was struck by the resonance between a mythic interpretation of the scientific account of the history of the universe and the Māori creation story, which begins with Te Kore, the empty realm that is full of potential. I experience the primordial and ever-new ground of emptiness as the deepest and most positive part of myself. Chellie points out that Covid-19 and the reality of climate change asks us to draw upon Te Kore. She says this requires us to go on a journey of discovery, explaining that the word "discover" can mean to pull apart.

> "A journey of discovery involves a fragmenting, so shafts of light can shine through the cracks and we gain new perspective. It's not the most comfortable place to be, but then true adventures encourage us to reimagine places in ourselves and in the world. This journey starts with ourselves – to inquire into our experience. And in the odyssey of discovery old maps won't be enough."

The thirteen-hour time difference between New Zealand and the UK in the summer months meant that I received emails in the morning about the London projects left behind. Amidst the challenges our colleagues were facing, I observed shafts of light breaking through due to the lockdown necessity of finding new ways to work. Our Voices of the Earth fellows moved on to a new project called Voices of the Universe. Whilst working remotely, our young fellows took the practice of thinking large and seeing small to new heights. The group was invited to imagine they were the universe going through its tumultuous and creative phases of evolution. This included the empty place before the big bang, the stars, the galaxies, the supernova and the sun, the earth and the wondrous array of life on earth. Creative writing in the first person was done by the fellows, on their own and simultaneously online using a Google document. Each person imagined how they might have felt being the universe as it made its way through epic twists and turns. The fellows recorded themselves on their mobile phones and posted the audio to the sound designer, who created a spectacular sound piece. As I listened to the final audio of the different lines spoken by the fellows combined with music, I heard humility and wonder in their descriptions of the scale and mystery of the universe and the intricacy of life on earth.

In the beginning there was nothing

What does nothing look like ?... I am nothing ... I am a vision forming

An intense explosion of brilliant light, unfathomable heat and uncontainable energy flashes out with the brilliance of who I am

From nothing to everything in an instant

You can't measure my depth or how far I stretch

I am a tidal wave of creation and destruction

I feel anticipation for things unseen and I challenge my strength into a vibrant explosion

From smoke, fire and dust I form

From eternal night I bring a new day

I am the one and the countless many and we spin through space as giants

We are the fiery jittering balls of light dotted across the galaxy

Have you seen the detail of everything inside of me, look at the sky, see the clouds so delicate and unique

Look at the sea, watch the intensity of colour, I am so deep that even light can't get through

Now look at your hands

Everything I do and have ever done is with the greatest intent

My colleague, Silvia Pedretti, has supported hundreds of young people on Global Generations projects to feel and express their best and biggest self. Silvia describes the sense of journey and discovery she observed in the Voices of the Universe piece:

> "This piece creates the right sense of fear and calm that the nothingness can create in our imagination. The audio feels like an adventure. To me, this is a highlight in these strange months of the pandemic and an example that the universe, this Old Story, can still support young people and their feelings after millions of years."

It is easy for any of us to feel self-conscious when we hear our own voice, and so it was encouraging to get the feedback from the fellows about what they had created after they listened to the audio. In many ways it is the effect of this work on the young people we have had the privilege to work with that has given my colleagues and I the confidence to keep exploring new opportunities for how this universal story might be expressed.

While in New Zealand, I joined the Global Generation team in our weekly update meetings on Zoom. I felt reassured that the spirit of wayfinding was alive and well. Due to the national call to grow back greener, lots of work was coming our way and our funds were in good shape. At the same time, I noticed that some of my colleagues were worn down and tired. To help the inevitable exhaustion of living through the pandemic, a much needed addition was brought to our meetings that addressed our wellbeing. For many years now, we have begun the meetings with time for being silent and still together, this is followed by a reading before each person shares highlights and updates from the preceding week. The staff team were now invited to share something they had done for their own wellbeing that week.

In preparing this chapter, I revisited our meeting notes. As I read of freshly washed bed sheets dried in the sun, swimming and singing, eating magnolia flowers, watching newts, seeing the sea for the first time in months, slowing down and practicing gratitude, I reflected on how small things really can make a difference. In these day-to-day steps of personal commitment, I felt gratitude for the relentless power of the human spirit that can be expressed in so many heart-opening, confidence-restoring, life-giving actions. Children's author Jennifer Morgan describes how in times of crisis, the universe gets creative.[7] Whilst a climate-changed world is not something any of us would welcome, this last year gives me faith that there is a politics of hope in terms of the strength and creativity of the human spirit, expressed in stories old and new, and perhaps it is the countless new ways the human spirit will express itself that we can look forward to with a sense of possibility.[8]

References

1. Spiller, C., Barclay-Kerr, H., and Panoho, J. (2015). *Wayfinding Leadership: Ground-Breaking Wisdom for Developing Leaders*, Auckland. Huia.

2. Greening Leighton (2020). (http://greeningleighton.org.uk)

3. Solnit, R. (2020). *A Paradise Built in Hell: The Extraordinary Communities that Arise in Disaster*, London. Penguin.

4. Riddiford, J. (2021). *Learning to Lead Together*, London. Routledge.

5. Global Generation. *The Stay at Home Garden*. (www.globalgeneration.org.uk/stayathomegarden)

6. Ruru, J. and Nikora, L.W. (Eds.). (2021). *Nga Kete Matauranga: Māori Scholars at the Research Interface*, Dunedin. Otago University Press.

7. Morgan, J. (2002). *Born with a Bang: The Universe Tells Our Cosmic Story*, Nevada City. Dawn Publications.

8. Sacks, B. (1997). *Politics of Hope*, London. Jonathan Cape.

Part 3:
Systemic Change

From Thinking to Acting

Responding to the Climate Emergency with our Minds, Hearts and Hands

Karen Scott

This chapter explores the disconnection of humanity from the natural world we inhabit and traces some of the roots and branches of that 'Great Disconnect'. It highlights how we must change our habitual modes of thinking in order for climate actions to be effective. Taking new action without new thinking may achieve some useful outcomes, but when both support and reinforce one another then sustainable, long-term change is more likely.

The chapter also considers how paradigm shifts in thinking, including perspectives that reconnect people with their place in the natural world and a willingness to accept uncertainty, can strengthen commitment to leadership in climate action.

The concepts in this piece draw on the ideas and work of general systems theorist and deep ecologist Joanna Macy and her colleagues, who developed the 'Work That Reconnects', Jem Bendell and Rupert Read's work on Deep Adaptation, Robin Wall Kimmerer's blending of Indigenous wisdom and Western plant science, along with Kathleen Allen's Regenerative Leadership, among others.

I'd also like to acknowledge and thank Dr Hanna Nuuttila, Marine Biologist, conservation scientist and fellow climate activist, for her kind generosity in reviewing a draft of this chapter and providing some very helpful comments and suggestions.

Modern thinking and the great disconnect

There is something profoundly wonky in our thinking about the place of humanity in the world – a place in which humanity is seen as disconnected from and superior to other species and the whole of nature. To be clear, I'm referring to the modern or 'Westernised' worldview and not the ancient wisdom of many Indigenous peoples, the world over, who have much to teach their younger siblings, about connection to place, ancestral lineage and the natural world.

In this paradigm, we've been sold a story of our separation from nature, which is evident, for example, in the Judeo-Islamic-Christian texts where humans are seen as above nature, created by God as something special. This deeply religious but culturally pervasive story has then been reproduced through the various lenses of sciences and the arts. It also underpins the neo-liberal capitalist economic systems that regard nature as 'not us', but rather a 'resource' or 'ecosystem service' for humans to both exploit and pollute, *'using Earth as a supply house and sewer for the Industrial Growth Society'* (Joanna Macy).[i]

Like the composite eye of a fly, there are many lenses through which we can perceive and tell the story of a fundamental human disconnection from the natural world. We can find evidence of and explanations for this Great Disconnect in diverse academic disciplines, spanning history, philosophy, religion, literature, science, psychology and education.

Part of the problem may be that academic schools of study have taken a siloed approach, attempting to dissect and understand a vast indivisible living

---

i   See, for example, Work That Reconnects Network. Foundations of the Work. (https://workthatreconnects.org/spiral/foundations-of-the-work/)

system through any given focused lens. Perhaps a fundamental question is not so much *'what do we know about x?'* or even *'how much is it possible to know about x'*, but *'is it actually possible to know, to wrestle 'knowledge' from a vast complex, unknowable cosmic living system?'*. I'll return to these themes of living systems and 'not-knowing', or uncertainty, later in this chapter.

Another aspect of the problem is the way in which human languages and thinking per se (or at least modern languages) appear to separate us from nature. The very process of naming, classifying and describing what our senses perceive in and around us, using words, mediates the direct sensory experience of being part of nature. Here's an example:

> 'There's a wood near us. I can't see the wood for the words. Probably the wood is wonderful. My intuition tells me it is. But unless intuition is knowledge, I really don't know. And even if intuition is knowledge, all that I get from my intuition is the generic assertion, "This wood is wonderful." I can't see any particulars. I can't get an uninterrupted view of a flower petal or the hair on a caterpillar's back. My words about petals and caterpillar hairs get in the way. I am appalled by the distance between a petal and the word "petal", by the dissonance between the word "hair" and a hair—let alone between the word "hair" and the hair. When I think I've described a wood, I'm really describing the creaking architecture of my own mind.'

Charles Foster[1]

Dr Robin Wall Kimmerer, a botanist and member of the Native American Citizen Potawatomi Nation, writes beautifully about the richness of learning the language of her Indigenous people. In this ancient language (and others of people who are deeply rooted in place) there is an emphasis on verbs and process words, pointing to relationships and movement. In contrast, modern English is riddled with nouns and object-subject splits, tending to emphasise fixity and separation. As noted by Kimmerer:

> 'A bay is a noun only if water is dead. When bay is a noun, it is defined by humans, trapped between its shores and contained by the word. But the verb wiikwegamaa—to be a bay—releases the water from bondage and lets it live. "To be a bay" holds the wonder that, for this moment, the living water has decided to shelter itself between these shores, conversing with cedar roots and a flock of baby mergansers. Because it could do otherwise—become a stream or an ocean or a waterfall, and there are verbs for that, too. To be a hill, to be a sandy beach, to be a Saturday, all are possible verbs in a world where everything is alive. Water, land, and even

a day, the language a mirror for seeing the animacy of the world, the life that pulses through all things, through pines and nuthatches and mushrooms. This is the language I hear in the woods; this is the language that lets us speak of what wells up all around us.[...] This is the grammar of animacy.'[2]

Another common problem in our thinking is 'shifting baselines' in science, where everything is measured by what we can see at the moment, overlooking how they once were, or may have been. In conservation science, for example, this might be assuming that the biodiversity we have now is somehow normal, so that what we ought to measure is any reduction or change in species populations in our current timeframe. This viewpoint fails to acknowledge the reality that we already have hugely eroded levels of species populations and habitats, so the baseline has shifted (for example, we already live with seas that have almost completely been overexploited).[ii]

The Fall

The Agricultural Revolution is thought to have begun about 12,000 years ago. It coincided with the end of the last ice age and the beginning of the Holocene era, forever changing how humans live, eat and interact – and paving the way for modern civilisation.

During the previous Neolithic era, hunter-gatherers roamed the natural world, foraging for their food. But when the dramatic shift occurred, it is thought by many scholars that foragers became farmers, transitioning from a hunter-gatherer lifestyle to a more settled one. This meant they were able to produce sufficient food that they no longer had to migrate to find it. Only then could they begin building permanent structures, developing villages, towns, and eventually cities.

In Daniel Quinn's philosophical novel 'Ishmael', he describes how the Great Disconnect began with agriculture and a world-view that saw humans as special masters of the world, separate from other animals and able to forge a path away from the natural processes that have sustained life since it arose.[3] Quinn describes how it is not 'human nature' to adopt such a pathway of destruction, but rather it has risen from the particular social model that has come to dominate the world, with many older tribal societies (mostly since annihilated) having a very different world-view.

---

ii   See, for example, http://media.longnow.org/files/2/REVIVE/Shifting%20Baseline_Pauly.
      pdf

Nature-connectedness and nature deficit disorder

There are many studies of the ways in which children (and hence adults) have become disconnected from the natural world, through systems like: anxious protective parenting, the dominance of screen-time in its myriad forms, mainstream education and the culture as a whole, amplified by the ever-present media.[iii]

Peter Senge, a general systems scientist and professor at MIT Sloan School of Management, has critiqued modern educational systems based on conventional assumptions about learning, with fragmented knowledge drawn on "machine-age thinking" that became a "model of school separated from daily life."

Specifically, he details "industrial age" assumptions about learning and schools, suggesting that "children are deficient and schools should fix them"; that learning is strictly an intellectual enterprise; that everyone should learn in the same way; that classroom learning is distinctly different than that occurring outside of school; that some children are smart while others are not; that schools "are run by specialists who maintain control"; that the way knowledge is taught is inherently fragmented; that schools claim to teach some kind of objective truth, and that school-based "learning is primarily individualistic and competition accelerates learning".[4]

We are thus educated from childhood to think of ourselves as being separate from nature, as individuals separate from any dynamic system, with little or no skills taught for daily living. We are not taught, for example, about growing food, caring for animals, making or mending things. These deficits in self-sufficiency keep most of us wedded to the continuation of the capitalist consumerist system, fuelled by an artificially created need to buy unnecessary 'stuff', and we become addicted to buying ever more, competing with one another to 'have the best'.

Another way in which modern education systems disconnect children from nature is through the way they use language. Most of the education systems, across the world, is based on teaching students to categorise, systemise and filter information. It teaches by rote – where memorising the name attached to a thing or the date of an event is more important than understanding the processes behind them. Where such processes are touched upon, the discourse is always in favour of a dominant narrative.

Controversial as this categorising pedagogy may be, many names for aspects of the natural world are disappearing – having been removed, for example, from the Oxford Junior Dictionary 2007 edition. This provoked a heated debate about the relationship between our imagination, our ability to have ideas about things, and our vocabulary.[5] Words such as acorn, blackberry, bluebell, conker and kingfisher were lovingly memorialised a decade later in 'The Lost Words' by wordsmith and nature lover Robert Macfarlane and artist Jackie Morris.[6]

Another nature-writer, Richard Louv, who coined the term 'nature-

---

iii   See, for example, https://tocaboca.com/magazine/nature-deficit-disorder/[7]

deficit disorder', has written about the extensive human costs of alienation from nature. This includes eroded use of our senses, attention disorders and various impairments.

He also writes about ways in which children are disconnected from place, from the land, and hence from connection to nature where they live. He points to what is needed to heal this rift – falling in love with nature and developing a passionate enjoyment of being outdoors:

> "Passion is lifted from the Earth itself by the muddy hands of the young; it travels along grass-stained sleeves to the heart. If we are going to save environmentalism and the environment, we must also save an endangered indicator species: the child in nature".[7]

Individualism: the separation of humans from community

Not only are we conditioned from childhood to think of ourselves as separate from nature, but this cognitive outlook is reinforced throughout our lives. Jem Bendell and Rupert Read offer a useful perspective about the disconnection in their book 'Deep Adaptation'.[8] They describe a false assumption in the dominant culture of the modern world – *'the idea that each of us is the separate autonomous origin of our awareness, values and decisions, and that it is good to become more autonomous'*.

They suggest that modern society is based upon an 'ideology of 'e-s-c-a-p-e', comprising our assumptions and beliefs in the following: **entitlement, surety** (another word for certainty), **control, autonomy, progress,** and **exceptionalism.**

> "The 'ideology of e-s-c-a-p-e' is a summary of mental habits that arise from, and maintain, restrictions on our affinity with all life – human and beyond. The acronym e-s-c-a-p-e is intentional and convenient, as the mental habits arise from a desire to escape from unavoidable aspects of our reality – impermanence and death – as well as our aversion to those realities, which arise because we experience our existence as separate mortal entities (Jenkinson 2016). These mental habits of e-s-c-a-p-e give rise to attitudes like individualism, nationalism, fundamentalist religiosity and selfish spiritualities, as well as systems like colonialism, capitalism and neoliberalism. They are also involved in processes of unconscious bias, helping to reproduce prejudices and oppressions of various kinds".[9]

The ideology of e-s-c-a-p-e

Entitlement involves thinking, *'I expect more of what I like and to be helped to feel fine.'*

Surety involves thinking, *'I will define you and everything in my experience, so I feel calmer.'*

Control involves thinking, *'I will try to impose on you and everything, including myself, so I feel safer.'*

Autonomy involves thinking and feeling, *'I must be completely separate in my mind and being because otherwise I would not exist.'*

Progress involves thinking and feeling, *'The future must contain a legacy from me, or make sense to me now, because if not, when I die, I would die even more.'*

Exceptionalism means assuming, *'I am annoyed in this world because much about it upsets me and so I believe I'm better and/or needed.'*

These thought patterns are deeply embedded both on a wider societal level and within our own conditioned comprehension of the world. They are purveyed by the education system, by culture, by the mainstream media, and by the overwhelming majority of our peers.

Nonetheless, there is an increasing awareness that something isn't quite right about this world view, that it is missing something; that we are even being lied to. Certainly, that if we keep stubbornly adhering to it, the natural world will be completely destroyed – and us with it. From these sentiments, we can look to alternatives; ones that do not necessarily have to be created afresh but instead have existed for a very long time, practiced by humans themselves for millenia. The opposite of 'e-s-c-a-p-e' is, for example, articulated by Bendell and Read as 'C-o-s-m-o-s' – a world-view that invites us to consider and develop qualities that can be seen as more heart-centred and connecting than the divisive qualities contained in the e-s-c-a-p-e paradigm. These are: compassion, openness, serenity, mutuality, oneness and solidarity.

In the next section, we're turning our lens towards further perspectives in human thinking that can shift the paradigm from a Great Disconnect to ways of thinking that (re)connect and join minds with hearts and hands.

'COSMOS'

Whereas the habit of **entitlement** involves thinking '*I expect more of what I like and to be helped to feel fine . . .*'

Compassion, in this context, involves sensing that '*I feel an active responsibility for any of my contribution to your suffering, without expecting to feel right, better or worse.*'

Whereas the habit of **surety** involves thinking, '*I will define you and everything in my experience so that I feel calmer . . .*'

Openness wishes '*I will keep returning to be curious about as much as I can, however unnerving.*'

Whereas the habit of **control** involves thinking '*I will try to impose on you and everything, including myself, so I feel safer . . .*'

Serenity involves allowing the feeling that '*I appreciate the dignity of you, myself and all life, however disturbing situations might seem.*'

Whereas the habit of **autonomy** involves thinking and feeling '*I must be completely separate in my mind and being, because otherwise I would not exist . . .*'

Mutuality involves remembering '*as this world has produced me and societies have shaped me, I will question all my understandings and ways of relating with others.*'

Whereas the habit of **progress** involves thinking and feeling that '*the future must contain a legacy from me, or make sense to me now, because if not, then when I die, I would die even more . . .*'

Oneness awareness involves sensing '*what is important is how I live more lovingly right here and now, without needing to believe that I matter or am improving.*'

Whereas the habit of **exceptionalism** means assuming '*I am annoyed in this world because much about it upsets me and so I believe I'm better and/or needed . . .*'

We are Gaia: Reconnecting with nature and the cosmos

"You didn't come into this world. You came out of it, like a wave from the ocean"

Alan Watts[10]

While we can trace roots of the story of the Great Disconnect back at least two and possibly twelve millennia, some branches of modern scientific and philosophical thought are now bringing us full circle back to the oldest creation stories, still surviving in Indigenous wisdom traditions across Earth.[iv]

General systems theory, gaia theory and quantum physics, for example, suggest that we are part of one vast living web of life, one interconnected conscious whole, in which every small thing affects everything else.[v]

> 'Quantum theory thus reveals a basic oneness of the universe. It shows that we cannot decompose the world into independently existing smallest units. As we penetrate into matter, nature does not show us any isolated "building blocks," but rather appears as a complicated web of relations between the various parts of the whole.'

Fritjof Capra, physicist.[11]

General systems theory was founded by Austrian biologist Ludwig von Bertalanffy who called it a 'way of seeing'. It now appears within many disciplines – including biology, sociology, linguistics, ecology and management theory – that life is a complex adaptive system with the capacity to self-organise, self-regulate and change from experience.[12] Rather than dissecting and looking for the building blocks of life, in a way that asks *'what is it made of?'*, general systems theorists look at the whole system – processes rather than pieces.

Living systems are seen to have generative emergent properties, where new possibilities arise that couldn't have been predicted from the properties of the 'separate' parts. A simple example here is the molecular structure and properties of water, H_2O – the astonishing outcome of combining the atoms of hydrogen and oxygen.

Living systems have many other interesting properties, of which 'the holonic principle' has particular relevance here. This says that every system is a 'holon', meaning that systems are 'nested' or fractal in nature. Each one is a whole system in itself, while also being comprised of subsystems and part of larger systems – from cells to bodies to ecosystems, to planets to galaxies.

---

iv   For example, this can be seen in the Christian biblical story of 'the Fall' and exile from the Garden of Eden, which is thought to have begun with the agricultural revolution, which some scholars attribute to the stabilising of climate some 10-12,000 years ago.[15]

v   For example, see https://www.scienceandnonduality.com/interest/physical-sciences[16]

Credit: Greg Rakozy

Each system is greater than the sum of its parts, dynamically organised and balanced, with feedback loops through which it can grow, evolve and maintain equilibrium. However, problems arise when feedback to the system is blocked or ignored, which can lead to 'overshoot', or 'runaway' – a loss of coherence, resulting in system collapse.

Applying this to the climate crisis, we've had many decades of feedback data from countless scientists and the more recent IPCC reports. The big question is whether we still have just enough time left to rebalance and adapt the system to a new level of equilibrium, or whether the tipping points we see now will inevitably lead to runaway collapse and the death of many existing living systems on Earth.

While some of these ideas may be relatively new in the academic world, they're far from new to humanity. Indeed, we can follow a spiral path back to some of the oldest creation stories, still known to many Indigenous peoples who can trace their lineage back through tens of thousands of years.

Regenerative leadership

One specific area of systems thinking that holds hope for transforming capitalism is in its application to leadership, management and organisational development, in corporations, governments, academic institutions and other sectors.

During an interview in the May 2021 Nature Summit Dr Kathleen Allen said '*if we're not experimenting and learning by listening to feedback, then we are atrophying*'.[13]

In a complex system, no single element, part or person can see the whole picture, so we need diverse perspectives from all parts of the system to bring feedback from their explorations. Applying this to an organisation, if you want to thrive and evolve you need to invite innovation and experimentation, observe what happens and learn from it, in order to complete the feedback loops and continue to thrive.

In nature, profit doesn't look like money; it looks like an ongoing evolution of the system into more complexity and sophistication, so that it can continue to flourish for future generations.

Leaders in government and other influential organisations would therefore be wise to encourage and reward innovation, which rests on not knowing, beginner's mind and learning from what works, as well as what doesn't work.

Actions that reconnect

In his book 'Blessed Unrest', Paul Hawken presented a mind-blowingly comprehensive *'manifesto of hope for the 21st century'*, cataloguing a vast global regenerative social movement that is *'restoring grace, justice and beauty to the world'*.[14] This encompassed sustainable, peaceful and equitable innovation across every conceivable area of human life, livelihood and society, including how humans interact with, tend, restore and regenerate the natural world.

Transformational endeavours such as these, nurtured and supported by connectedness with nature, can be seen as a virtuous circle. Pro-ecological, pro-climate activism feeds connectedness with nature and vice versa, leading to improvements in wellbeing for individuals, communities and ecosystems. While some people are motivated by such innovative and inspiring initiatives, others – as suggested by Christiana Figueres and Tom Rivett-Carnac, the driving forces behind the Paris Agreement – may be galvanised by a sense of responsibility to the whole:

> 'We can no longer afford the indulgence of feeling powerless. We can no longer afford to assume that addressing climate change is the sole responsibility of national or local governments, corporations or individuals. This is an everyone-everywhere mission in which we all must individually and collectively assume responsibility. [...] Whoever you are, you are needed now in every one of your roles.'[15]

However, some of the feedback loops in the great systems of humankind are currently blocked. As we shall see later in a case study with the Welsh Government in the UK, there are understandable reasons why many human individuals and institutions have not been acting as quickly and effectively as they should.

So, we're turning our focus now towards decades-old empowerment approaches that support us in fully facing and responding appropriately to the vast predicament humanity and natural ecosystems are in.

Active hope

> "Your opponents would love you to believe that it's hopeless, that you have no power, that there's no reason to act, that you can't win. Hope is a gift you don't have to surrender, a power you don't have to throw away"

'Active Hope' is a term coined by Joanna Macy and Chris Johnstone in their book of that name.[16] It's a way of tending to our longing for things to change for the better. It has little to do with anticipated outcomes, but is more of a process that engages our moral imagination and our heart which may be yearning for more truth, justice, love and compassion in the world.

If we gave up this kind of hope, we might dwell in despair, apathy, resentment, or some other bleak, dark place. To be clear, this isn't about *having* hope, or being hopeful (filled with hope), which might be naive, given the state of the world we're living in. We can think of hope in terms of *what we do and what motivates us*, rather than being a quality that we either do or don't have.

In essence, Active Hope is about taking action to support the future we hope or long for in our world. Of course, we often encounter challenges to this sense of active, authentic hope. Many of us also feel powerless or overwhelmed and increasingly so in recent times. It's not unusual to sometimes be overcome with despair, depression, anger, or denial (a natural enough protective 'blocked feedback response' to our overwhelming global situation).

Feelings of powerlessness are a common emotional response to world problems. Many activists (and perhaps sustainability professionals too) start out with a sense of power – a sense of being able to really make a difference in the world, especially alongside others. But it's not uncommon for people to become disillusioned or completely burned-out, especially when we're not careful to look after ourselves, or find opportunities to express and be witnessed in how things really are for us.

The work that reconnects

The Work That Reconnects (WTR) is an empowerment process that harnesses the power of Uncertainty and strengthens our desire and capacity for Active Hope.

The practices in a typical WTR workshop or session follow a spiral path of four stages:

First stage: Gratitude

Reciprocity is a powerful motivator: the experiences we have of receiving from others increase our desire to give back. When we pay attention to what we love in our world and the many ways we receive, from the natural world in particular, we may feel inspired to express our love and gratitude for life by giving something back.

Second stage: Acknowledging our painful feelings about the world

The dominant 'culture' of the Global North would have us avoid uncomfortable feelings, neither expressing them nor even recognising them in the first place. This can lead us to turning away from looking too closely at painful issues, and perhaps to really struggle when we do face them without appropriate support. Listening to each other share our concerns and feelings can strengthen our ability to face and respond well to our global predicament. And then we can draw energy from our emotional reactions, rather than being overwhelmed by them.

Third stage: 'Seeing with new eyes' (aka *'seeing anew with ancient eyes'*)

In this stage, we reframe the way we think about power. If we believe an issue is beyond our power to do anything about it, this can fuel feelings of resignation, apathy or powerlessness. The 'seeing with new eyes' part of the spiral changes the story of power, seeing it as something that happens through us, through our choices and actions, in an interconnected, interdependent way. It also frames our place in the world in terms of a larger sense of self (sphere of influence) and within the context of a longer view of time.

For example, when we think of ourselves as being an integral part of a vast living system, or a cell in the larger body of Earth, we can discover a new sense of agency and power. This view of power is not that of competing interests, with some people having 'power over' others, but one that is rooted in values of compassion, connection and courage. This *'power-with'* perspective draws on general systems theory where 'the whole is greater than the sum of the parts' and where emergent properties that we can't predict can bring about wondrous results.

Could people in the 1960s have imagined same-sex marriage, a Black president of the USA, or the ending of apartheid in South Africa, for example? Having a longer view of time and a sense of the individual self as part of a greater system can free us from the limitations and constraints of the e-s-c-a-p-e paradigm. When we look beyond the short-term, beyond the individualistic vantage point, new possibilities for re-imagining the world can open up.

Fourth stage: Going forth and giving our unique gift of Active Hope
Here we explore and practice the skill of visioning future possibilities that may inspire and motivate us, and consider achievable action steps we can take in that possible future direction. Active Hope is a three-step practice that we can learn (like any skill). It's a particular way of looking at:

- where we are
- where we want to go
- how we can strengthen ourselves for the journey there

This practice supports the narrative of a Great Turning, the great adventure of our time that's taking place alongside the narratives of Business-as-Usual (which is part of, and is leading to, The Great Unravelling). We have the power to choose which of those epic stories we want to get behind. And we also have the power to choose what we're willing and able to do, or be, to play our own part in that story.

Piloting the work that reconnects with civil servants in Welsh government

There's a newly emerging edge where the Work That Reconnects (WTR) is being brought to sustainability professionals and others in corporate organisations, including public sector bodies.

The approach outlined above was tested in a small pilot study with employees of the Welsh government in 2020. Lessons from the pilot study have been shared with the global community of WTR facilitators and, at the time of writing, steps are being taken towards a similar offering to the Scottish government in 2021, in the lead up to COP26.

Six years ago, the National Assembly for Wales (now known as 'The Senedd') passed ground-breaking legislation, based on the 17 UN Sustainable Development Goals (SDGs), placing them at the heart of public policy and decision-making. This requires Welsh government and 43 other public sector bodies in Wales, such as health boards and local government, to consider the impacts of their policy decisions on future generations (under the 2015 Wellbeing of Future Generations Act).[17]

The UN's Sustainable Development Goals recognise that ending societal problems, such as poverty, can't be done in isolation from strategies that improve health and education, reduce inequality and support economic growth, all alongside tackling climate change.

In brief, the Act 'requires public bodies in Wales to think about the long-term impact of their decisions, to work better with people, communities and each other, and to prevent persistent problems such as poverty, health inequalities and climate change. The Act is unique to Wales attracting interest from countries across the world as it offers a huge opportunity to make a long-lasting, positive change to current and future generations'.[18]

A key way in which the Welsh government is responding to the Act is through an innovative 20-year sustainable development behavioural and culture change programme in which employees (and members) are learning from leading-edge behavioural science. This programme is informed by the view that policy makers 'can't separate emotion from reason. Better information about citizens' emotions and greater emotional literacy could improve policymaking.[19]

Evaluation is carried out by academics from universities across the UK and has so far considered: the embedding of coaching across Welsh government; flow and change; attention in leadership; use of mindfulness and behavioural insights to improve decision making; stakeholder engagement, and co-production in public services.

The pilot WTR workshops were framed as supporting delivery of the

Wellbeing of Future Generations Act, while also being a resource for the personal resilience of sustainability professionals and their colleagues. In total, 44 people took part in four runs of the workshops, of whom 36 worked for the Welsh government and eight were external partners.

Being a relatively small sample, we relied on narrative data to identify the elements that most impacted participants. One practice that was particularly noted by participants was based on an exploration of the medieval story of Parsifal and the Fisher King (see next page).

Parsifal and the Healing Question

Parsifal, a knight of King Arthur's court, is on a hero's quest. When finding himself lost in a wasteland, he comes across a regally dressed man who is fishing from a boat on a lake. This is the Fisher King, who invites him to stay the night at his nearby castle. Parsifal is welcomed and treated courteously, with a great feast prepared for his arrival. On entering the banqueting hall, he sees the Fisher King lying on a bed, apparently suffering great agony from a wound in his groin that will neither heal, nor from which he can die. His kingdom, which is barren and described as 'the Wasteland', reflects the state of its sovereign in lacking the ability to regenerate.

Parsifal notices that no one mentions the state of the Fisher King or the Wasteland, but rather everyone goes about their business as though nothing were amiss. So, being a chivalrous knight, Parsifal doesn't mention or enquire about the king's suffering either.

It turns out that the king, the land and the people are enchanted and only a Holy Fool or Innocent can break the spell by asking 'the healing question'.

After being admonished by a crone named Cundry for failing in his quest, following many more years and adventures, Parsifal finds himself back at the castle of the Fisher King. Now led by the wisdom of following his own heart, rather than societal conditioning, Parsifal approaches the Fisher King and (in this version of the tale) asks the powerful question: *'What ails thee?'*

The simple, compassionate act of asking the question had an immediate, powerful and transformative effect. The king regained his health and the land began once again to flourish and bloom, the spell having been broken.

This story contains the theme of uncertainty, namely getting lost and not knowing the right question to ask (until maturity and wisdom have been earned). It contains other powerful themes too, not least that of the 'blocked response': a feedback loop in a system that can't be completed as it's neither recognised nor acted on.

The Parsifal exercise invites workshop participants to consider seven common kinds of blocked feedback response, or forms of denial, in the face of overwhelming data.[20] These are:

- I don't believe it's that dangerous.

- It isn't my role to sort this out.

- I don't want to stand out from the crowd.

- This information threatens my commercial or political interests.

- It's so upsetting, I prefer not to think about it.

- I feel paralysed- I'm aware of the dangers and don't know what to do.

- There's no point in trying to do anything, it won't make any difference.

Several participants reported 'aha moments', or insights, when they recognised these forms of denial in themselves and others. Some confirmed in later follow-up conversations that this exploration had brought them more empathy and understanding of colleagues who appear to be in denial of the magnitude of the global predicament we face.

Here's a quote from one of them:

> 'I have really been able to see the blocked responses in people, things like 'it's too big'. I'm starting to see that if everyone plays a role, no matter how small, we'll start to see a difference. Now that I'm aware of the blocked response, rather than being annoyed with people, I can step back and recognise that's just where they are, without judging them. And I know that the blocked response isn't the end of the story. Overall, I'd say I'm calmer and less reactive. I've also been looking into behavioural science and neurology and putting some of this into practice. I am trying to get the message out about these workshops, via my networks, and letting them know this can help them influence others in a positive way.'

Welsh government WTR workshop participant

This example from the case study illustrates how an empowerment tool such as the WTR can shift thinking and action, enabling participants to see how their place in the system matters, inspiring a sense of agency and leadership.

The motivating power of uncertainty

The COVID-19 pandemic has shown us that human structures, such as governments and corporations, really aren't in as much control as they might like to think they are. When they are not acting for their own benefit, nor for those who put them in power, they seem incapable of responding adequately to global emergencies. Unlike COVID-19, there is no vaccine for climate change. The impacts are not solely economical and cultural, but existential.

Those of us who take an active interest in climate action may be all too painfully aware of the 'Great Unravelling' narrative of our times. From this perspective, we are witnessing the sixth mass extinction of species, alongside climate collapse, the COVID-19 pandemic, late-stage capitalism, social division and many other global ills.

At the same time, it's possible to see things from new (and ancient) diverse perspectives. When we turn the lens of awareness, we can also see inspiring examples of a 'Great Turning' narrative: permaculture and regenerative farming, intentional communities, carbon-free cities, global uprisings of young people, massive reforestation projects, the revival of earth wisdom traditions, the mindfulness movement, ocean clean-ups and local skills-based currencies. There are countless seeds of 'the more beautiful world' springing up globally, in many local communities, and in pioneering institutions. Moreover, in many cases, changes in thinking generate new ways of acting, and vice versa – with permaculture being one such example:

> 'Through paying greater attention to the complexities, cycles and subtleties of natural systems, permaculture can invite us into a fuller sense of ourco-being with nature. As such, it aligns with reducing our sense of separation from the natural world and therefore the restoration of our sense of inter-being.' (Rupert Read, Deep Adaptation, 2021)

Despite these signs and pathways of hope, it must be born in mind that the The Great Turning and The Great Unravellingnarratives are present at the same time, alongside a third 'Business-as-Usual' story that is often conveyed by the mainstream media and many dominant cultural institutions. While someone reading a book on climate adaptation may be well aware of the Great Unravelling as the inevitable end-game of Business-as-Usual, the mainstream narrative still being told by corporations, dominant world powers and the mainstream media is: *"Keep buying, keep burning fossil fuels, keep partying on (with no need to wear a mask now!), keep calm and carry on with 'normality'."*

The Great Unravelling and the Great Turning

The 'Great Unravelling', also referred to as 'end stage capitalism', is a term used by Joanna Macy and colleagues that refers to the system collapse of the modern human world and its institutions, as we know them, along with climate derangement, threats to ecosystems across the planet and the mass extinction of countless species. [28] The mass media presents us with many fear-fuelling glimpses of this narrative, alongside their preferred story of 'Business-as-Usual'.

In contrast, the 'Great Turning' describes a great revolution that we can see signs of when we look *anew with ancient eyes*. It's a great transition from the modern world's 'industrial growth society' to a 'life-sustaining society', informed by the ancient technologies, practices and wisdom of Indigenous peoples, as well as emergent new thinking and acting. The Great Turning is thought to be on a par with the previous great agricultural and industrial revolutions of human society and like those may not be obvious to people living in its midst, but become more apparent with hindsight.

Three mutually reinforcing dimensions of the Great Turning are:

1. Actions to slow the damage to Earth and its beings.
2. Analysis and transformation of the foundations of our common life.
3. A fundamental shift in worldview and values. [21]

Surrendering to The Great Unravelling or forging a new path through The Great Turning is dependent on how we think and act. Society, and every individual within it, is locked into patterns of thought and action that are based on centuries-old dogmas. Many of these serve no purpose whatsoever, save from maintaining the power of elites, whose positions are reliant upon widespread social and environmental exploitation.

The 'power of the elite' concept is also why civilisations in previous times have succumbed and collapsed. [22] Since the elites are so far removed from the damage they're causing to people and ecology, they power ahead without changing and cause their own demise in the process. We've seen clear recent examples of this with the 'billionaire space race', in summer 2021. This had three of the richest men on the planet in a narcissistic contest to see who can be the first to build a rocket for a leisure trip into space, with further plans to colonise Mars, at great cost not only to themselves but to the future of humanity, the climate and ecosystems. [vi] We also see very worrying evidence of this 'system

---

vi   See, for example, https://www.doubledown.news/watch/2021/july/26/why-jeff-bezos-space-dream-is-humanitys-nightmare-george-monbiot [32]

overshoot' in the tipping point reached by clearance of the Amazon rainforest, which is now believed to be emitting more carbon than it absorbs.[23]

As worrying as the situation appears to be, uncertainty about the future can take us beyond despair and anguish. It can also bring us increased awareness. Uncertainty is counter-cultural, since the dominant culture of the modern world is built on certainty, knowing, planning and control. And not only is this cultural but hard-wired into our neurobiology.

Neuroscience and trauma therapy tell us that different regions of our brain and neurology regulate different emotional states, needs and behaviours, such as the need for safety, security and control, desire-fulfillment, and connectedness. The good news is that we can learn the basics of how our neurology works along with simple practices to help us overcome trauma and regulate our nervous systems, creating the right conditions for feeling safe, connected and ready to face the many uncertainties of life.[vii]

Of course, the capacity to learn these principles and practices depends on having access to affordable information, training and/or therapy. It also depends to some extent on our basic physical needs for safety and security having been met. Assuming we have the basic human requirements of shelter, clean water, adequate food, connection with others and protection from physical conflicts (increasingly rare privileges in our current global predicament, which those of us who have them can no longer take for granted), then we have the potential to expand our ability to be with uncertainty. This evolutionary shift can free our moral imagination and creative energy, so that we can lean-in and fully face the predicament of these times, consider what kind of future we hope for and then take action towards making that longed-for future more likely for future generations.

---

vii   See, for example, the work of Peter Levine, Stephen Porges, Judith Herman, Bessel van der Kolk

A personal view of uncertainty

Credit: Robert Anasch

In an interview with Joanna Macy, I was struck by the idea that we don't know whether we're death doulas, attending the hospice beds of a dying world with a dying humanity, or whether we're midwives attending the birth of a more beautiful world. In this interview, Joanna also says:

> *"Leadership means being able to have that loving attention to the reality of the situation, that you can live with that uncertainty and that you can ask the people around you to take risks for what they most care about. We have to ask people to give up the comforts of their old opinions. We have to ask people to give up the comforts of their old antagonisms and the comforts of their old worldviews, and to bet everything on the adventure of life going forward. Leadership is to evoke people's reverence, appreciation and gratitude for the miracle of life."*

The truth is that we don't know, and we can't really know, exactly which way things are heading in the future. And they seem to be spiralling in both directions, with plenty of evidence of both the Great Unravelling and Great Turning happening at the same time.

If only we could zoom out and see the bigger picture of Life on Earth, with all the instances of inspiring activism the world over, like a fractal zoom perhaps, it might blow our uncertain hearts and minds wide open and strengthen our sense of Active Hope.

I'm learning to see and hold in my heart both destruction and regeneration happening at the same time. I'm learning to remember that it's both/and, not either/or.

Whether we place our energy and focus in witnessing and grieving the death of all we love, or in actively co-creating the new paradigm, or whether our particular calling is to attend to both of these stories at the same time, it seems to me that to fully embrace our uncertain future, we need these same deeply human qualities:

-gratitude

-presence

-connection

-compassion

-courage

-acceptance

-and above all,

LOVE

References

1.   Foster, C. (2021). Against Nature Writing. Emergence Magazine. (https:// emergencemagazine. org/essay/against-nature-writing/)

2.   Wall Kimmerer, R. (2013). Braiding Sweetgrass: Indigenous Wisdom, Scientific Knowledge, and the Teachings of Plants. Milkweed Editions.

3.   Quinn, D. (1992). Ishmael. New York. Bantam Books.

4.   Senge, P. (2004). The Fifth Discipline. New York. Doubleday., Senge, P. (2001). Schools That Learn. New York. Doubleday.

5.   The Guardian. (2017). The Lost Words by Robert Macfarlane and Jackie Morris review sumptuous.

6.   Macfarlane, R. and Morris, J. (2017). The Lost Words. London. Hamish Hamilton Press; Greater Good Magazine. (2017). How Modern Life Became Disconnected From Nature.

7.   Ibid.

8.   Bendell, J. and Read, R. (2021). Deep Adaptation: Navigating the Realities of Climate Chaos. Cambridge. Polity Press.

9.   Ibid.

10.   Watts, A. (1973). Cloud-hidden, Whereabouts Unknown: A Mountain Journal. New York. Random House.

11.   Fritjof, Capra. (1975). The Tao of Physics: An Exploration of the Parallels Between Modern Physics and Eastern Mysticism. Boston. Shambhala.

12.   Wikipedia. Systems Theory. (https://en.wikipedia.org/wiki/Systems_theory)

13.   The Nature Summit. (https://thenaturesummit.com), Kathleen Allen. (https:// kathleenallen.net)

14.   Hawken, P. (2007). Blessed Unrest: how the largest movement in the world came into being, and why no one saw it coming. New York. Viking.

15.   Figueres, C. and Rivett-Carnac, T. (2020). The Future We Choose: Surviving the Climate Crisis. London. Manilla Press.

16.   Johnstone, C. and Macy, J. (2012). Active Hope: How to Face the Mess We're in Without Going Crazy. California. New World Library.

17.   Welsh Government. The Well-being of Future Generations. (https://gov.wales/well-being-of-future-generations-wales)

18.   Future Generations. Well-being of Future Generations (Wales) Act 2015. (https://www. futuregenerations.wales/about-us/future-generations-act/)

19.   European Commission. (2021). Understanding our political nature: how to put knowledge and reason at the heart of policymaking. (https://ec.europa.eu/jrc/en/facts4eufuture/ understanding-our-political-nature)

20.   Johnstone, C. and Macy, J. (2012).

21.   Work That Reconnects Network. Three Stories Of Our Time. (https://workthatreconnects. org/spiral/the-great-turning/the-global-context/)

22.   Brown, M. and Macy, J. (2019). Coming Back to Life. New Society Publishers.

23. The Guardian. (2021). Amazon rainforest now emitting more CO2 than it absorbs. (www. theguardian.com/environment/2021/jul/14/amazon-rainforest-now-emitting-more-co2-than-it-absorbs)

Environmental Education

Educating for a Sustainable Future

Vitalie Duporge and Olivia Copsey

Introduction

Global environmental change is the defining feature of our times and demands a widespread and collective re-examination of our social, political and economic systems. In order to do so, it is necessary to develop appropriate educational frameworks that address environmental issues and enhance environmental literacy across all communities. Indeed, as UNESCO (2021) states, 'Learning must prepare students and learners of all ages to find solutions for the challenges of today and the future.[1] Education should be transformative and allow us to make informed decisions and take individual and collective action to change our societies and care for the planet'. However, while education can be seen as an important vehicle for both raising public awareness and encouraging civil action toward a more sustainable future, there is also an urgent need to clearly define the types of teaching methodologies, curriculum content and practical skills that are being prioritised and whether they are appropriate for addressing the multiple challenges (such as biodiversity loss, species extinction, rampant consumerism etc.) that are likely to continue to characterise the state of our shared planet in the coming decades.

Indeed, we must re-examine the types of social values and behaviours that are being encouraged within modern and mainstream education frameworks and begin to question whether school and university institutes are best equipped to understand and act on the issues of climatic and environmental change, or whether alternative practices of education and community dialogue are also needed. Finally, we must ask whether current education practices are enabling students to develop their own voice and agency in order to face the demands of a changing planet, and how democratically involved schools and universities should be in shaping our environmental future.

Many of these important issues have come to light as a result of recent events such as the 'Friday for Future' school walk-outs taking place across Europe and spreading globally, wherein dissatisfied students have been increasingly demanding more serious responses from education institutes towards tackling environmental collapse. Overall, there is an evident and widespread frustration with the lack of engagement with topics related to climate change and sustainability that are rarely taught in classrooms. There is also a feeling that teachers are largely ill-equipped to navigate the urgency of the global environmental situation or to provide actionable opportunities for students to do something about it.

How, then, can education systems better meet the needs and demands of their pupils and of a rapidly changing planet? In order to navigate these multiple questions and concerns, this chapter will begin by providing a brief history of the environmental education movement as it has developed in the Global North, before discussing two relevant case studies that demonstrate alternative models for engaging students in the issues related to climate change and environmental degradation, both within mainstream institutions and frameworks (the eco-schools movement) and beyond it (the eco-village movement).

A history of environmental education

Although pre-dated by conservation and nature-education initiatives, a widespread environmental education program emerged in the Global North from the 1960s onwards, spurred on by seminal publications that sought to reveal the devastating effects of industrial agriculture (see for example Rachel Carson's *Silent Spring*) as well as the influence of radical political pressure groups such as Greenpeace and Friends of the Earth. During the 1970s, the United Nations Environment Program (UNEP) was established and a number of international conferences were held which advocated for the need to increase environmental knowledge and skills, positioning environmental education as an important issue of concern. During this time, the environmental education movement was defined as an attempt to: a) increase awareness of economic, social, political and ecological interdependence; b) provide people with the opportunities to acquire knowledge, skills and values for protecting the environment; and c) encourage new patterns of ecologically-minded social behaviours.[2] Commitments to environmental education also spurred practices of outdoor learning and field study wherein students are encouraged to engage practically with nature-based experiences (see, for example, UK Forest Schools).

Later on in the 2000s, against the backdrop of an increasingly urgent climate crisis and a push to tackle global poverty, the environmental education project was subsumed and transformed into education for sustainable development. Essentially, education for sustainable development has focused on many of the same areas as Environmental education in terms of increasing environmental knowledge and awareness, but has also framed development as a key end goal. At the same time, higher education institutes have been increasingly positioned as key intervention points for instilling environmental values into student bodies. This has led to a plethora of university-led sustainability-focused subject areas (in areas such as sustainable architecture and design, renewable technologies and environmental policy and politics) as well as a range of on-campus greening initiatives (such as plant-based food policies, recycling centers, cycle-to-work schemes).[3]

Despite its widespread application, however, many people have become increasingly critical of pursuing environmental education via mainstream frameworks and via the concept of 'sustainable development' as neither of these questions the logic of endless growth nor leaves space for the inclusion of alternative perspectives and approaches (such as those deriving from Indigenous and degrowth groups).[4] Additionally, a growing understanding of the role that many modern and formal education systems have played in the trajectory of unsustainable development has prompted several movements that are helping to shift environmental learning away from the domain of mainstream education.

For example, a number of grassroots and community-led initiatives (such as transition town networks, cooperative agricultural projects, climate activist groups and co-housing schemes) have begun to provide alternative learning opportunities that engage with social and environmental issues in non-formal, collective and practice-based ways. At the same time, a range of autonomously-run higher education institutes have recently developed ecologically-focused education initiatives that are approaching sustainability topics via more holistic and less economically-driven forms (see 'The Ecoversities Alliance', Schumacher College in Devon, UK, and the online-based Gaia University).

These modern and alternative education practices not only demonstrate that environmental learning can take place across a whole host of arenas, they also reject the more traditional top-down instructive methodologies found in mainstream education institutes wherein the dissemination of information is thought to lead to increased awareness and understanding. In fact, the underlying problem with this approach is that it requires set pathways and predetermined solutions to sustainability problems that we now understand to be deeply complex and few simple solutions exist which meet both the needs of environments and the local people who depend on them. Additionally, top-down approaches to education raise questions over the 'politics of knowledge', i.e. who is providing information on sustainability issues and who has most to gain from any behavioural or attitudinal outcomes. Asserting more bottom-up models of education can therefore be seen as a crucial step toward developing more democratic involvement in tackling environmental issues.

To conclude, although there is a rich history of engagement with environmental issues via education, there are still many pressing challenges and factors to consider in terms of defining the types of methodological approaches, settings and contents that are most effective for creating a sustainable and just future. This chapter will now focus on two important examples that illuminate possible future avenues for doing sustainability education differently: the eco-schools and the eco-village movements.

Eco-schools: A transformative model for mainstream educational change

Many educational for sustainable development (ESD) professionals believe that to achieve sustainable development, mainstream education systems need to transform on a conceptual, structural and cultural level. Experience from the international Eco-Schools programme suggests that this is possible from the bottom up.

Eco-Schools was a concept developed in 1992 as a response to the UN Conference on Environment and Development in Rio de Janeiro. The Agenda 21 document coming out of the Rio conference suggested that youth-led environmental protection and development was key (United Nations, 1992). A new model for the mobilisation of action-based learning was initially developed through a Danish collaboration between NGO and municipality, and soon extended to the world to promote student and teacher engagement in environmental and sustainability education. From modest beginnings in a few European countries, the programme has expanded to effect change in some 59,000 schools in 68 countries across the globe.

Eco-School Committee for leadership
Representative of the school community it directs and facilitates the sustainability of the whole institution and develops future sustainability leaders.

1

7 Eco Code of Values
The Eco Code is a statement of values and demonstrates the internalization of a sustainability culture in the whole institution.

2 Sustainability Review to identify issues
Understanding the biophysical environment, auditing its level of sustainability and identifying the need for improvements.

6 Informing and Involving
for partcipation
Publicity and awareness raising to keep the school stakeholders and wider community involved and iformed.

3 Action Plan to address
sustainability issues through ESD
Prioritising plausible actions, setting specific and achievable targets with completion dates and responsibilities.

5 Curriculum Linkages to
align with curriculum standards
Sustainability embedded in curriculum standards, subjects and non-formal learning spaces and contexts.

4 Implementation,
Monitoring & Evaluation
Implement the change, check progress towards set targets and make ammends where and when necessary.

Figure 1

Today, the programme employs a simple Seven-Step process (Figure 1) that guides participating schools to plan and implement learning and change based on their own specific sustainability challenges. The nature of each of the Seven Steps and the order in which they are implemented allows students to engage on a journey of incremental change through active learning, building confidence and action competence as they discover their own ability to transform their communities and surroundings. The steps are intended to be flexible enough to accommodate any school context and environmental theme, while being rigorous enough to bring about change. The Seven Steps are learner-centred by design with teachers acting as facilitators. Teachers do not just provide instructions and assess progres, but are also co-learners as they investigate local challenges with their students and help to co-create solutions.

For example, in Uganda the eco-schools seven-steps have been integrated within a rights-based Education for Sustainable Development (ESD) methodology focusing on developing action competences with schools as a hub for whole-community participation in action-based learning. Learners, parents and community members are involved in development and leadership of sustainable natural resource management and micro-projects that promote sustainable community development. The micro-projects are varied and often highly innovative, using locally available resources and local knowledge. Among many examples are included rainwater harvesting projects, sustainable agriculture and agroforestry, sanitation, waste management and income generating micro-enterprises. These shared projects unite schools with their local communities and build collective competences. The collaborations form a two-way process which result in improved pedagogies and learning outcomes, development and transference of critical skills, and ultimately, practical improvements to conditions in the schools and local communities.

In common with traditional environmental education programmes, the basis of the Eco-Schools approach is a process of connecting and contextualising learning and knowledge to the real environments and communities in which they are based. Using engagement with local issues and individuals increases the learners' abilities of critical reflection, collaborative problem solving and action on local challenges. Teacher Didus Gumisiriza, 2nd deputy head at St. Kagwa school in Western Uganda explained the transformation in teaching and learning that the Eco-Schools seven-step process brings about:

> 'We had traditional methods of teaching with chalk, nowadays there is emphasis that the children must use their environment in the learning. They help make learning materials, learning in the environment they learn to conserve it. Their education will be practical and will help them impact their community (e.g. tree planting, growing), hands-on skills that will help them create their own jobs.'

However, the incremental Eco-Schools methodology soon moves beyond the confines of environmental education to address social issues and development challenges affecting the learners, their families and local communities. Alex Kaamu, Ugandan primary year 3 teacher at Queen of Peace Eco-School on the outskirts of Kampala outlines the educational approach behind this process:

> 'I believe in innovation – what will really affect the community and the children? Around here there are too many needy people. We assessed the community to see what they need and we teach the children relevant skills to take home (e.g. urban farming on verandas, fuel-less cookers) and the children have told us stories of success.'

St Kagwa school in Western Uganda has seen several benefits since using the Eco-Schools methodology. Learners have made lasting changes in their homes and communities, and developed more self-confidence. Parents Caroline Arinaitwe and Mujuni Genensoo particularly noticed a difference in their children's ability to express themselves and communicate with adults:

'The children are bold and strong in asking questions and petition over environmental degradation through their parliaments to higher levels. Parents are now up in arms to protect the environment through community committees for environmental protection.' - Mujun

The Eco-Schools learning approach entails a shift within mainstream education towards bottom-up processes that involve discourse and critical reflection, with actions taken based on this. The experience of Ugandan Eco-Schools suggest that processes of implementing environmental learning can potentially play a transformative role in helping to reorient wider educational policy and practice towards a more holistic view. Nevertheless, there is still space for formal curriculum learning which can still be consistent with a bottom-up approach if all information is viewed critically, and conclusions drawn based on assimilation of given facts, community perspectives and the students' own knowledge.

As explained by Stephen Omoding – P7 science teacher, St Alloysius, Uganda:

'Learning as a process is not about passing exams. The children exhibit a different quality. They ask questions like 'Teacher how?' that was formerly not there. They have a new interest in the learning and retention of the learning.'

The stories told in Ugandan Eco-Schools mirror several others told in other countries operating Eco-Schools around the world. They promote a new role for mainstream education institutions in facilitating the adaptation of humankind towards a sustainable and resilient future. However, this role is no longer one of instruction. Instead, it requires widespread understanding by teachers, curriculum developers and education institutions that societal adaptation is a collective rather than an individual process which relies on the incorporation of system properties including local and Indigenous knowledge, community interests, environmental health and local livelihoods. In the end, the Eco-Schools movement shows that it is possible for educators, parents, community members and students to be co-developers of their own context-specific and place-based knowledge, and that this has the potential to solve even the most urgent challenges.

Ecovillages: Laboratories for lower-impact living

While the Eco-Schools movement therefore provides a promising approach to tackling sustainability in new and transformative ways via existing education institutions, there is also significant effort taking place outside of mainstream contexts. One notable example of this is the ecovillage movement, which is simultaneously committed to offering groups of people the chance to live as low-impact as possible, as well as elaborating alternative models of environmental education for the general public that are specifically place-based and eco-centric.

Figure 2: Permaculture gardening in Findhorn ecovillage in Scotland, UK. **Credit:** GEN EU.

The ecovillage first emerged around the 1960s in tandem with the 'back-to-land' movement and has been defined as 'an intentional, traditional or urban community that is consciously designed through locally owned, participatory processes in all four areas of regeneration (social, culture, ecology and economy) to regenerate their social and natural environments'. To this end, ecovillages have typically adopted organic gardening principles, aimed for self-sufficiency in food or supplemented it through local networks, attempted to produce their own renewable energy, recycle and repurpose as many resources as possible, implemented cooperative self-governance and non-hierarchical forms of decision-making, and lived communally with the sharing of resources and tasks. Across the world today, ecovillages constitute a diverse archipelago of set-ups: from farming communes with sustainable practices; eco-architectural and experimental towns; spiritual communities with pro-environmental infrastructures, and villages in the Global South organised around ecological traditions. Although historically, geographically and politically diverse, the global ecovillage network is unified around a common worldview that is grounded in a holistic understanding of the planet as a sacred living organism, of which humans are an inter-related part.

Figure 3: Volunteers using appropriate renewable technologies in Los Portales ecovillage in southern Spain. **Credit:** GEN EU.

As experimental centres for social, economic, political and environmental change, education initiatives have been a feature of ecovillages since their inception. From the early 2000s, however, an increasing number of ecovillages have begun to offer sustainability-focused education programmes to the general public through which to explore radical ecological perspectives and sustainable living techniques. Driven and delivered through the Global Ecovillage Network (an umbrella organisation for ecovillages across the world) and Gaia Education (an online learning provider) these have taken the form of accredited courses such as the Permaculture Design Course and the Ecovillage Design Education course, as well as a range of internship placements, youth exchanges, school visits and immersive volunteer/resident programmes through which participants engage with ecovillage life for a sustained period of time. A number of publicly accessible workshops and seminars have also proliferated in recent years offering short-term and skills-based projects in areas such as appropriate technology, soil science, conflict-resolution and food sovereignty. Additionally, there have been an increasing number of school and university field trips to ecovillages across the world.

Figure 4: Sunseed Desert Technology ecovillage in southern Spain - Volunteers digging in the organic gardens (left) and solar panels on the roof of the main house that provides electricity for the community (right).

Through their learning models, ecovillages can be said to provide a practical sustainability classroom or 'laboratory' within which to explore alternative environmental narratives and experiment with alternative lifestyle practices that are aimed at both shifting human relationship with the planet and lowering individual carbon footprints.[5] To do this, ecovillages typically adopt non-formal and interactive pedagogies as well as a trans-disciplinary curriculum (see Figure 3) that provides an experiential and holistic learning process in which participants are directly involved in the development of their knowledge and skills for living sustainably in all its dimensions.[6]

Additionally, being an inherently place-based site of environmental learning, ecovillages have been said to offer a unique opportunity to be physically immersed in an eco-centric culture and spatial landscape within which to experience first-hand what a more sustainable human community looks and feels like.[7]

Figure 5: Sociocratic decision-making processes in Seiben Linden ecovillage in Germany. **Credit:** GEN EU.

Figure 6: The Ecovillage Design Education course curriculum that seeks to address the four key areas of sustainability (Gaia Education, 2020)

In this way, much like other grassroots groups that aim to tackle social and environmental change, ecovillages engage in learning processes that are practical, bottom-up and which prioritise collaborative dialogue and exchange.

Indeed, as Chloe, a 30-year old former European Solidarity Corp volunteer at Sunseed Desert Technology describe:

> 'Ecovillages are there to educate people, they are there to show people how to live an alternative way of life...they show you how to get in touch with yourself, others, nature, emotions. In an ecovillage you don't sit at a table and learn from a teacher...if you want to eat, you learn how to do it practically.' – **Chloe**

For many, the opportunity to experiment and live-out alternative modes of being with the environment can also be a deeply transformative experience, allowing them to reshape their norms and behaviours around production, consumption and decision-making:

'Living in an ecovillage totally changed my life. Things like using a compost toilet, prioritising renewable technologies, cooking for big groups, engaging in sharing circles, showed me what I am capable of. My relationship to products changed. After living in Sunseed I started to make my own products for cleaning, buying second-hand clothing and sharing resources between friends' - **Ellie**

'I was taught practical learning experiences... how to grow food, how to process food, how to make medicine, how to live together as a group. My habits changed in the way that I connected with nature... I started to feel more gratitude for water, for sun, for heat... my way of feeding myself changed, I started to forage, to consume less and to make do with what I had.' - **Chloe**

In fact, living in an ecovillage can also go beyond an education in environmental issues, towards teaching participants how to engage with community life and share time, resources and experiences, as Simone, a garden volunteer in Angsbacka ecovillage in Sweden describes:

'The diversity of the people here is incredible. All the knowledge that people have gathered during their lives, they bring to the village and share with the rest of the community. If you wish to learn a craft or a new skill, there is always someone to support you. In particular, having skilled gardeners who can teach you how to relate to the environment is a big benefit of living in an ecovillage... I believe having a community is a great benefit for mental health, as a growing number of people around the world face loneliness and screen addiction.' - **Simone**

Beyond providing an alternative space for living out low-impact lifestyles, ecovillages can therefore be said to offer an important space in which to reassess our everyday values and behaviours in relation to food, mobility, waste and cleanliness and to develop new skills and patterns of living that are more communal and ecologically oriented. In this way, they offer a deeply practice-based and immersive approach to thinking through sustainability – one that can complement more mainstream and formal approaches.[8]

Figure 9: Eco-construction in Arterra Bizimodu ecovillage in northern Spain. **Credit:** GEN EU.

Figure 8: Sharing communal food in Sunny Hill ecovillage in Slovenia. **Credit:** GEN EU.

So, where to next?

Both the Eco-Schools and eco-village movement offer important examples of the various ways in which educating for a sustainable future can be thought through and brought about. What is unique to both approaches is the commitment to developing learner agency via bottom-up approaches and to moving beyond theory toward actually experiencing and practicing patterns of lower-impact living through everyday action. Arguably, both of these characteristics are hugely important if we are to equip students with the ability to address ecological collapse in courageous and resilient ways. Indeed, while initiatives within mainstream frameworks are useful for developing theories and knowledge around the science and technology of climatic and environmental change, it is arguably movements like Eco-Schools and eco-villages that are providing a base from which to understand first-hand what a more sustainable society can look and feel like. Learning from, experimenting with and building on different models of environmental education such will be crucial in the coming decades.

References

1. UNESCO. *Education for Sustainable Development.* (https://en.unesco.org/themes/education-sustainable-development)

2. Wals, A. E. J., Brody, M., Dillon, J., and Stevenson, R. B. 2014. *Convergence Between Science and Environmental education. Science.* 344(6184), pp. 583-4.

3. Jickling, B. and Sterling, S. (eds). 2017. *Post-Sustainability and Environmental education: Remaking Education for the Future.* Switzerland. Springer Nature.

4. Wals, A. E. J. and Jickling, S. 2002. *Sustainability in Higher Education: from Doublethink and Newspeak to Critical Thinking and Meaningful Learning. International Journal of Sustainability in Higher Education.* 3(3), pp.221-232.

5. Burke, B.J. and Arjona, B. (2013). *Creating Alternative Political Ecologies Through the Construction of Ecovillages and Ecovillagers in Colombia,* Nova Iorque. *Environmental Anthropology Engaging Ecotopia: Bioregionalism, Permaculture and Ecovillages.* Berghahn Books, pp. 235-250.

6. Greenberg, D. (2010). *Ecovillages-Academia. Beyond You and Me: Inspirations and Wisdom for Building Community.* Permanent Publications, pp. 236-242; Global Ecovillage Network. (https://ecovillage.org); Mychajluk, L. (2017). *Learning to Live and Work Together in an Ecovillage Community of Practice. European Journal of Research on the Education and Learning of Adults,* 2, pp. 179-194.

7. Roysen, R. and Cruz, T.C. (2020). *Educating for Transitions: Ecovillages as Transdisciplinary Sustainability 'Classrooms'. International Journal of Sustainability in Higher Education,* 21(5), pp. 977-992.

8. Waerther, S. (2014). *Sustainability in Eco-villages: A Reconceptualization. International Journal of Management and Applied Research,* 1(1), pp. 1-16.

PROUT

Filippo Basso and Dada Vedaprajinananda

Summary

Integrated rural development (IRD) projects are small or large-scale operations in developing countries with a coherent set of socio-economic goals. They were widespread in the 1960s and 1970s, mostly abandoned in the 1980s, but restarted with success in the 2000s. In the last 30 years, several examples of small-scale grassroots IRD projects have been addressing a relevant subset of Sustainable Development Goals (SDG) in an integrated fashion.

Ananda Valley is a grassroots IRD project in a rural area in central Portugal. It is a model project, part of a broader programme known as Master Units (MU), comprising a series of developmental village projects worldwide. Several elements that are central to the ecovillage movement are key aspects of MUs – their multi-pronged approach to development, including environment, farming, coops, small industry, social service and other socio-economic projects to benefit the local communities in which they function. With particular emphasis on rural community needs, MUs embrace most SDG goals in a holistic way.

The Progressive Utilisation Theory (Prout) is the primary economic framework through which MUs are implemented. Prout is an integral socio-economic theory offering alternative ways to organise the local economy in a sustainable manner. Central concepts of Prout include economic democracy, balanced utilisation and rational distribution of resources, revitalization of local culture, decentralised planning, and a social contract guaranteeing everyone's basic needs.

The wellbeing of nature cannot be sacrificed to meet the goals of profit margins. The goal of a Master Unit is not simply the welfare of human beings but the welfare of all living beings. Similarly, to maintain social balance and harmony, one must ensure both the individual as well as collective wellbeing of society. MUs therefore strive to nurture the holistic development of each community member – physically, intellectually, emotionally, culturally, ethically and spiritually.

Integrated development projects

In the field of rural development, the concept of *integrated development projects* usually refers to programmes in Africa or Asia which are large-scale operations with a coherent set of socio-economic goals. The main concept, common in most of the discussions around IRD in this period, was that, in order to develop deprived areas, it was essential to address a larger set of interdependent topics, such as education, infrastructure, access to finance, health and, as a central theme, rational agriculture, featuring increased productivity.

In the 1980s these projects were mostly abandoned, due to a vast literature evaluating 10-20 years of implemented projects in developing countries, showing a critically low efficiency of IRD pilot projects. Project success was not achieved, in varying degrees, and the expected results were far from satisfactory. The question is: was the concept behind IRD inherently wrong, or was the particular design of the projects not able to cope with the specificities and difficulties of a large-scale integrated approach?

Edoardo Masset analyses the causes of these failures and a new wave of integrated development approaches.i Some of the causes were identified in the design as being very often top-down, with an over-simplified modelling, scarce knowledge of the context and solutions, and high operational complexity. It became evident that it was too difficult to manage cross-sectorial and cross-agency projects using standard governing methodologies. Subsequently, a new wave of smaller-scale IRD projects, endowed with a more inclusive and participatory agile management, showed how the lack of efficiency of the first wave of IRD projects could have been avoided, while proper monitoring and evaluation can help to identify and correct pitfalls in a rigorous way. In the last 30 years, several examples of small-scale IRD projects have been addressing a relevant subset of Sustainable Development Goals (SDG) in an integrated fashion, with more appropriate design and implementation, leading to promising results.

The IRD concept, in which each project has specific characteristics and differences in design and implementation, was tested also on the European continent, taking advantage of previous investigations, pitfalls and good practices. Small-scale projects, dealing at the same time with multiple and inter-related development aspects, may look difficult to manage, but they offer one of the most important learning experiences in terms of resilience and sustainable regeneration practices.

Master units

In the 1960s and 70s several non-governmental organizations and movements tried to start IRD projects or programmes in developing countries, with their own well-defined characteristics and distinctive features. In the same years, a practical small-scale IRD concept was designed and developed, under the name of **Master Units**, by a worldwide socio-spiritual organisation and movement founded in Jamalpur (Bihar), India, by Prabhat Ranjan Sarkar. With a widely distributed presence – established in more than 180 countries across the world – based on a practical philosophy and personal development lifestyle and the all-around transformation of society, this organisation began to implement Master Unit projects, starting in developing countries, with a maiden project in India. Master Unit projects (MU) were created in several developing countries in this first phase, with the focus only of developing the prospects of the more impoverished classes, who were often exploited and existing at a survival level. This was especially the case in nations like India where the caste system was strong and hate crimes are rampant.[i] These first MU projects attempted to address deep social imbalances in the rural areas and

---

i   As reported for example by the 'Crime in India-2019' report of the National Crime Records Bureau.[2]

were sometimes met with violent resistance from entrenched interests, since they entailed tackling head-on corruption, caste suppression and exploitation.

The first MU and an example for many other developing projects is Ananda Nagar (literally, The City of Bliss), situated in the north-eastern part of India, in the heart of Rarh, one of the most underdeveloped regions of India. Due to the ideological and service-minded approach of the organization, such reactions didn't inhibit the growth of these MU projects. Instead, they evolved into a **second phase**, taking root in other countries outside of India, with a larger base of integrated disciplines. Nowadays the Master Unit concept is present on every continent, with several model projects in countries such as India, Brazil, Taiwan, Russia and the United States, and at least one strong MU per country in places like Denmark, Portugal, Brazil, Poland, Argentina, Italy, Ireland, Vietnam and Thailand.

In addition to Integrated Development goals, MUs are also focused on spiritual goals that include self-realisation and service to the surrounding community and to the planet. A number of projects overseen by distinct departments are ideally included and developed in a MU, from the environmental and ecological aspects to the artistic and cultural ones. MUs also include social services, disaster relief and preparedness, together with the study of socio-economic systems that can better direct the collective movement of society. The total number of departments intended to be activated and represented inside a MU amounts to 40, highly integrated and working in cooperation; sometimes only a subset of the most important departments will be active and structured with an independent team and well-defined responsibilities.

A somewhat different concept, more general in its scope and often confused with the idea of the MU, is defined by the term 'ecovillage'. In the 90s, Robert Gilman proposed a definition that became the standard for many years: 'a human-scale full-featured settlement in which human activities are harmlessly integrated into the natural world in a way that is supportive of healthy human development and can be successfully continued into the indefinite future'.3 In his foundational article of 1991, Gilman emphasizes that this is not a process of 'going back' to the traditional agricultural village model; rather, a true eco-village is a specific post-industrial phenomenon, drawing on lessons from humanity in the past, but not trying to return to any previous period or way of life. The Global Ecovillage Network (GEN) is a growing network of approximately 10,000 regenerative communities and projects, where people learn how to live with greater ecological awareness and harmony. The GEN approach is process-centered, empowering communities of any kind, be they intentional or traditional, or even of urban origin, and harnessing the collective intelligence and experience for its development, integrating social, cultural, economic and ecological dimensions in a regenerative perspective. Master Units are a special kind of ecovillage, created around spiritual goals and actively promoting the creation of a very diverse and inclusive network of service activities for the surrounding community and the planet. Master Units are not built to create a beautiful oasis in the middle of problems, or as closed paradise-shaped niches created by communities of people with a common vision. Instead, MUs are intended to be easily adopted, are consciously designed and developed to actively support the local community, and approach the world with a regenerative approach.

There are several frameworks upon which MUs are based, with their own scope and related methodologies. Here we will highlight only a couple of them: neohumanism and Prout. Neohumanism is an ethical approach to life, rooted in the understanding that all existence is bound together; that we are all interconnected through systemic relationships and deep interactions. It can also be defined as the extension of the underlying spirit of humanism to everything and everyone, animate and inanimate. It finds its expression not only inside MU projects but also in numerous educational projects all around the world, kindergartens, schools, colleges and research institutes. Distancing itself from the 'rhetoric of belonging' and oversimplified methodologies, the neo humanistic education (NHE) system places full responsibility for change onto us, transforming individuals into active citizens, bound to explore their own potentiality and to expand their understanding of who we are and why we are here. Consciousness itself becomes the chief protagonist, allowing for no distinction based on race, sex, caste, religion or even species. In its specific implementations it develops a synergy between morality, individual responsibility and rational process. Prout is the acronym for the Progressive Utilisation Theory, a new socio-economic model based on self-reliance of each bioregion, through cooperatives, environmental balance and universal spiritual values.

A detailed look at Prout

Credit 1: Anada Valley project.

Humanity stands at the brink of a critical juncture. Immense disparities of wealth, global pandemics, extinction of species and climate change have created a crisis unprecedented in our recent history.

To overcome these developments, we will have to use intelligence, wisdom and love. However, our dilemma is that the present economic system, capitalism and its related political structures, places the life and death decision-making regarding these problems in the hands of people who are primarily seeking to enrich themselves or their backers. Intelligence, love and wisdom have little or no role to play in their deliberations.

Is there a way out? Is there an alternative to capitalism? Can we get the human household in order and create a world where all people (and not just a few) live with dignity, have their basic needs fulfilled and are free to reach their highest potential? The adherents of Karl Marx's

theories tried to create an alternative to capitalism in the 20th century but their efforts were, in most respects, unsuccessful.

At the height of the Cold War, when the clash of communism and capitalism was intense, an Indian philosopher named P.R. Sarkar put forward an alternative social and economic theory: the Progressive Utilisation Theory (Prout). Sarkar said that the application of this theory could bring prosperity and social justice to the world, overcoming the problems of both capitalism and communism.

Sarkar's socio-economic approach for development outlined in Prout draws inspiration from neohumanism. Prout proposes a cooperative, decentralised and democratic approach to economics rooted in cardinal human values and love for all living beings.

Economic democracy

Success of a political democracy depends on several factors – morality, education, and socio-politico-economic consciousness of the electorate. In the absence of any of these aforementioned factors, political democracy becomes a farce. Such a system is a tool in the hands of a few politicians with vested interests, who form a nexus with capitalists and delude the public with false promises of putting an end to economic exploitation to win elections. Common people are deprived of any decision-making power over their socio-economic circumstances in political democracies.

Economic democracy, on the other hand, requires that common people be made guardians of their own economic destiny. In economic democracy, there is a bifurcation of political and economic power. Common people are empowered to make their own economic decisions and draw up economic plans to meet local needs. Political leaders, as administrators, legislate policies and remove obstacles in the way of implementing economic democracy. The primary goal of economic democracy is to build and grow strong self-reliant local communities.

When local people assume control of managing their economic needs, they are guided by an intimate knowledge of local natural resources available to them. They are better judges of economic potentialities in their region, and they can plan economic activities to use these resources in a sustainable and responsible manner due to a sentimental bond they have with theentire natural ecosystem of the region, such as the rivers, mountains and forests. Thus, economic democracy ensures activities in a region cause minimal impact on natural ecosystems. This will provide the flora and fauna a greater opportunity to thrive and offers a solution to many man-made crises like deforestation, depletion of natural resources, climate change and extinction of species.

Prout's economic democracy is based on the following requirements that will assist in the holistic well-being of human beings and the natural world:

1. Minimum requirements of a particular age, including food, clothing, housing, education and medical care, must be guaranteed to all. This socio-economic security will enable people to meet their physical needs, and develop their intellectual, artistic, and other subtler potentials in order to advance the development of society.

2. Increasing purchasing capacity must be guaranteed to every individual so that they are able to purchase their minimum requirements. Adequate and increasing purchasing capacity is ensured through easy availability of minimum requirements, stable prices, employment of local people in local industries, progressive and periodic increase in wages, and by planning the economy efficiently to increase collective wealth.

3. Power to make all economic decisions is in the hands of the local people. Local people decide, based on their collective necessities, what kind of agricultural and industrial commodities to produce, how much to produce and how these commodities are equitably distributed.

4. Outflow of capital and raw materials from a region must be curbed by preventing outsiders or a 'floating population' from participating in economic decisions and profiting from local economic activities. P.R. Sarkar defines 'local people' as those individuals who have merged their own socio-economic interests with the socio-economic interests of the region in which they reside.

Prout recognises economic liberation as the birth right of every individual and it must be guaranteed to everyone irrespective of one's gender, race, faith, ethnicity or nationality. Economic liberation is achieved through economic democracy. Economic liberation, consequently, leads to the utilisation of human potentialities in other areas of human existence – intellectual and spiritual pursuits, art, science, social service, etc. People who are liberated from the shackles of economic exploitation are free to use their physical, mental and spiritual energies in subtler pursuits and to contribute to the welfare of all living beings. Hence, economic democracy is not only essential for economic liberation of human beings but also for universal well-being.

Decentralised economy

Prout's vision of 'economic democracy for economic liberation' is fulfilled by a system of economic decentralisation. A decentralized economy materialises Prout's core tenets of maximum utilization and rational distribution of resources. For economic democracy to become a reality, economic policies adhering to these principles of decentralised economy must be implemented.

1. **Resources of a socio-economic region must be controlled and managed by local people.** These resources must be used not only to meet the minimum requirements of local people but also to achieve the economic prosperity of that region. Outsiders should not be allowed to interfere in production and distribution.

2. **Production must be for consumption, not for profit.** When commodities are produced for consumption of a socio-economic region, then that very region becomes a readily available market for sale of these commodities. Goods produced locally are sold locally. This keeps money circulating in the local markets and instils dynamicity in economic life.

3. **Production and distribution should be organised through cooperatives.** In a decentralised economy, most industrial and agricultural production and distribution will happen through mid-sized worker-owned cooperatives embedded within the community. This form of local ownership helps maintain employment and democratises the work place as well. When economic activities of a local region are entrusted with cooperatives, they flourish without fear of big corporations monopolising their markets. Local people begin to accept the idea of an economy run by cooperatives wholeheartedly.

4. **Local people must be given first preference for employment in local economic enterprises.** One of the basic requirements for economic democracy is the guaranteed minimum requirements of life. Prout suggests this requirement be satisfied by employing everyone who is able to work. Employment must be the means of providing a sufficient and ever-increasing purchasing capacity. Decentralising the economy will increase local hires by local cooperatives and businesses, and thereby achieve the goal of 100% employment of the local region.

5. **Commodities which are not produced locally should be gradually removed from local markets.** The aim of a decentralised economy is to develop local industries, create local employment and produce goods based on the collective necessity of the region. Commodities that are not locally produced do not contribute towards achieving this goal. There are many benefits to not allowing outside goods in local markets: local economic enterprises grow, distribution of local goods consumes fewer resources, and outside forces will be thwarted from manipulating local markets.

In a centralised economic structure, the economy is controlled either by a small group of capitalistic individuals and institutions, or through state capitalism. Profits take precedence over people and environment and are concentrated in the hands of a few individuals and institutions. This leads to wealth inequality and economic exploitation. Furthermore, capitalists rarely reinvest their profits for the development of the regions in which they are taking advantage of cheap resources – cheap labour, energy, raw materials and transportation. Their motive is to produce goods and services at a minimum cost of production and extract maximum profits.

Profit-oriented systems of organising economic activities have failed to solve the problems of economic exploitation and ecological exploitation and have brought our planet to the brink of destruction. A decentralised economy, as proposed by Prout, pays close attention to managing resources responsibly for all-round welfare of human beings, and all species, thus ensuring sustainable economic growth.

Three-tiered economy – small businesses, cooperatives, key industries

One way to move towards the goals of economic democracy and the best use of resources would be to organise our economic enterprises into three tiers.

1. The private sector

This tier would include small businesses and enterprises that employ few people and do not deal with essential needs. Small restaurants, repair shops, custom fabrication and other similar activities are examples of enterprises in this sector. These businesses are most efficiently run privately by individuals, partnerships or families. This sector is where private enterprise would thrive and not harm the larger society.

2. The cooperative sector

When enterprises grow larger, employ more people and start to deal with the necessities of life such as food, shelter, clothing, education and medicine, then individual ownership and management becomes problematic because the needs of the wider community and the employees are often neglected by owners seeking to maximise their personal profits. At that point, a good arrangement for medium-sized businesses is the cooperative. In addition, exclusive private ownership of enterprises producing and distributing vital necessities can result in outcomes that are not beneficial to society. A recent example in the US came when one private pharmaceutical company hiked the price of a drug from $13.50 to $750 per pill.

All the workers in a cooperative are shareholders and they elect a managing board. Each worker has some say in determining the direction of the co-op, but the managing board handles operational decisions. A large portion of an economy could be run by cooperatives and this would help establish economic democracy.

It is not uncommon that industrial firms are bought by foreign owners, and when these owners decide that one of their foreign holdings is unprofitable, they can simply decide to shut down a factory. The workers of that factory have no say in this decision made by a small board of directors based in a foreign country. Those workers have the right to vote in political elections in their country and thus could be said to enjoy political democracy, but they would have to sit silently on the side-lines while their economic livelihood was being determined undemocratically by a few people in another country.

Worker-owned cooperatives substitute this form of absentee ownership with local ownership – -building enterprises that are directly tied to the needs of the people working there and the surrounding community.

Worker-owned businesses exist all over the world. In the US there are close to 400 worker-owned cooperatives with a total yearly turnover exceeding $400 million, and in the Basque region of Northern Spain the Mondragon Corporation, a federation of worker-owned cooperatives, employs more than 70,000 workers and has a yearly turnover in excess of 12 billion Euros.[4]

Building up a cooperative sector amidst a capitalist system will be one of the biggest challenges in implementing the three-tiered economic model. Already existing large-scale capitalist enterprises enjoy advantages of scale and can offer their goods at lower prices, for example. That is why Sarkar suggests that the government should provide 'protective armour' in the form of exemption from sales tax, duties, etc., this sort of help would enable cooperatives to thrive.[5]

3. The public sector (key industries)

There are economic activities which run on a larger scale and with wide-ranging impacts on the greater economy. Transportation, communication, mineral extraction and generation of power are some of the large-scale enterprises which require a form of ownership and management that is neither private nor cooperative. Sarkar has called these 'key industries'. We could also call this the public sector because this is the area of activity that affects everyone and in which we all have a common interest. According to Prout, these enterprises should be managed by the local state government. If there is no strong local government (as might arise in unitary political systems where there are no state or provincial governments) a public board could be set up in that geographic area to run the project. Sarkar emphasises that in cases where governmental bodies manage the key industries, these bodies would be immediate, local governments, and not central governments.

Balanced economies and regional self-sufficiency

In today's world, there are great disparities in economic development between regions and localities. Within a single country economic activity is often centralised around manufacturing centres, while other areas, usually rural, remain underdeveloped and less prosperous. With fewer job opportunities in the rural areas, young people flee to the cities. The underdeveloped areas are not only economically disadvantaged but suffer from less activity and development in the arts, culture and education.

The current centralized capitalist economy leads to all kinds of social and economic problems. Young people deprived of economic opportunities become alienated, crime spikes in overcrowded urban areas and people are forced to leave their native areas in search of jobs elsewhere.

The best way to reverse this situation is to develop some industries and supporting services in rural areas. Self-reliant local economies ensure that there are economic opportunities right at people's doorsteps. In this way, no one is forced to leave their native land, excessive congestion of urban areas will be avoided, and strong regional centers will provide employment and services to previously neglected rural areas. On the international level, the task of implementing decentralised and balanced economic development is of prime importance.

The present world has developed very unevenly. The commercial and industrial revolutions began in Europe in the 1600s and 1800s respectively. Europe and the US developed their industries and commerce rapidly, colonising large parts of Africa, Asia and South America. In the 1960s the colonised areas achieved *political* independence. We put emphasis on the word political, because in most cases the former colonies did not achieve economic independence. Multinational corporations (based in developed countries) owned the valuable mineral extraction enterprises and other industries of these newly independent countries. Profits of these foreign-held assets were sent abroad and not used in the development of the newly independent countries.

P.R. Sarkar said that a country with a balanced economy should employ a certain portion of its population in agriculture, another portion in the sector that provides equipment for agriculture, and another portion in a sector that finished, or added value, to the raw agricultural produce. The rest of the population could be employed in manufacturing and services. A country or a group of countries in a geographic region with a diverse and balanced economy would become prosperous and provide economic opportunities to local people.

In addition to this, the encouragement of balanced economic planning and implementation could help developed countries as well. Due to current trade policies, the US, for example, no longer manufactures many goods, and this has brought unemployment and blight to previous industrial areas. In addition, the country also finds itself in a difficult position when global supply chains are disrupted by unforeseen developments (like pandemics or war).

In a more just world, developing nations and less prosperous regions would be assisted to build up their new industries and move towards more diverse economies. If one country does not have enough resources or a topography suited towards building a self-sufficient unit, it could join with other nearby countries to form a self-sufficient economic zone. P.R. Sarkar envisioned the creation of self-sufficient economic zones based on common economic, linguistic, cultural and geographical features to create prosperity in all parts of the world. As the different economic zones of the world reach parity, it might be possible, one day, to envision a world that is one economic zone.

Walk the talk – Ananda Valley project in Portugal

Many beautiful MU projects around the world are serving as pilot projects, each with the specific experience of the community and the culture it is deeply connected to. A special MU was born in the last 10 years in the Iberian peninsula, right near the Biogenetic Nature Reserve of Serra da Estrela, the largest mountain range and nature conservation area in Portugal.

Figure 2: Ananda Valley premises and surroundings. **Credit:** Anada Valley project.

The Ananda Valley (AV) project was born from a solid background: skilled volunteers from six complementary associations with different skill sets and clear methodologies tested in Portugal and in several other parts of the world. Deep ecology, sustainable agriculture, vegetarianism, life-long learning, art, social service and social activism are the focus areas of these non-profit associations, with a few more ready to join. In 2010, in the midst of a national economic crisis, the ideal place was discovered to develop a vibrant settlement. It sought to create a service hub and a research centre where individuals, moving together, can fully realise their potential for inner growth, in harmony with nature and the surrounding community. Looking at the Iberian peninsula and specifically at the interior and more isolated/remote areas in central Spain and Portugal, all share critically exacerbated problems:

- **Social:** high levels of desertification, an aging population, brain drain, difficulty in attracting and keeping young generations;
- **Environmental:** threats caused by large-scale operations in low population areas but providing some employment;
- **Personal:** depression, illiteracy, difficulty in expressing one's full potential (creative, interpersonal, active citizenship) due to living at 'survival level'.

Figure 3: Someof the volunteers in Ananda Valley. **Credit:** Anada Valley project.

In a fully integrated way, and with very limited resources, the Ananda Valley started as a grassroots multidisciplinary project, with very limited support from external entities, in a community-centric way. The integrated rural development approach has been present since the beginning, putting aside quick achievements in one field, in favour of developing the whole project as a Master Unit. The process was not easy or simple, but many of the participants feel strongly that these first intense steps helped to create the inner strength needed to develop such a special project.

At the moment not all the departments of a full-fledged Master Unit are present. Project members organise themselves in several 'focus areas', such as:

- **Volunteers and trainees** – one of the fundamental goals of the project is to inspire and spread the ideas and the lifestyle developed in the project to other cities and countries, pollinating and changing the lives of several hundred youths and individuals every year;
- **Events** – lifelong informal and non-formal learning with a flow of regular events, ranging from social to environmental, and including youth exchanges, music and art festivals, meditation retreats and vegetarian residential courses;
- **Microvita** – a department focused on vegetarian and conscious food production, (mainly in the form of agriculture), processing, distribution and catering for special events, such as the famous Portuguese summer festivals, and volunteer-based vegetarian restaurants in nearby cities;
- **MU City Centre** – activity centres have been formed in nearby cities, often connected with vegetarian restaurants, where people may learn about our courses, workshops and concerts, exposing them to other residential activities at AV;
- **Ecotourism** – intended as a conscious tourism effort, bringing visitors on a journey which is not only physical, and helping them to live and learn to deal with nature in a different way. This activity also helps to financially support the non-profit organisations at AV;
- A few other departments are in development but do not yet have a stable team, namely the neohumanist education department, with a vision of a kindergarten and school system, based on neohumanist education principles; the housing coop department, which will allow more residents to come and live in a Residential Area, already well-identified on the overall map; and the Health and Wellness department, focused on alternative health systems with a scientific method.

Figure 4: Neohumanist education activities during the Ananda Festival of Bliss. **Credit:** Anada Valley project.

The direct experience of some Ananda Valley members shows that this integrated and interdisciplinary way of forming a community is more challenging and complex than starting a mono-focus project. It may create more internal friction, and it is apparent that the projects are not developing at the same speed as those of an ecovillage mainly focused on one topic. Still, such integrated systems have in general a higher degree of resilience, while allowing a fuller expression of the potentialities of each individual.

Those who helped to start the AV project were all coming from organised grassroots entities or informal groups, dealing with specific aspects of societal needs and offering detailed approaches to address those needs with a service-minded spirit. One of the co-founders of AV is a socio-spiritual organisation and movement, based on a practical philosophy for personal development and the all-around transformation of society, rooted in ancient yogic practices and the tantra tradition. An environmental association registered in 2020, but active since the beginning of the AV project, rallied those interested in supporting a more ecological lifestyle and activities, ranging from ecosystems conservation and preservation, environmental education, regenerative lifestyle and environmental advocacy. Art and culture is certainly a strong component of AV, and each year the Ananda Festival of Bliss is held.

Another co-founding NGO is dedicated to local development, both in impoverished areas in Portugal and in other developing countries. It has a history dating back more than 25 years in Portugal, helping both with community services and in relief operations after catastrophes. Another group organised since the beginning of the AV project is working on systemic socio-economic solutions to support both people and the planet (see section on Prout). It focuses on practical and integrated approaches, such as people-centered economics, environmental sustainability and a new model of prosperity. Another group of AV members has gathered around the topic of 'food', leveraging one of the basic needs of human existence that has a huge impact on the planet but can also be the source of regenerative solutions.

Many are the lessons learned from this developing project. As in other approaches to IRD, grassroots small-scale rural development project dynamics can be better understood after many years of trial and error, with an iterative process of identifying and fine-tuning the best options for each individual project. The 'integrated' component may seem a difficult goal to achieve in the first years of the project; in our case it took more than six years to form specialised teams around the various focus areas, instead of relying on a small group of multi-tasking members. This may also be due to the lack of initial capital. The volunteer-only based approach of AV evolved over the years into a more balanced combination of both volunteers and staff, allowing long-term operations to grow more consistently. Internal challenges such as the existence of different approaches and external situations like the 2020-21 pandemic were difficult, but ultimately contributed to creating a more healthy, resilient and adaptable project. In IRD projects, as well as in every attempt to create more regenerative solutions, there is a clear need to nurture and support the systemic relationships and interactions of the components of the project, the quality of the iterative generation of internal knowledge, and the information flows inside the overall system. Several of these techniques have traditionally not been found in academic educational systems, although the situation is changing, and approaches such as permaculture, regenerative design and sociocracy are increasingly being studied in universities and research institutes.[6]

Principles such as 'Integrate rather than segregate', 'Use and value diversity', or 'Use edges and value the marginal' are studied as ecosystem patterns, and can suggest that small-scale community-led IRD projects are inherently more resilient than big governmental IRD projects. Principles such as 'Observe and interact', 'Apply self-regulation and accept feedback', 'Use small and slow solutions', or 'Creatively use and respond to change' could refer to some of the possible pitfalls of the first implementation of IRD projects. In broad terms, an integrated approach can be shown to enhance organisational resilience as it contributes to the development of traits, capabilities,and attitudes supportive of the three stages of the resilient process: anticipation, coping and adaptation.[7] While there is not much literature available on the relationship between diversity and resilience in ecovillages, it is widely recognised in several European projects. The same concept transposed to the relationship between biodiversity and system stability is well studied, with for example Michel Loreau describing the main mechanisms that endow biodiversity with the capacity of stabilising ecosystems.[8]

Another approach that is often associated with integrated rural projects is regenerative design or regenerative sustainability. A more recent process-oriented whole-systems approach to design – considering natural, social, or economic systems as complex dynamic systems – advocates the importance of biomimicry, and, in the words of Daniel Wahl, of 'diversity and redundancies at multiple scales, to facilitate positive emergence through paying attention to the quality of connections and information flows in the system'.[9] With a very practical approach, it pays attention to several similar solutions, helping to identify limits and possibilities of each in order to improve the desired outcomes. Raymond Cole explores the concept of regenerative design and what it means in relation to 'green' and 'sustainable' design, showing that 'green' intends to reduce the negative impacts that are often associated with 'development'; the sustainable design viewpoint is trying to take another step forward, finding solutions that are reducing these impacts to the amount that we can meet the needs of the current generation without depleting the resources of future generations.[10] Regenerative design starts from these approaches and takes an extra step, using biomimicry techniques, feedback loops, whole-systems thinking, continuous learning and transformation. It is not only a quantitative improvement, but a perspective shift that can also be seen as the transition from a 'narrative of separation' to a 'narrative of interbeing', causing regenerative, resilient, and flourishing eco-systems as a natural output.

Figure 5: Lifelong learning activities inside the dome near the river. **Credit:** Anada Valley project.

While few ecovillages reject the role of science, technology, and rational thinking, MUs actively embrace scientific methods. Ananda Valley recognizes research centres and academia as important partners in finding new solutions, validating alternatives and overcoming dogmas about alternative solutions. Even if the holistic approach and spiritual base of Ananda Valley are very open to promoting synthetic solutions that can originate in a more creative way, a strong practice in Ananda Valley is the balance between an intuitive approach and a rational confirmation, analysis, explanation and empirical experimentation. In the last two years AV, through its various entities, began stricter cooperation with a local university, Universidade da Beira Interior (UBI), with the Centre of Functional Ecology in Coimbra, together with the Polytechnic of Turin and with other European research centres. Daniel Wahl expresses this healthy synergy as the capacity to 'acknowledge multiple ways of knowing, neither dismissing the reductionist scientific perspective nor the participatory holistic perspective'. This viewpoint is present in all aspects of AV: a continuous learning experience, cultivating as virtue the 'attitude of an apprentice – acknowledging that nature in all its forms has so much to teach us'.

Figure 6: Multiple ways of knowing - healthy blending of nature and technology. **Credit:** Anada Valley project.

References

1. Masset, E. (2018). *Integrated Development, Past and Present. IDS BULLETIN-INSTITUTE OF DEVELOPMENT STUDIES*, 49(4). (https://bulletin.ids.ac.uk/index.php/idsbo/article/download/2994/Online%20article?inline=1)

2. Namboodiri, U. The Indian Express. (1997). *Basu Govt still suppressing facts on Margi massacre.* Archived from the original on 12 March 2010. (https://www.hvk.org/1997/0597/0001.html)

3. Gilman, R. (1991). *A Quarterly of Humane Sustainable Culture. IN CONTEXT, 29.*

4. Community Wealth. (https://community-wealth.org/)

5. Sarkar, P.R. *Dicsourses on Prout.* (https://anandamargabooks.com/books/discourses-on-prout/)

6. Holmgren, D. (2002). *Permaculture. Principles and Pathways Beyond Sustainability.* Hampshire. Permanent Publications.

7. Duchek, S., Raetze, S. & Scheuch, I. (2020). *The role of diversity in organizational resilience: a theoretical framework.* Business Research, 13(2). (https://doi.org/10.1007/s40685-019-0084-8)

8. Loreau M, de Mazancourt C. (2013). *Biodiversity and ecosystem stability: a synthesis of underlying mechanisms.* Ecology Letters, *16.* (https://doi.org/10.1111/ele.12073)

9. Wahl, David C. (2016). *Designing Regenerative Cultures.* UK. Triarchy Press.

10. Cole, Raymond J. (2012). *Transitioning from green to regenerative design. Building Research & Information*, 40(1). (https://www.tandfonline.com/doi/abs/10.1080/09613218.2011.610608)

Localisation vs Globalisation

Steven Gorelick, Anne Chapman and Alex Jensen

'Localised economies are created by and for the people who live there. Rather than subscribing to a global mono-cultural model, localised economies respect local cultures and needs, while allowing for the free exchange of knowledge and ideas across borders. In fact, localisation requires international cooperation and collaboration to address global problems like climate change, and to forge agreements to scale back the rapacious power of global corporations and banks.'

- Local Futures

* * *

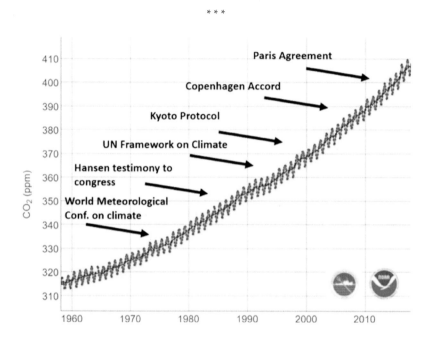

Track of CO2 emissions with a note of previous COPs and protocols **Credit:** Local Futures.

As explored in Chapter 1, COP member states have consistently failed to cut CO_2 emissions by the amount required to prevent catastrophic climate change. The only effective dips to emissions have been due to economic slowdowns: the first following the 2008 financial collapse and the second a result of the COVID-19 pandemic. This points to a simple truth: the fastest and most reliable way to reduce GHG emissions is to make fundamental changes to the economy. The question is: how can it be transformed in ways that actually improve people's lives – providing the huge environmental benefits we need without enormous social and economic costs?

Localisation offers a way to lower GHG emissions while increasing quality of life. Here's how:

1. Eliminating unnecessary transport

In today's global economy, trade is no longer about obtaining goods that can't be produced locally or regionally, nor is it about exchanging surpluses. Instead, it is about maximising profits within a global economic system that ignores social and environmental costs. One result is that a lot of today's trade is simply 'redundant', with goods sourced from thousands of miles away when an identical product is available next door. This is particularly true in the global food system. Britain, for example, imports and exports 15,000 tons of waffles annually, and exchanges 20 tons of bottled water with Australia; supermarkets on the Citrus Coast of Spain carry imported lemons while local lemons are left to rot on the ground; and Canada simultaneously imports and exports greenhouse tomatoes.[1]

In some cases, heavy subsidies for fossil fuels and other resources needed for global trade – combined with the exploitation of abysmally low wages abroad – leads to foods being shipped to the other side of the world just to shave a few cents off the cost of production or to add a few cents to the sales price. The US seafood company Trident is typical: to save on labour costs it ships about 30 million pounds of fish annually to China for filleting, and then ships the fish back to the US for sale.[2] For reasons that should be clear, we refer to this as 'insane trade.'

Trade in manufactured goods is not as likely to be insane as trade in food, but globalisation has increased transport distances in this sector as well. The parts in a typical iPhone, for example, have travelled a total of 500,000 miles before reaching the end user.[3] Among the many effects of the COVID-19 pandemic was to reveal how vulnerable to disruption these long supply chains are.

These are among the reasons that the volumes and tonnage – and thus the energy footprint – of global trade have grown so rapidly during recent decades. The total volume of goods and resources traded around the world has increased by a factor of 2.5 during the past 30 years (roughly corresponding to the period of corporate-led globalisation).[4] The total volume transported globally was 32 times greater in 2009 than it was in 1950.[5]

If globalisation is allowed to continue on its current trajectory, the energy required for global trade – and the consequent emissions – will continue to rise. By 2050 trade volumes are expected to increase more than fourfold; average hauling distances will grow by 12%, and CO_2 emissions related to global freight transport will increase by 290%.[6]

Putting an end to insane trade is probably the fastest and easiest way to reduce GHG emissions. But despite the clear correlation between long-distance transport and rising GHG emissions, climate negotiators have never considered reducing even insane trade as a climate-stabilising strategy. In fact, the opposite is true: the commitments made by nations under the Paris climate accords, for example, don't include emissions from international aviation and shipping,[7] and so no nation has any incentive at all to reduce them. In other words, the economic benefits of needless transport will continue to be given to the trading corporations, while the costs are shifted to the environment and future generations.[8]

2. Sufficiency above consumerism

High levels of consumption in the 'developed' countries are a major factor not only in GHG emissions but in many other forms of pollution, as well as in resource depletion. Environmental destruction is telling us that those consumption levels are too high, but the economic models on which the global economy is based require constant growth. Whenever there is an economic slowdown, in fact, governments typically intervene by lowering interest rates, cutting taxes, or taking other steps to "stimulate consumer spending".

In the 'less-developed' parts of the world it is presumed that a continued push for economic growth will eventually enable standards of living to approach the levels found in Europe and North America. But the developed countries are already using far more than their share of resources, while placing a much greater burden on the Earth's ability to absorb wastes like greenhouse gases. For the rest of the world to consume and pollute at the same pace would require almost four additional planets.[9] (Actually even more planets would be required: by the time 'development' enables people in the global South to reach Northern levels of consumption, those levels will presumably have risen still further.)

One way that economic globalisation increases consumption is by imposing a consumer monoculture. Every day, people around the world are bombarded with media images that present the modern, Western consumer lifestyle as the ideal, while implicitly denigrating local traditions and land-based ways of life. As a result, millions of people are abandoning traditional local foods for highly processed junk food,[10] while local wool, flax and cotton is giving way to imported designer jeans and polyester. In the process, the use of energy-intensive resources is going up, along with pollution and greenhouse gas emissions.

Even in the North, cradle-to-grave advertising and planned obsolescence enable marketers and technological "innovators" to create a never-ending stream of new needs among people who already have more "stuff" than the vast majority of the global population. For the individual, this consumption treadmill ultimately leads nowhere: studies have shown that once basic needs are met – a condition long ago reached in the global North – further increments of consumption don't actually leave people any happier, and in fact have the counterproductive effect of eroding well-being.[11]

If running ever faster on the consumer treadmill ultimately erodes long-term well-being, localisation offers the prospect of genuine improvements in quality of life for the vast majority. In healthy local economies, people are deeply connected to both community and the natural world – connections that psychologists recognise as fundamental wellsprings of happiness.[12] Those connections can be made without the material throughputs that consumerism requires, enabling improvements to be made in quality of life at the same time that environmental impacts are reduced.

For example, a study of the Dancing Rabbit Ecovillage in rural Missouri showed that, compared to national US averages, residents produce only 18% as much municipal solid waste, drive 10% the number of miles, consume 6% as much fuel, and use only 23% as much water. Despite using far fewer resources, 81% of Dancing Rabbit members rate their level of happiness at 7 or above on a scale of 1 to 10, with 10 being most happy.[13] This finding is confirmed by a survey of the members of almost 200 intentional communities worldwide. Researchers found that 80% of residents felt their quality of life was "better" or "much better" since joining the community.[14]

In ecovillages, the interdependence of residents is acknowledged and celebrated.
Credit: Dancing Rabbit Ecovillage

3. Making food a sink of carbon rather than a source

The global food system is a major part of climate change: estimates of the food sector's contribution to GHG emissions range from 19-29 percent.[15] The globalisation and industrialisation of the food economy is responsible for a large and growing portion of that total. This is because:

- **Globalisation leads to needless trade in food,** described above, and increases the distance between producers and consumers. By shrinking 'food miles', localisation reduces transport-related emissions.[16]
- **The global food economy requires far more processing and packaging than local food systems:** in the US for example, more than one-third of the energy used by the food system is used for packaging and processing.17 A significant proportion of the roughly 170 million tons of plastic packaging produced each year worldwide – most of it intended to be disposed of after a single use – is used in the food industry.[18] When consumers are buying direct from farmers, on the other hand, the need for packaging and processing all but disappears.
- **Globalisation is structurally linked to agricultural monoculture.** Because global marketers need massive amounts of a few globally-

traded commodities, it is far more 'efficient' to source those foods from a few giant monocultural farms than from hundreds of diversified farms.[19] Monocultures rely heavily on agrochemicals and mechanised equipment – both of which result in significant GHG emissions. They also degrade soil, depleting it of the ability to sequester carbon. Regenerative agriculture, on the other hand, enables soil to absorb a large proportion of the excess carbon in the atmosphere. Local food economies are structurally suited to regenerative agriculture practices.[20] That's because local economies don't need huge amounts of single commodities, but rather a diversity of foods – which provides an economic incentive for farmers selling locally to diversify their farms.

This connection can be clearly seen in those parts of the global South where farmers have been able to resist inroads from industrial agriculture. Most of them produce for their own families, and sometimes for regional or local markets. Their farms are small, highly diversified, and – though the farmers themselves may not describe them this way – are based on regenerative agro-ecological practices. In Odisha, India, indigenous farmer Sunamain Mambalaka grows more than 80 crop varieties on her 5-acre farm, including locally adapted varieties of millet, sorghum and rice – all while improving soil health and fertility.[21] She is typical of small farmers worldwide, who are collectively responsible for feeding 70% of the world's population.[22]

Farms in Ladakh have fed the local population sustainably for centuries.
Credit: Local Futures

- In the global North those practising regenerative agriculture often develop ways to sell directly to consumers, through farm shops or via the internet, to increase the price they can get for their outputs as well to find markets for their diverse range of products. For example, Gabe Brown, a farmer in North Dakota who is one of the pioneers of regenerative agriculture, sells his 'Nourished by Nature' products from a trailer at farmers markets. In the 1990s, Brown's Ranch produced wheat, oats and barley along with beef whereas now they produce over 30 products, including pork, lamb, chicken, eggs, grains, fruits, vegetables and honey on their 5000 acres. These multiple enterprises, where often the waste from one enterprise becomes the input into another (for example the waste from screening grains is fed to the chickens) are key to increasing profitability per acre. This, Brown says, is what farmers should focus on, rather than yield.[23]

- **Globalisation is leading to dietary changes that exacerbate GHG emissions.** The mimicking of Western patterns of consumption mean that global meat consumption is expected to double by 2050,[24] most of it sourced from factory farms that are major contributors to climate change: factory-farmed broiler chickens, for example, produce seven times more GHG emissions than backyard chickens.[25] At the same time, huge supermarket chains have trained Northern consumers to eat foods produced thousands of miles away that are out-of-season locally. These perishable foods are not only produced on monocultural farms, but many also require refrigeration and air transport, adding to their carbon footprint. What's more, globalisation has enabled transnational food corporations to spread highly processed, plastic-packaged junk food into parts of the world that previously relied on more nutritious and home-cooked foods, in the process exacerbating both public health and waste crises, and increasing the energy footprint of food. The global sale of packaged foods jumped more than 90% from 2002 to 2012, with 2012 sales topping $2.2 trillion.[26] While the global food system is homogenising diets worldwide, local food systems promote a diversity of food preferences that are attuned to local soils, climates, and cultural traditions.

Industrial, processed food have made huge inroads in the global South.
Credit: Anaxila, CC BY-NC-ND 2.0

- The changing diets in the global North are one reason why a country like the UK now imports so much more of its food than it did 60 years ago – people in the UK eat pasta made in Italy rather than our local potatoes, and we import sunflower, olive and soya oil, rather than using the fat from UK livestock, which now has to be incinerated.[27] This leads to calls to increase outputs - as if increasing output from UK farms would reduce our imports. In reality, increasing production just puts further downward pressure on the prices that farmers receive and the inputs of artificial fertilisers, herbicides and pesticides required degrade soils, increase water and air pollution and destroy wildlife.[28]
- The global food system destroys rainforests and other wild ecosystems. Many of the planet's carbon-sequestering natural ecosystems are being destroyed to make way for monocultural production for global markets: Brazil, for example, is converting large swaths of the Amazon to soybean production for export to industrial animal feedlots, while Indonesia's rainforests are being displaced by palm oil plantations, mostly destined for processed junk food products. As Brazilian activist Camila Moreno points out: "If you really want a mechanism to avoid deforestation, dismantle agribusiness. This is the main driver of deforestation in the entire South".[29]
- The global food system robs people in the global South of the ability to feed themselves. In the global economy, food goes to the highest bidder, rather than the hungriest child. In rural parts of Kenya, for example, 38.8% of the population lived in poverty in 2016; meanwhile,

much of Kenya's best agricultural land was devoted to growing black tea and cut flowers for export to Europe and North America, rather than feeding hungry people at home.[30] This is not a problem unique to Kenya: a recent study showed that 550 million people in Asia, Africa, and Oceania could be fed from land that has been taken over by foreign governments and corporations – mostly for exported food and biofuel crops.[31] Local food systems, by contrast, focus on feeding local people first, before trading any surpluses. Much of the food grown in local food systems – especially in the global South – remains outside the formal money economy and therefore adds nothing to GDP or the bottom lines of global agribusinesses. But if the goal is to improve people's quality of life while reducing GHG emissions, there is no better place to start than by strengthening local food systems.

Growing potatoes, Peru. **Credit:** Suma Yapu

4. Replacing energy-intensive technologies with human labour and skill

Globalisation is both scaling up and speeding up the economy – two trends that put a premium on energy-intensive technology while devaluing human labour. Robots are increasingly relied upon to do factory work that was once done by people – a trend that is spreading to every other sector of the economy, including farming.

The mainstream narrative is that all this is happening because of efficiencies of scale. However, these technologies are *not* more efficient when all the costs are taken into account. Because the price of energy doesn't include its ecological costs – including greenhouse gas emissions – it becomes artificially cheap to use more and more of it. It has been estimated that the direct and hidden subsidies for fossil fuels alone amount to $10 million per minute.[32] At the same time, governments provide a wide range of subsidies, many of them hidden, for energy-dependent technologies. Tax breaks, tax credits, accelerated depreciation and other subsidies are provided to companies that invest in technology; hiring workers, on the other hand, means paying costly payroll taxes that make human labour artificially expensive.

Because local economies serve much smaller populations than the global economy, they do not justify massive expenditures on robots and other energy-intensive equipment. Instead there is a premium on place-based knowledge and human skill. In the global North the mega-farms of industrial agriculture tend to employ a lot of immigrant labour because the working conditions are poor, or the work is seasonal. In contrast, the diversity of enterprises on a farm mean there is more likely to be year-round work and the continual experimentation and learning characteristic of regenerative agriculture make that work more interesting. So Greenham and Link (2020)[33] argue that in agroecological enterprises what are 'operatives' in industrialised agriculture become 'knowledge workers' whose know-how is essential in the experimentation, fine-tuning and learning processes that increase productivity in these farming systems (p.49-50).

One of the authors of this chapter has written about this with regard to his own small farm, where the only cash crop (blueberries) is sold and bartered locally. The crop is too small to justify investments in expensive equipment and, instead, knowledge and skills are prized: "When our family picks blueberries, we know what each of the several varieties we grow look and feel like when they're perfectly ripe: berries that aren't quite ready will be left for the next day's picking, when they'll be larger, juicier and better-tasting. But the mechanical blueberry-picking machines favoured by large growers can't make such distinctions: they simply shake the entire bush and catch whatever berries drop." Not only is the quality reduced, so is the yield: a University of Florida study showed that because mechanical blueberry harvesting bruises a lot of good berries and harvests many under-ripe ones, it yields 13% less marketable fruit, with additional losses from both ripe and immature fruit dropped on the ground by the harvester.[34] Despite resulting in lower quality and smaller yields, the mechanical harvester is considered more 'efficient', simply because it requires less labour.

5. Stemming the tide of energy-intensive urbanisation

The consumer culture that globalisation promotes is increasingly urban. At first glance, high-density urban living might appear to reduce per capita use of resources. But this is only true when compared with life in the grossly inefficient suburbs, which are themselves a product of urbanisation. Compared to more genuinely decentralised towns and villages connected to a surrounding localised economy, urbanisation is extremely resource-intensive.

One reason is that virtually every material need of urbanised populations must be brought in from elsewhere, requiring vast energy-intensive infrastructures to do so. For example, almost all the food consumed by city dwellers must be grown for them, typically on giant, chemical and energy-intensive farms. All this food must then be brought into the cities on roads purpose-built to accommodate huge trucks. Similarly, providing water involves enormous dams, man-made reservoirs, and aqueducts stretching into distant hills and mountains. Energy production means huge, centralised power plants, coal and uranium mines, along with thousands of miles of transmission lines.

Urbanisation is also linked to significant increases in consumerism. A report by the McKinsey Global Institute points out that "the shift to cities is creating waves of new consumers who promise burgeoning markets for businesses." This may be good for global corporations, but for the environment and the climate it is a disaster. Among other things, the flood of new urbanites will require a near doubling of the current amount of commercial and residential floor space (an area equivalent to the size of Austria) and a 250% increase in port infrastructure to meet rising container shipping demand.[35] Most of this construction requires concrete, a material with a huge carbon

Urbanisation is linked to greatly increased resource consumption. **Credit:** John Page.

footprint: according to a BBC report, "if the cement industry were a country, it would be the third largest emitter in the world, behind China and the US."[36] Studies show that even in the global North, urbanisation adds to people's carbon footprint. In Finland, for example, annual GHG emissions by a resident of Finland's biggest city, Helsinki, are almost 40% higher than emissions by rural residents.[37]

Because rural towns and villages are more connected economically to the surrounding landbase, they are places where localisation initiatives can take root quickly if they are given government support. By improving the vitality of rural life, localisation can help stem the tide of rapid urbanisation. This alone would provide enormous opportunities for GHG reduction.

* * *

As Local Futures has argued more fully elsewhere,[38] a shift in direction from global to local is not only the most sensible response to climate change, it would simultaneously address the many other social, environmental and economic problems we face: poverty and unemployment, pollution, the erosion of democracy, the loss of cultural and biological diversity, rising levels of senseless violence, fundamentalism, and more.

Nonetheless, the negotiators at climate talks have studiously avoided any discussion of economic localisation, no doubt at the direction of political leaders back home. Without pressure from below, those government leaders – who are heavily influenced by corporate campaign donations and lobbying – cannot be counted on to take the lead. But if people across the world join forces to apply massive pressure for a shift from global to local, the corporate spin can be reversed, and *real* solutions to the climate emergency can be pursued.

	GLOBALISATION vs LOCALISATION	
TRANSPORT	• Separates producers and consumers, so almost all goods travel further • Promotes redundant trade	• Shortens distance between producers and consumers, so less transport needed
CONSUMERISM	• Requires endless growth, fueled by endless consumption • Pulls people away from self-reliance • Creates new "needs" and planned obsolescence	• Reduces consumption by answering real psychological and spiritual needs for community and connection • Reduces artificial needs, advertising, and corporate influence
FOOD AND FARMING	• Requires monocultural production, which is chemical and energy-intensive • Increases GHG footprint through factory animal farms • Promotes redundant trade, multiplies food miles, and increases need for processing, packaging and refrigeration • Encourages dietary changes in global South, including new emphasis on meat • Encourages expectation of out-of-season foods year-round in rich countries	• Encourages agro-ecological, diversified production, which is less energy- and chemical-dependent, and provides carbon sinks • Integrates livestock in a productive and sustainable way • Reduces need for packaging, refrigeration, and transport • Encourages diets that are locally-adapted and seasonal, making use of what grows best in particular ecosystems and microclimates
ENERGY	• Replaces human labor with energy-intensive technology, thereby adding to both unemployment and pollution	• Makes more use of human labor and knowledge, with less need for energy-intensive technology
URBANISATION	• Promotes the growth of megacities and suburban sprawl • Requires huge energy-intensive infrastructures • Centralizes production and job opportunities, encouraging rural populations to abandon low-impact lifestyles	• Promotes more decentralized living patterns • Brings people closer to the sources of their basic needs, so less need for huge infrastructures • Decentralizes production and job opportunities, revitalizing villages, towns and smaller cities, where energy needs and consumption pressures are lower

References

1. "The Problem with Redundant Trade" (2013) Deconstructing Dinner, October 9, http://deconstructingdinner.ichannel.ca/the-problem-with-redundant-trade-2/.

2. Yeoung, Choy Leng (2005) "NW salmon sent to China before reaching U.S. tables", The Seattle Times, July 16, http://www.seattletimes.com/business/nw-salmon-sent-to-china-before-reaching-us-tables/.

3. Humes, Edward (2016) "Your iPhone's 500,000-mile journey to your pocket", Wired, 12 April https://www.wired.com/2016/04/iphones-500000-mile-journey-pocket/

4. Giljum, S., Dittrich, M., Lieber, M., and Lutter, S. (2014) 'Global Patterns of Material Flows and their Socio-Economic and Environmental Implications: A MFA Study on All Countries World-Wide from 1980 to 2009', Resources 3, 319-339.

5. WTO & UNEP (2009) Trade and Climate Change: A Report by the United Nations Environment Program and the World Trade Organization, Geneva: WTO Publications. https://www.wto.org/english/res_e/booksp_e/trade_climate_change_e.pdf

6. International Transport Forum (2016) "The Carbon Footprint of Global Trade", Organization for Economic Cooperation and Development.

7. United Nations Pan-European Programme (PEP), http://www.thepep.org/chwebsite/chviewer.aspx?cat=d10..

8. WTO & UNEP (2009) Trade and Climate Change: A Report by the United Nations Environment Program and the World Trade Organization, Geneva: WTO Publications. https://www.wto.org/english/res_e/booksp_e/trade_climate_change_e.pdf

9. Global Footprint Network (2015), "Living Planet Report 2014 Facts", http://www.footprintnetwork.org/en/index.php/GFN/page/living_planet_report_2014_facts/.

10. Dehghan, Saeed Kamali (2019) "Coke, crisps, convenience: how ads created a global junk food generation", The Guardian, 26 December. https://www.theguardian.com/global-development/2019/dec/26/coke-crisps-convenience-how-ads-created-a-global-junk-food-generation

11. Simms, Andrew, Victoria Johnson and Peter Chowda (2010) "Growth isn't possible: Why we need a new economic direction", Schumacher College and New Economics Foundation, http://www.neweconomics.org/publications/entry/growth-isnt-possible.

12. Belton, Teresa (2017) "The many reasons why less is more for the people choosing modest lives"https://theconversation.com/the-many-reasons-why-less-is-more-for-the-people-choosing-modest-lives-75554; Monbiot, George (2018) "The town that's found a potent cure for illness – community", The Guardian, 21 February, https://www.theguardian.com/commentisfree/2018/feb/21/town-cure-illness-community-frome-somerset-isolation

13. Lockyear, J. (2017) "Community, commons, and degrowth at Dancing Rabbit Ecovillage", Journal of Political Ecology, Vol. 24

14. Ibid.

15. Vermeulen, Sonja J. et al (2012) "Climate Change and Food Systems", Annual Review of Environment and Resources, Vol. 37: 195-222, November, http://www.annualreviews.org/doi/abs/10.1146/annurev-environ-020411-130608.

16. Local Futures (2019) "Insane Trade Factsheet", https://www.localfutures.org/programs/global-to-local/insane-trade-short-film-factsheet/

17. Pimentel D. (2006) "Impacts of organic farming on the efficiency of energy use in agriculture", An Organic Center State of Science Review, Organic Center, August, http://organic.insightd.net/reportfles/ENERGY_SSR.pdf.

18. Jowit, J. (2011) "Global hunger for plastic packaging leaves waste solution a long way off", The Guardian, 29 Dec. http://www.theguardian.com/environment/2011/dec/29/plastic-packaging-waste-solution.

19. Altieri, M. (2009) "Agroecology, Small Farms, and Food Sovereignty", Monthly Review, July 1. https://monthlyreview.org/2009/07/01/agroecology-small-farms-and-food-sovereignty/

20. Lin et al. (2011) 'Effects of industrial agriculture on climate change and the mitigation potential of small-scale agro-ecological farms', CAB Reviews: Perspectives in Agriculture, Veterinary Science, Nutrition and Natural Resources 6, No. 020; GRAIN (20) 'Food, Climate Change and Soils: The Forgotten Link', in Wake up before it is too late: make agriculture truly sustainable now for food security in a changing climate, UNCTAD 2013 Trade and Environment Report.

21. GRAIN (2021), "Agroecology vs. climate chaos: Farmers leading the battle in Asia", March 10 https://grain.org/en/article/6632-agroecology-vs-climate-chaos-farmers-leading-the-battle-in-asia

22. ETC Group (2017) "Who Will Feed Us" (3rd edition) http://www.etcgroup.org/sites/www.etcgroup.org/files/files/etc-whowillfeedus-english-webshare.pdf

23. Brown, G. (2018) Dirt to Soil: One Family's Journey into Regenerative Agriculture, Chelsea Green.

24. GRAIN (2015) "Trade Deals – Boosting Climate Change: the Food Factor", October, https://www.grain.org/article/entries/5317-trade-deals-boosting-climate-change-the-food-factor.

25. Ibid.

26. Norris, J. (2013) 'Make Them Eat Cake: How America is Exporting Its Obesity Epidemic', Foreign Policy, 3 September. http://foreignpolicy.com/2013/09/03/make-them-eat-cake/.)

27. See p. 23 of Fairlie S. (2010) Meat a Benign Extravagance, Permanent Publications

28. For a discussion of this issue see p. 23 of Chapman, A. (2020) A Just Transition in Agriculture , Green European Foundation.

29. Moreno, Camila (2009), interviewed on Democracy Now, 18 December, "Environmental and Indigenous Activists Criticize Proposed Deal to Save Rainforests", www.democracynow.org/2009/12/18/environmental_and_indigenous_activists_criticize_proposed.

30. Xinhua News (2019) "World Bank lauds Kenya for reducing poverty rates", 4 Dec http://www.xinhuanet.com/english/2019-12/04/c_138603343.htm; Export.gov (2019) 13 Aug 13, https://www.export.gov/apex/article2?id=Kenya-Agriculture

31. Carrington, D. (2014) "Land taken over by foreign investors could feed 550m, study finds", The Guardian 27 June. https://www.theguardian.com/environment/2014/jun/27/land-grabbing-food-biofuels-crops)

32. Carrington, D. (2015) "Fossil fuels subsidised by $10m a minute, says IMF", The Guardian, 18 May http://www.theguardian.com/environment/2015/may/18/fossil-fuel-companies-getting-10m-a-minute-in-subsidies-says-imf

33. Greenham, T. and Link, M. (2020) Farming Smarter; the Case for Agroecological Enterprise. Food, Farming and Countryside Commission.

34. Gorelick, S. (2013) "7 billion for dinner? Here's how to feed them", Local Futures blog, November 24. https://www.localfutures.org/7-billion-for-dinner-heres-how-to-feed-them/

35. McKinsey Global Institute (2012) "Urban World: Cities and the rise of the consuming class" https://www.mckinsey.com/~/media/McKinsey/Featured%20Insights/Urbanisation/Urban%20world%20Cities%20and%20the%20rise%20of%20the%20consuming%20class/MGI_Urban_world_Rise_of_the_consuming_class_Full_report.ashx.

36. Rodgers, Lucy (2018) "Climate change: the massive CO_2 emitter you may not know about", BBC News, 17 December 17. https://www.bbc.com/news/science-environment-46455844.

37. Ketcham, Christopher (2020) "Cities and Green Orthodoxy", Counterpunch, 27 September. https://www.counterpunch.org/2020/09/27/cities-green-orthodoxy-and-the-future-of-sustainable-development/

38. Norberg-Hodge, Helena (2019) Local Is Our Future, Local Futures, East Hardwick, VT.

Visioning the Future as an Act of Subversive Democracy

Ashish Kothari[1]

---

1   This article builds on 'Collective dreaming: Democratic visioning in the Vikalp Sangam process', *Economic and Political Weekly*, vol. LIV no. 34, Aug 2019.

Caught with its hubris-filled pants down, humanity is probably as far away from utopian thinking as it has ever been. Immediate survival, whether from COVID-19 or unemployment and unrest, appears to be on top of everyone's mind. And yet, what better opportunity than a collective global crisis to do some collective visioning of the kind of future we want? I start here with one such vision of the future, and then describe two ongoing processes that could help us move towards such a vision.

A borderless, bioculturally governed South Asia

In the book Alternative Futures: India Unshackled (2017), my co-editor KJ Joy and I report on an imaginary speech made by Meera Gond-Vankar in 2100, looking back at a century of transformation. Among the many changes she noted was the following: "Everything I've described above has been remarkable. But perhaps the most noteworthy has been the change in our relations in South Asia. While India, Pakistan, Bangladesh, Nepal, Bhutan, Sri Lanka, and China still retain their 'national' identities, boundaries have become porous, needing no visas to cross. By the middle of the twenty-first century various oppressed nationalities of the twentieth and early twenty-first century in the region could choose their own political future. Local communities have taken over most of the governance in these boundary areas, having declared *shanti abhyaranyas* (peace reserves) in previous conflict zones like Siachen, the Kachchh and Thar deserts, and the Sundarbans (the last had become a serious arena of water and land conflict due partly to the climate crises, during the 2030s and 40s). The same applies to the Palk Strait, with fishing communities from both India and Sri Lanka empowered to ensure sustainable, peaceful use of marine areas. A Greater Tibet has become a reality, self-governed, with both India and China relinquishing their political and economic domination over it and rather extending a helping hand where necessary. In the Greater Thar, communities of livestock herders in both India and Pakistan have been similarly empowered for self-governance. In all these initiatives, narrow nationalism is being replaced by civilisational identities, pride and exchange, a kind of *swasabhyata* (own ethnicity) that encourages respect of and mutual learning between different civilisations and cultures. Both nomadic communities and wildlife are now able to move freely back and forth, as they used to before these areas became zones of conflict and were dissected by fences. In short, the trans-boundary elements of nature and resources in the region – like water, forests, migratory species – are being increasingly brought under a regional public good framework of governance."

Getting there: envisioning and acting

To be sure, this vision seems to be far from being realised at present. Nation states have become ever more insular, and we have the renewed belligerence of the Chinese state on India's northern borders adding to the continued tension with Pakistan. Internal colonisation and aggression continues, or has worsened in some parts of the region, such as in the Kashmir region where the Indian state revoked its relatively autonomous status in 2019.

Humanity has been confronted with such seemingly intractable situations before. The great European war (otherwise known as WWII) was about as bitter and murderous a conflict as could be imagined. Yet Europe subsequently unified as no other continent has done; leaving aside the fact that the 'economic' integration has been pretty disastrous for many, the fact that visa-less travel and cross-border employment became possible between nations that were at war with each other just a few years before is pretty remarkable. Why can't that happen in South Asia?

Community resilience in the face of crises

Even as COVID-19 created mass suffering among already marginalised sections of society, it has also thrown up new forms of citizens' solidarity actions and demonstrated the resilience of communities that have mobilised themselves for various purposes:In Telangana, over 4,000 *Dalit* and adivasi[1] women farmers, part of <u>Deccan Development Society</u>, have transformed a state of hunger, malnutrition, gender and caste oppression into achieving *anna swaraj* (food sovereignty). In COVID-19 times, these women fed landless families in their villages, contributing 10kg of food grain per family to the district relief measures, and daily feeding 1,000 glasses of nutritious millet porridge to health, municipality and police workers in nearby Zaheerabad town.

In Kachchh, the village of Kunariya set up a crisis management team, used social media to raise awareness about COVID-19, and facilitated a full health survey. Three hundred and sixteen needy families, including those of visually impaired and differently abled individuals, single women and other marginalised people, were assured all basic necessities using *panchayat* (village council) funds or local donations. Over the last few years, dynamic facilitation by its *sarpanch* (elected village head) Suresh Chhanga has enabled Kunariya to move towards <u>greater public participation</u>, including women's empowerment, in governance of local affairs. After COVID-19 hit, Kunariya is now envisioning the local production of all basic needs.

---

1   *Dalits* are the 'lowest' caste in traditional Hindu hierarchy, once also called 'untouchables' or 'outcastes'. They have been systematically oppressed, assigned the most undignified jobs, and considered 'impure', and subjected to systemic marginalisation that continues in many forms today. *'Adivasi'* (original inhabitant) is the term used for India's Indigenous or tribal peoples, about 7% of its population.

- Several villages in eastern Maharashtra have obtained community rights under the Forest Rights Act 2006, overturning two centuries of centralised government control and exploitation of their forests by outside contractors. Apart from helping to sustain domestic needs (including forest foods, medicinal plants, and culturally and spiritually important sites), sustainable harvesting of forest produce has earned villages substantial income, part of which has gone into community funds. In settlements like Rahu in Amravati district, together with Kukdale and Salhe in Gadchiroli district, these funds are being used to help returning migrant labour or landless people obtain basic relief materials. In the Korchi region of Gadchiroli, 90 villages have formed a *Mahagram Sabha* (a federation of village assemblies) towards greater self-rule and economic self-reliance also as a way to stop destructive mining.
- Kuthambakkam village near Chennai has demonstrated how small-scale manufacturing (e.g. of solar fan-bulb kits) and grain processing have helped families avoid having to migrate for work. Its ex-*sarpanch* Elango Rangaswamy has created a solar-powered way of making disinfectant, which he says can be set up cheaply in any village for both employment and disease prevention.
- In the Adi village in Upper Siang region of Arunachal Pradesh, the local institution (*kebang*) used a traditional practice of restricting movement during certain festivals and rituals, to enforce quarantine and lockdown even before the government declared it (as did many other Adi villages). The village has faced no food scarcity issues as mixed cropping of jhum (shifting cultivation) and home gardens (alongside long-term storage traditions for food grain, smoke-dried meat and fish) have ensured adequate food availability.

Deccan Development Society women at mobile fest, Pastapur, Telangana (India), Feb 2020. **Credit:** Ashish Kothari.

In all these and many other examples,[2] the single most crucial element of resilience is the ability of communities to take collective decisions for themselves. Democracy has been deepened in each of these communities, well beyond the neo-liberal electoral drama that we indulge in once every five years. Communities have taken control over one or more critical elements of their life – the visioning of what they want their present and future to be, building on their past – whether it is regarding food production and distribution, or local ecosystems on which their livelihoods are based, or their health or local markets.

Some (even if partial and imperfect) vision of swaraj (self-rule)[3] has been achieved based on explicit or implicit prefigurative dialogue and discourse, and with plenty of asking-doing-learning-doing-asking spirals. As a result, dependence on the state and on faraway markets has been reduced or even eliminated. In all these examples, there has been some movement towards tackling internal inequities: some faced by women, Dalits, children or other marginalised sections of society, though many are so entrenched they will not go away without a fight.

Such radical democracy (it is strange I have to qualify democracy in this manner since its original meaning, power of/by the people, should be radical enough!) is a subversion of normal structures of power. These communities even challenge the notion of 'power-over' and argue for 'power-with' or 'power-to', rendering the concept and practice of power less hierarchical and competitive, and more equitable and solidarity-based (Kothari and Das, 2016).

From individual to collective visioning

Prefigurative actions by communities and collectives at various levels are important in themselves, especially as they occur at the human scale. For this reason, I think people are wrong in scoffing at 'local' actions as being insignificant. But they are right in observing that, by themselves, they will not bring about the macro or systemic changes we require. For this, we need to create a critical mass of various kinds, and this entails coming together across regions, cultures, ideologies and imaginaries.

In a significant part of people's movements and civil society, there is an increasing restlessness about being in a constant state of protest. Many of us have been fighting systems – including those based on patriarchy, capitalism,

---

2   See dozens of stories and case studies at www.vikalpsangam.org, and in Kalpavriksh, 2017; Kothari and Joy, 2017; and Singh, Kulkarni and Pathak Broome, 2018; see also about 60 stories of COVID-19 time resilience from various parts of India in a series called Extraordinary work of "ordinary" people: beyond pandemics and lockdowns, https://vikalpsangam.org/article/extraordinary-work-of-ordinary-people-in-multi-language-translation/

3   *Swaraj* is an ancient Indian term, revived during its independence struggle against British colonial rule by Mahatma Gandhi. However, its meaning is much deeper than national freedom: it entails a deep democracy, with an assertion of individual and collective autonomy along with responsible behaviour towards all others so their autonomy is not undermined.

statism, casteism, racism and other forms of power asymmetry. All are ecologically devastating, economically iniquitous and socially disruptive. This includes, in its most visible form, the current system of 'developmentality', an ideology that assigns all countries or peoples as being 'higher' or 'lower' based on homogenous criteria like GDP or financial size of economy, and forces or encourages all to take the path that the industrial West has taken (Deb, 2009; Shrivastava and Kothari, 2012). It is a struggle that has to continue, especially in today's times when regressive forces are emerging stronger than ever.

But we also need to put our energies into collective prefigurative visioning and actions, building on what communities and collectives are already attempting. Even as we get better at saying 'no', we need to come up with what we are saying 'yes' to. Resistance that attempts to save existing ways of life (*adivasi*, peasant, pastoral, fishworker, artisanal) is very much part of how to say 'yes'. But it is not enough, because in many of these ways there have been inequities and marginalisations of their own: patriarchal dimensions being nearly universal, casteism featuring prominently in India. Another reason is that many of these ways of life are no longer able to meet basic needs or legitimate aspirations. Witness, for instance, the mass distress among small-scale or artisanal farming, fishing, traditional crafting and pastoralist communities, even in pre-COVID times (Shrivastava and Kothari, 2012). There is a real need for addressing issues of deprivation and injustice, across the world, and that cannot come only from protest and resistance. Constructive, creative alternatives for meeting needs and aspirations have to be revived from the past and created anew. And such scattered actions on grounded alternatives have to be enabled to come together.

Vikalp Sangam: collective envisioning in India

In 2014, an initiative began to try to address a number of questions at a collective level. The underlying question was: if we don't want patriarchy, capitalism, statism, casteism and racism, then what do we want? What solutions are emerging to tackle real poverty, hunger, energy insecurity and other deprivations? How do we achieve them without destroying the earth, or without creating further inequities and inequalities?

Answers to these questions have been attempted over many generations and in many parts of the world. However, movements along these lines have often been divided or fractured on lines of sectors, generations, urban-rural, classes, and so on. The agro-ecology movement (internally quite diverse) has grown as a response to the destructive chemical-dependent 'green revolution' model propagated by governments and corporations.[4] Movements for individual human or collective community rights have obtained legislation providing a

---

4   Among the substantial literature on these subjects are books and articles by Vandana Shiva, Devinder Sharma, Bharat Mansata, Kavitha Kuruganti, Rajeswari Raina and Claude Alvares. A review and visioning of the subject is under publication by Mansata et al., 2017.

range of protective or assertive rights – against discrimination, and instead towards information, education, food, employment, forest resources, health, child and women's empowerment.[5] But not so common are attempts at intersectionality, bringing different movements together.

Democracy Vikalp Sangam, Rajasthan, India, Oct 2019. **Credit:** Ashish Kothari.

In the climate movements, there have been strands that do not actively seek a common cause with, say, the anti-racism or worker rights movements. Typically in India, many environmental action groups have not reached out to those struggling on the rights of women and the differently abled, even less so with *Dalit* movements, despite the growing evidence that environmental problems affect these sections often more than others,[6] and conversely that their empowerment can be a powerful force for ecological revival and conservation (such as in the case of the Chipko movement, or the *Dalit* women farmers' agricultural revolution through Deccan Development Society).[7] Urban groups do not often work well with rural ones and there can remain significant gaps between ways of thinking and doing between old and new generations. The fact that we all are victims, in one way or the other, of the system(s) mentioned above has only recently begun to be realised. To address these issues, a process called Vikalp Sangam (Alternatives Confluence) was initiated in 2014 as a platform to share, collaborate and collectively evolve alternative futures. It involves physical gatherings (there have been 20 so far,

5   See, for instance, Roy et al., 2017; Gopalakrishnan, and http://www.righttofoodcampaign.in

6   There is considerable eco-feminist literature on the relationship between women and environment, including varying perspectives by Vandana Shiva and Bina Agarwal in the Indian context, see Shiva, 1988 and Agarwal, 1994; on the neglect of *Dalit* issues by environmentalists, see Sharma, 2012.

7   For several examples of *Dalit*, women's and other marginalised sections mobilising to protect the environment, see www.vikalpsangam.org.

at regional levels or on themes,[8] providing spaces for cross-sectoral or inter-cultural exchange among practitioners, thinkers, researchers and theorists (these are not necessarily mutually exclusive categories!). It also involves extensive documentation and outreach of alternative initiatives, collated into a website. An e-list connects several hundred people, including those who have participated in the Sangams. During the COVID-19 period in 2020 and early 2021, several online dialogues and presentations have been organised since physical gatherings were not possible.

Human chain demonstration against mega-dams on Indravati river, Hemalkasa, Maharashtra, India. **Credit:** Ashish Kothari

In general, the Vikalp Sangam (VS) initiative attempts to:help document, understand and make more visible ongoing practical and conceptual alternatives in all fields of human endeavourprovide a platform for people working in these to come together for sharing, learning and collaborating, especially across sectors

- be a forum for collective visioning of a better future and pathways to it
- contribute to the possibility of a critical political mass that can more effectively challenge and change the system or systemic forces mentioned aboveThe third objective, *collective visioning*, has been perhaps the most important, innovative and subversive element. It attempts to break out of our modern-day inability or unwillingness to envision utopias. Comparing it to the grand task of preparing a constitution for a newly emerging nation would be rather hubristic, but in a sense it is a similar attempt at bringing the visionary voices of many sections of Indian society, over many years, into a common agenda. And in doing this, it has sought to learn from and bring up grassroots voices, while also recalling and learning from historic greats like Gandhi, Marx, Ambedkar, Tagore and Phule.

---

8   see http://www.vikalpsangam.org/article/vikalp-sangam-reports#.WxjYtC2B1E6

This aspect of VS's visioning is crucial. Most of academia and civil society, especially those belonging to the urban and middle classes, assume that 'expertise' is located only in such classes. The written word dominates the oral; increasingly, the digital trumps the written too. This means that most of 'folk' knowledge and wisdom, worldviews and conceptual frameworks, remains 'hidden' to the world of formal 'intellectuals'. The farmer, the pastoralist, the fisher, the industrial worker, the craftsperson ... these are considered 'practitioners', whereas those who study them are the 'intellectuals' and 'theorists'.[9] In India this is likely exacerbated by the caste and gender hierarchies, built on the strong belief that *Dalits* and other 'lower' castes, and women in general, are not capable of (or should be kept away from) intellectual conceptualisation.

Another possible reason for the neglect of 'folk' ideologies and concepts is their marginalisation in official processes of planning and visioning. Overwhelmingly, governmental processes of planning at various levels involve only officials, academics and urban civil society members. Agricultural and fisheries planning and visioning does not involve farmers and fishers; forest sector planning and visioning does not involve forest dwellers; educational planning does not involve students, and so on.

The VS process tries to consciously involve and enable people from communities, both rural and urban, in various activities. At the first Sangam (referring to physical confluences that are part of the process) in Timbaktu (Andhra Pradesh) in 2014, Kalpavriksh introduced a note In Search of Alternatives: Key Aspects and Principles for discussion. This was based on our understanding of on-ground processes of resistance and transformation, including the kinds of strategies and principles that are contained in them. It includes wisdom expressed by 'ordinary' people in communities and movements. The document (translated into several Indian languages) has since been discussed by over 1,000 people.[10]

One of the most important parts of this visioning is the search for clarity on what is an alternative. At a time when so many corporations are 'greenwashing' their products as 'natural' or 'eco-friendly', governments are claiming to be climate-friendly and even 'well-being' oriented, many people seem to think that simply directing their garbage for recycling makes them a responsible citizen. Vikalp Sangam makes it clear that an initiative is alternative when it challenges and helps change the fundamental conditions of inequity and unsustainability, including the structures of patriarchy, capitalism, statism, racism, casteism and anthropocentrism.

The VS vision document describes what kinds of transformations are taking place or need to take place in five spheres of life: political, economic, social, cultural, ecological and – at the centre of this – ethics and principles. It is in

---

9   There seems to be little written about this in academic circles, though it is a frequent topic of discussion in civil society. Some related issues are dealt with by Shambu Prasad, 2011 and authors in Basole, 2015.

10   http://www.vikalpsangam.org/about/the-search-for-alternatives-key-aspects-and-principles/

the political sphere that it envisages rescuing democracy from its currently form (with power centred on political representatives and bureaucrats, and participation pivoted around intense electoral competitiveness), transforming it to *swaraj*, or 'radical' democracy, where communities grounded in their own reality are at the centre of power. In this way, political relations are transformed from 'power-over' into 'power-to' or 'power-with'. Decision-making is also respectful of ecological and cultural connections, in bioregional or eco-regional landscapes. This is what helps us reimagine political boundaries within and between nation states, such as what Meera Gond-Vankar spoke about at the beginning of this chapter. And this goes hand-in-hand with economic democratisation, struggles for social justice and equity, preserving cultural and knowledge diversity, and sustaining the earth that sustains us.

Possibly VS's most important component is a clear statement of ethical values and principles, which are at the foundation of alternative initiatives, either implicit or explicitly stated. In the examples I have briefly described above, communities have been able to achieve a great deal based on principles like collective responsibility and sharing. There is a focus on solidarity and reciprocity, diversity, freedom and autonomy, respect and responsibility, living within and with nature, dignity and inclusiveness, and others. A crucial extension of this is that instead of 'upscaling' successful initiatives (a typically capitalist or statist approach, unfortunately adopted by many NGOs also), the strategy is to 'outscale' them, with thousands of distributed initiatives learning principles from each other and adopting them to their own unique contexts, then networking to create a bigger scale. This is happening, for instance, with regard to sustainable, biologically diverse agriculture, or decentralised water harvesting or more direct forms of democracy.

A very interesting part of the VS process has been the porosity of conventional ideological boundaries. Several Sangams have had participants with strong Gandhian, Marxist, feminist, *Dalit*, *adivasi*, nature rights and other perspectives, which can often be in contestation with each other. Yet there has been an atmosphere of working out these differences and building on the commonalities, based especially on a collective agreement on the above-mentioned ethics and values. This could be because the Sangam space has an atmosphere of positivity given its core subject matter, so participants coming into it are aware in advance that it is a space for constructive dialogue. But perhaps most important is how experiences from the ground are impossible to silo-ise into ideological or sectoral boxes; the experience of a *Dalit* woman farmer breaking out of caste and gender and class barriers and achieving food sovereignty lends itself magnificently to holistic, out-of-the-box ideologies. She would much rather not be classified as being part of a Marxist, or a Gandhian or an Ambedkarite revolution, but perhaps all rolled into one ... and much more!

National Vikalp Sangam, Udaipur, 2017. **Credit:** Ashish Kothari

One outcome of the VS process that also lends itself to democratising spaces is the 'Alternatives Transformation Format'.[11] This is meant to be used by actors within an initiative where transformations towards justice and sustainability are being attempted. It can be done with or without external facilitation, enabling actors to see how holistic, coherent and comprehensive their initiative is. It has been used for a two-year study of transformations among handloom weavers in Kachchh (Kothari et al., 2019) and sporadically by organisations for some critical self-reflection.

The latest from the VS stable is a national networking process to respond to the huge crisis of livelihoods created by COVID-19 (or rather, by the callous nature of the lockdown imposed by the Indian state). Called Vikalp Sutra,12 this links to several dozen national or regional organisations (including those working for immediate relief and rehabilitation, and those working for many years on generating and sustaining dignified livelihoods). Apart from an intense focus on livelihoods and worker rights, the Sutra process also hopes to conceptualise and advocate for fundamental changes in economy – towards greater self-reliance, open localisation, circularity, local exchanges, producer control and well-being. The Sutra process endeavours to be non-hierarchical, horizontally distributed, with a light coordination structure; again, a core principle of democratic functioning.

Finally, the fourth objective of VS – to create a political critical mass for transforming the structures of power and decision-making – has enabled some spaces for democratisation. Advocating policy shifts for certain regions (e.g. Kashmir, Ladakh) or in certain sectors (e.g. food and agriculture) are elements

11   http://www.vikalpsangam.org/static/media/uploads/Resources/alternatives_
transformation_framework_revised_20.2.2017.pdf .

12   https://sutra.vikalpsangam.org

of this, but more ambitious are attempts to push 'people's agendas' at a national level, such as a manifesto[13] issued in the context of the 2019 general elections, and a statement on long-term measures that should be taken in the context of the COVID-19 pandemic and lockdown.[14] In 2020, it also linked with several other movements on the Jan Sarokar process and in sessions of a Janta (People's) Parliament, bringing together citizens' views on the government's performance in various sectors and advocating alternatives.

Village Mapping at Kunariya, Kachchh, western India. **Credit:** Kunariya Panchayat

13   https://vikalpsangam.org/article/peoples-manifesto-for-a-just-equitable-and-sustainable-india-2019/

14   https://vikalpsangam.org/article/vikalp-sangam-core-group-statement-on-the-need-for-creative-long-term-alternatives-in-view-of-COVID-19-28-march-2020/

Global transformations

A transformation towards justice, equity, sustainability cannot happen in India alone. Economic globalisation has interconnected peoples and countries like never before, and global crises with climate, biodiversity and inequality blithely disregard national boundaries. Visioning and democratisation movements have to link with similar processes elsewhere, creating a global critical mass.

In the same imaginary speech quoted at the beginning of this chapter, Meera Gond-Vankar went on to observe:

> "The people of India and the rest of South Asia have been significant movers of an increasingly borderless world ... the gradual dissolution of rigid nation state boundaries. South Asia learnt from the mistakes of blocks like the European Union, with its strange mix of centralisation and decentralisation and continued reliance on the nation state, and worked out its own recipe for respecting diversity within a unity of purpose. This is heavily based, as mentioned above, on community-based governance in areas of what were formerly nation state boundaries. Peoples' movements across South Asia were key actors towards devising the democratic Global Peoples' Assembly that, sometime in the mid-2000s, began to replace the United Nations. This Assembly has a series of governance mechanisms that do not give permanent or long-term power to any people or individual, are accountable to direct democracy and eco-regional units on the ground, and are meant exclusively for absolutely essential functions such as governance of the global commons (the seas, the atmosphere, and so on), and facilitation of equitable and sustainable cultural and economic relations.
>
> Indeed, let us acknowledge that the transformations in South Asia are not entirely its own doing ... It was only when we realised that we could learn enormously from peoples' initiatives across the world, just as they could learn from us that transformations could be made more effectively and widely. Still, I guess we could take some pride in having been instrumental in starting (with others) the Global Alternatives Sangam, which ran for some decades till it was incorporated into the Global Peoples' Assembly."

A number of attempts are being made to bring together progressive movements across the world. One, emerging from the Vikalp Sangam process (and other similar ones such as Crianza Mutua[15] in Mexico), is the Global Tapestry of Alternatives (GTA)[16]. This is a non-hierarchical, convivial platform for *weaving*: exchange, mutual learning, collaboration and collective visioning, to challenge the dominant patriarchal, capitalist, statist, racist and anthropocentric system. The aim is to demonstrate that it is possible to live in ways that promote justice, equity and ecological wisdom. It stresses learning from Indigenous people and other local communities, along with radical counter-movements emerging within industrialised societies.

Begun in mid-2019, the GTA process has been endorsed by networks, movements and several prominent individuals, spreading across all continents. It is setting up exchanges, dialogues, mutual learning and mapping to support on-ground action with several partners, building on the experience of networks like Vikalp Sangam and Crianza Mutua.

Conclusion: the democratic potential of collective visioning

At its core, democracy should be about 'ordinary' people, unshackled from blind faith in conventional structures of power, individually and collectively taking stewardship of their past, present and future. The above describes some modest attempts at trying to provide platforms to enable this. As I observed elsewhere, an attempt like VS is:

> "a celebration of the ability of 'ordinary' people to innovate, persevere, collaborate and find solutions to what may seem intractable problems. It puts back faith in communities and individual citizens, who are not waiting for 'experts' and 'sarkar' to lead the way to sustainability and justice. But it also shows that transformative initiatives can come from anywhere, from civil society and communities, from government officials and research institutions, from social enterprises and businesses. It shows further that the visioning of a better society, of a future we want to strive towards, is not the prerogative of formal 'experts'. It can be done by putting together the wisdom, knowledge and experience of people anywhere. People in different stages of life, in whatever culture and livelihood, at whatever level of learning and education, in nature or in the farm or in classrooms. People who have shown themselves capable of doing the most extraordinary things."

---

15 https://globaltapestryofalternatives.org/newsletters:01:index#crianza_mutua_in_mexico

16 https://globaltapestryofalternatives.org

To be sure, one can never confidently state that such processes will change society in fundamental ways. In the early 2000s many of us were involved in a nationwide exercise to prepare India's National Biodiversity Strategy and Action Plan (NBSAP). Over 50,000 people participated, through various modes of interaction, and produced about 100 local, state, regional and thematic plans, all culminating in the national one. Unfortunately, the Ministry of Environment and Forests rejected its outputs (Kothari and Kohli, 2009). But the process created a momentum that many local communities and groups carried forward, e.g. through a significant expansion in food sovereignty and biodiversity related exercises by Dalit women farmers of the Deccan Development Society in Telangana, or biodiversity celebrations and enterprise-based livelihoods among women by Vanastree of Uttara Kannada, Karnataka.[17] It also created a large body of information and analysis, made publicly available.[18] And it created lasting connections between communities and civil society, even individual government officials, that have spawned other constructive collaborations for visioning and action.

Indus, on way to Alchi, Ladakh, India. **Credit:** Ashish Kothari.

It is the *process* that is important, as much if not more than the final outcome. The combination of grounded action and lofty visioning, even utopian thinking, frees us from the confines of what the dominant system tells us is 'possible'. In this sense, the dreaming of alternative visions and thinking of pathways to get there is deeply democratic, taking us that much closer to swaraj and freedom.

17　See 'Deccan Andhra' substate biodiversity action plan at http://www.kalpavriksh.org/index.php/conservation-livelihoods1/72-focus-areas/conservation-livelihoods/biodiversity-and-wildlife/national-biodiversity-strategy-action-plan/225-bsaps-ftp-sub-state; see also http://ddsindia.com, and http://vanastree.org.

18　For the full documentation arising from this exercise, including a detailed process document, see http://www.kalpavriksh.org/index.php/conservation-livelihoods1/biodiversity-and-wildlife/national-biodiversity-strategy-action-plan.

References

1. Agarwal, Bina (1994). *A field of one's own: gender and land rights in South Asia*. Cambridge England New York, NY, USA: Cambridge University Press

2. Basole, Amit (2015). *Lokavidya perspectives: a philosophy of political imagination for the knowledge age*. Varanasi: Aakar Books and Vidya Ashram.

3. Deb, Debal (2009). *Beyond developmentality: constructing inclusive freedom and sustainability*. London: Earthscan.

4. Gopalakrishnan, Shankar (no date). Rights legislations and the Indian state: understanding the meaning of the Forest Rights Act [online]. Academia. Available at: https://www.academia.edu/360289/Rights_Legislations_and_the_Indian_State_Understanding_the_Meaning_of_the_Forest_Rights_Act?auto=download

5. Kalpavriksh (2017). *The search for radical alternatives: key elements and principles* [online]. Kalpavriksh. Available at: https://kalpavriksh.org/wp-content/uploads/2018/12/AlternativesframeworkbookletPawaniAnjitha.pdf

6. Kothari, Ashish and Das, Pallav (2016). Power in India: radical pathways', in Nick Buxton and Deborah Eade (eds.) *State of power 2016*. Transnational Institute, pp. 182-199. Available at : https://www.tni.org/en/publication/state-of-power-2016

7. Kothari, Ashish and Joy, K J (eds) (2017). *Alternative futures: unshackling India*, Delhi: Authors Upfront.

8. Kothari, Ashish and Kohli, Kanchi (2009). National biodiversity action plan, *Economic & Political Weekly*, vol xliv no 20, May 16.

9. Kothari, Ashish, Venkataswamy, Durgalakshmi, Laheru, Ghatit, Dixit, Arun, Trivedi, Kankana and Mulay, Radhika (2019). *Sandhani: weaving transformations in Kachchh, India: the full report*. Kachchh: Kalpavriksh, Pune, Khamir, Bhuj and Vankars. Available at: https://vikalpsangam.org/wp-content/uploads/migrate/Vikalp%20Sangam%20Case%20Studies/sandhani,_kachchh_full_report,_final,_english,_2019.pdf

10. Mansata, Bharat, Kuruganti, Kavitha, Jardhari, Vijay and Futane, Vasant (2017). Anna swaraj: a vision for food sovereignty and agro-ecological resurgence', in Kothari, Ashish and KJ Joy (eds), *Alternative futures: unshackling India*. Delhi: Authors Upfront.

11. Prasad, Shambu (2011). *Knowledge swaraj, agriculture and the new commons: insights from SRI in India*. Paper presented at the panel on Knowledge Commons And Knowledge Swaraj: The Missing Connection at the IASC (International Association for Study of Commons), Jan 10-14, 2011, Hyderabad. Available at: https://www.researchgate.net/publication/232219274

12. Roy, Aruna, Dey, Nikhil, and Kashyap, Praavita (2017). 'Allowing people to shape our democratic future', in Kothari, Ashish and KJ Joy (eds), *Alternative futures: unshackling India*. Delhi: Authors Upfront.

13. Sharma, Mukul (2012). Dalits and Indian environmental politics. *Economic and Political Weekly* vol xlvil no 23, June 9.

14. Shiva, Vandana (1988) *Staying alive: women, ecology and survival in India*. Delhi: Zed Press.

15. Singh, Neera, Kulkarni, Seema and Pathak Broome, Neema (2018). *Ecologies of hope and transformation: post-development alternatives from India*. Pune: Kalpavriksh and SOPPECOM.

16. Shrivastava, Aseem and Kothari, Ashish. (2012). *Churning the Earth: the making of global India*. Delhi: Viking/Penguin India.

Commons-based Monies for an Inclusive and Resilient Future

Ester Barinaga, Andreu Honzawa, Juan J. Ocampo,
Paola Raffaelli & Leanne Ussher

There is a Chinese proverb that goes "the fish is the last to know water" – a visual metaphor that succinctly conveys how blind we can be towards what we see every day. It describes our inattention to the obvious; our inability to question because we have never confronted a different way of perceiving, the normalised patterns of thought concerning phenomena we encounter regularly. This lack of ability to grasp a phenomenon characterises our relationship with money.

Money, for most of us, is experienced as a "thing" – one either has it or does not, an asset one always wants more of. We are taught that money is neutral to the inner workings of the economy, that it merely serves to grease the wheels of commerce.[1] Immersed in such thinking, many progressive policymakers root our sustainability plight in the individual behaviour money seems to elicit – the constant search for profit for money's sake. Blind to the internal architecture of money, this argument tends to centre on the vice of corporate greed that exploits nature, oppresses workers and transforms citizens into consumers).[2] The solution under such analysis implies that monied capitalist behaviour must change. Ignoring altogether the monetary system itself, for such scholars and policymakers, reform comes in the form of individual resistance: as eco-friendly consumers, we are to reduce our levels of material and energy consumption to minimise social and environmental damage[3]; as oppressed workers, we are to organise work through trade unions or the cooperative ownership of the means of production)[4]; as inhabitants of the Earth, we must care for all livelihoods, biodiversity, and promote production processes that rely on waste and recycling instead of on newly extracted or non-local natural resources.[5]

Ignorant of money's internal design, these strategies look past how the form money takes shapes the behaviour they so want to change. A pattern of thought that sees money as an asset blinds us both to the malleability of the monetary architecture and to money's institutional capacity to organise the very system of production and distribution that green policymakers and activists insist on transforming. Implicitly building their analysis on an assumption that money is neutral to the inner workings of the real economy, they disregard the very element of the system that gives the economy its boundary, shape, dynamic and rhythm. While urgent, such solutions are bound to remain inoffensive and marginal because the monetary infrastructure that surreptitiously steers the economy towards over-exploitation and degradation is kept intact.

With the increasing frequency of financial and economic crises, and with the growing impotence of orthodox monetary policy to stabilise our monetary system, our understanding and assumptions around money are changing. Emergent critical lessons that contradict the traditional view of money include: that money can be supplied freely alongside deflation (see Japan from early 1990s until now); that newly issued money can be used to stabilise not only banks during financial crises but small businesses and individuals as during the COVID-19 lockdown; that a currency can be manufactured privately by non-state and non-bank actors (see Bitcoin). These radical changes tipped the fishbowl and revealed water to the fish. Among both money activists, teachers and scholars, there is a growing desire to educate the public on what money is.[6] **The primary task is to show that money is in fact a political and social technology, an infrastructure that humans design and implement to coordinate the economy and to organise society.**[7]

In contrast to traditional conceptions of money as a public good, an asset created by governments for its citizen's benefit, these activists and scholars conceive of money as a commons.[8] Armed with this new understanding of money, communities, citizens and grassroots groups around the world set to make their own complementary monies – often referred to as local or community currencies.[9] In reimagining contributions and appropriations, in reorganising communal participation, and in rethinking relations between not just creditors and debtors but members and resources in a community, organisers of local monies hope to build more inclusive, resilient and sustainable interactions between producers, consumers, third-party actors, governance institutions and resource systems.

Not all reorganisations of money are, however, equally conducive to a sustainable future. Trapped in a dominant understanding of money as a commodity (a publicly or privately produced 'thing') and caught in monetary designs and practices intrinsic to such an understanding, many complementary currency initiatives risk reproducing the ills of today's national monies. To steer away from such risks, it is important to first understand the root of those ills. Only then will we be able to design monies that enable us to overcome the monetary origin of our unsustainable present. Entire books have been written on the shortcomings of our current conventional monetary system, identifying the many features that lead us to unsustainable and unequal societies.[i] This chapter will focus only on those that guide most local communities when reclaiming, redesigning and implementing complementary currencies.

Problems with today's national money

The story of money that many believe is the story of gold. Gold is seen as an intrinsically valuable commodity, that people dug up and gave to goldsmiths for safe keeping in exchange for an inventory receipt. The inventory receipts became the 'means of payment,' money that was used around town to trade for goods and services and clear accounts. If the gold bullion was minted into coins – like the *florin* in AD1252 Florence – then gold was money. But given gold's scarcity, it was the inventory receipts issued by reputable goldsmiths that was the more common form of money and 'as good as gold'. According to this story, goldsmiths discovered early on that they could issue more receipts than what they stored in gold. By lending or spending receipts independent of gold, goldsmiths – later banks – offered an elastic supply of money as needed by the community.

---

i   For the reader interested in learning more about the monetary design roots of our growing inequality and unsustainable plight.[10]

Today's monetary system is built on the goldsmith's story. To the story's two forms of money – gold coins and bullion first, 'receipts for gold' second – a third was added – 'receipts for gold receipts.' Non-bank financial companies could store bank 'receipts for gold' (invested in treasury bonds or money market mutual funds) and issue their own inventory receipts – called repurchase agreements or 'repos'. Each layer of financial innovation serves as money to clear accounts between different sets of users with their own institutional arrangements. Central banks became the primary holders of gold in the 20th century, representing their sovereigns and issuing central bank reserves for settlement between other central banks. Private commercial banks held gold inventory receipts (later digital central bank reserve receipts) to settle payments with each other, and issued their own bank (deposit) receipts. And financial firms used bank money or other securities to clear accounts between each other, and in the process they issued their own 'receipt on receipt' or 'repos'.[ii]

In a system with such an elastic monetary supply, each form of money is more expansive than the reserve upon which it is based, building a money pyramid, which can expand in layers vertically or in supply horizontally.

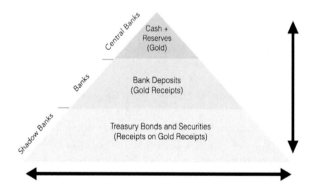

A simple 'money hierarchy' stylised upon Mehrling (2013), and Gabor & Vestergaard (2016), using gold as fictional meme.[11]

While our national monetary systems no longer rest on gold, this hierarchy of money remains a fair description of today's national monies.[12] Modern day central bank reserves are *digital entries* in a central ledger. Another central bank reserve is cash (paper notes and coins), but this is not the primary money we use. Rather, private bank money (bank deposits) makes about 97% of the money circulating in an economy.[14]

Anthropologists, historians, economists and legal scholars have repeatedly shown that the goldsmith story is not an accurate description of the history of

ii   See Gabor and Vestergaard 2016 for their discussion on repurchase agreements, shadow bank money, and the hierarchy of money.[13]

money. Money's history is far more pluralistic, with historical epochs and currency designs that run the gamut from money specifically as a commodity, to money only used for clearing, and some combination of the two.[15] And yet, that story continues to shape contemporary national money in at least five problematic ways. Recognising these architectural problems is the first step to develop 'monetary awareness' on which to rethink, redesign and repurpose money.

1. Unstable pro-cyclical dynamics

Not all layers of money are equally accepted for final payment, their 'moneyness' varies over the business cycle. During the business cycle upswing, demand for credit expands. Expecting the economy to grow, bankers and financial actors become less risk averse, increasing leveraging and expanding the money supply with it. When hopeful or in the context of booming business cycles, financiers create credit that fuels price rises, incites consumer demand and secures employment, boosting even more economic growth. But the expansion of leverage sows the seeds of the financial bust.[16] When the fear of over-leverage (and consequent debt defaults) takes over, there is a 'flight to quality' (conversion to higher order money) which contracts the money supply. Gloomy about the economy or in the context of recession, bankers and financial actors reduce credit, thus worsening the downward spiral of decreasing prices, tapering consumer demand and raising unemployment.

Leveraging and lending when confident and tightening when fearful, the spirits, sentiments, and profit calculations of financial actors seal the fate of the real economy (made of people of flesh and bones) into a pro-cyclical behaviour that intensifies booms and busts. As the saying goes, 'a banker is a fellow who lends you his umbrella when the sun is shining and insists upon its return as soon as it starts to rain'. The supply of commercial bank money contracts in a recession, making the recession worse, and expands in an economic boom, fuelling greater leverage and liquidity. It is these dramatic shifts by the financial sector that make hierarchical monetary systems inherently unstable. It is for this reason that central banks have the mandate, but often struggle, to stabilise business cycles (in particular of the fragile financial sector), with counter-cyclical policies.

2. Prone to leakages

A characteristic of today's money is that its desirability is dependent on its convertibility between layers and on its movement across circuits. National monies are often forced to adopt a one size fits all 'free market' approach, which ties them to 'free capital mobility' or convertibility – domestically and internationally. Such principles may also apply to free trade in products and free movement of labour. While such freedom may lead to more efficient allocations of money, people and resources in a static sense, they also imply greater inequality and instability for communities that are on the losing side. For example, money and labour tends to move from locations with lower rates of return, and low value-added industry or opportunity in the periphery (rural areas and the global South), to centres with higher rates of return and advanced, high value added industry and services (urban financial centres and the global North).[17] The periphery struggles to keep the very money and resources it needs to build capacity and opportunity for an inclusive and sustainable economy.

Most communities try to compete for these 'hot money flows', lowering taxes to attract investors and turning to export-led growth in competition with the global centres. But there is a fallacy of composition that all communities can become winners; instead, there is a 'race to the bottom'. While it is important that a community can "export" enough to pay for its "imports" (within a nation or between nations), the adoption of mantras like 'open borders' and 'easy capital convertibility' usually supports the centre rather than the periphery and can miss the point of adopting a more democratic and demand-led growth from within the peripheral communities.[18] A simple image visualises the problem cogently:

The less money circulates, the less economic activity there is.

The more money circulates, the more economic activity there is.

Credit: Social Trade Organisation (STRO)

3. Competing functions of money

By design, today's national money fulfils *competing functions*. First, it serves as a 'unit of account', a common measure of value to facilitate comparison of value across commodities and aid the clearing and settlement of positions. Under bilateral barter, two people might agree that one good is worth twice as much as another good. For multilateral barter to be possible, one of the goods has to perform the unit of account function. Far better to use an abstract measure – like inches, centimetres or dollars – to serve as a counting measure. Lacking a common unit of measurement, parties will find it extremely difficult to compare economic values.[iii]

Tightly tied to the first is money's second function as a means of final payment or 'medium of exchange'. This function frees traders from immediate reciprocity of a good for another good (barter) which requires a difficult 'double coincidence of wants'. Money allows the exchange of a good now, for a 'promise' that can be redeemed for a good provided by someone else at a later time.

The third function of most national monies brings the compatibility and peaceful fluidity of the first two functions to a halt.[iv] As a 'store of value', money is given a price, an interest rate that prompts users to hoard it and be less willing to spend it for goods or services. Saving money is a leakage into the monetary circuit, reducing its availability to circulate in the real economy and leaving those who cannot save with less income. In other words, the rational behaviour of an individual or household to save money for a rainy day, if generalised across the community, translates into the entrenchment of inequality and decreased general resiliency.[20] The store of value function thus worsens money's capacity to act as a medium of exchange.

4. Undemocratic money

Most of our national money, we saw, is produced by for-profit financial firms, which provide an elastic yet pro-cyclical and erratic supply of money. This system, where banks can freely create new lower order money at little cost, readily empowers some and excludes others from access to fresh money.

Based on a deep understanding of the political economy of the monetary circuit, Kalecki's insight is startling: "workers spend what they get and capitalists get what they spend".[21] Aggregate bank lending in a closed circuit equates to an equal rise in bank deposits. The

---

iii   Indeed, this is one of several arguments used to debunk the myth of barter as the origin of money. See Graeber 2011.[19]

iv   The choice of "peaceful" to characterise the fluidity of credit-debt money is a direct reference to David Graeber's historical analysis of money arrangements. In his book *Debt: The first 5,000 years*, he argues that "credit systems tend to dominate in periods of relative social peace, or across networks of trust (whether created by states or, in most periods, transnational institutions like merchant guilds or communities of faith); in periods characterized by widespread war and plunder, they tend to be replaced by precious metal".[22]

limited power of workers and stagnating wages means that all growth in such deposits leads to higher profits to firms and their bankers, but not to higher wages for the working class. Steady consumption growth yet declining real wages explains why household debt rose in the lead up to the 2008 financial crisis.

There is no reason why the production of money must be limited to banks and non-bank financial companies. Why should money should go to the highest bidder (justifying interest) and why should firms' profits are grow while wages stagnate? These outcomes reflect the power relations in the system between those that produce money and earn interests and profits versus those that earn wages.

5. Treating money as a thing

The goldsmith story highlights the extent to which money is treated as a commodity, an asset with intrinsic value that serves to back the next lower order of money. This fractional reserve banking approach requires that a lower order money is convertible (possible to sell) *at par*, 1:1, with some higher order money. Treated as a thing that can be converted/sold, financial actors package lower layers of money and resell it for its leveraging capacity. But, as we saw above, it is in the hoarding and leveraging individual behaviours that such an understanding of money provokes that we find the instability of our current monetary system.

And yet, money is no mere commodity that individuals can save and financial actors can leverage and resell. At least not per se. That individual economic agents can relate to money as if it was a commodity hinges on the set of rules, design features and arrangement of actors into which money has been institutionalised. The infrastructural capacities of money originate not in some intrinsic monetary value but, rather, on the way relations among economic actors have been engineered throughout the process of creating, distributing, moving and withdrawing money.[23]

Designing money that overcomes the problems of today's national monies requires us to break free from our contemporary monetary illusions. Seeing beyond the money-thing, into the institution that money is, jolts the fish out of the water. If money is a man-made institution, it can surely be remade.[24] This time, from the grassroots; this time, from a different understanding of money. Welcome to the world of local complementary currencies.[v]

---

v   While this chapter focuses on the remaking of the monetary system from the bottom up, several movements are calling for redesigning the governance of today's monetary institutions from the top. Modern Monetary Theory (MMT), Sovereign Money (or 100% money) and Positive Money are the most salient of these movements. On MMT, see Wray

Reconceptualising money as a commons

Moving from an understanding of money as an asset that some have and others don't, to an understanding of money as a commons to serve the many is possibly the most consequential lesson the fish drew. Money ceases to be seen as a thing that is privately owned and that ought to have intrinsic value. Instead, as has long been known by economists, bankers and policymakers, money starts to be understood as fabricated, a record of account with no limit, a tool we use to incentivise action, an institution for the coordination of the economy; a socio-technical arrangement to coordinate our economic life together.[25,26] The economic crisis that ensued after the financial collapse of 2008 is evidence that, while the financial elite had mismanaged the production of money, it was the many who were suffering the consequences. The trillions of dollars issued by central banks and spent by federal governments the world over following COVID-19 manifests that money is a collective good. These epochal events attest that money had been institutionalised as an asset for financiers to buy, leverage and resell, but that really it is an infrastructural system enabling the everyday flow of economic life. Ultimately, it is the tension between individual gain and collective good that has been made visible. Referring to natural resources, this tension has been dubbed "the tragedy of the commons".[31] The fish now saw that money, too, was a commons.

Elinor Ostrom won the Nobel Prize in Economics in 2009 for her work on the commons. She defined a "common-pool resource" – Ostrom's preferred term – as "a natural or man-made resource system that is sufficiently large as to make it costly (but not impossible) to exclude potential beneficiaries from obtaining benefits from its use".[32] A key distinction underlies that definition, that between resource system and resource units. A resource system is "what *generates* a flow of resource units or benefits over time"; resource units are "what individuals *appropriate* or use from the resource systems".[33,34] Fisheries, grazing fields and forests are classic examples of resource systems. Individuals do not appropriate the resource system – the river; they however appropriate the resource units – the fishes – flowing through the system. While the resource system is accessible to the many, while the many benefit from a healthy river, it is the individual that benefits from the unit he has fished. The distinction makes apparent that it is in the interest of the collective to maintain the health of the system, but that it is in the self-interest of the individual to catch yet another fish. Hardin (1968) saw "the tragedy of the commons" in the individual incentive to appropriate resource units well beyond the resource system's capacity to regenerate itself; that is, well beyond what we today would call the resource's "tipping point".[35] The tragedy of the commons, he argued, resulted in over-fishing, overgrazing and over-logging.

2012, Kelton 2020.[27] On 100% money, see Benes and Kumhof 2011.[28] On Positive Money, see Jackson & Dyson, 2012.[29] Others have called for the urgent need to reform not so much national monetary institutions as the international monetary system.[30]

Seeing money as a commons translates into distinguishing the monetary system that generates the flow of monetary units from the monetary units that individuals appropriate and accumulate.[36] In this perspective, units consist of the coins and bills in your pocket, along with the digits recorded in your bank account. The monetary system, in turn, consists of the socio-technical arrangements underpinning the accounting process through which money is created. Today's monetary socio-technical arrangement includes private commercial banks as well as central banks, money market dealers as well as financial technologies, regulations as well as dominant ideas about money. Understanding money as a commons renders recurrent financial crises as a tragedy of the money commons, where mis-management of monetary units culminates in the system's breakdown. It obviates that, at the root of today's economic inequality, there is a mismatch between the collective interest for a monetary system that serves us all, and the accumulating interest of individual financiers and rentiers positioned at the centre of the system.

Hardin, and mainstream economics, traditionally gave two solutions to the tragedy of the commons, both related to the ownership regime of the resource. The first solution gives ownership to the state who, through government regulations, ensures the quality and capacity of the resource. The second solution is through the market, and gives ownership to private individual economic agents in whose interests it is to keep the quality and capacity of the resource system. In a similar fashion, suggestions for addressing the troubles of our monetary system have followed either a laissez-faire market logic or the logic of an interventionist state. The first defend the creation of money by many competing private commercial banks and advocate for markets that, they argue, would lead to the self-regulation of banks and financial actors and 'reliable' money.[37] The latter favour stronger government intervention in money matters, both through re-regulation of financial actors and through a Central Bank that more closely controls the money supply.[38]

Ostrom's Nobel prize was granted for how she challenged such dominant solutions to the tragedy of the commons. She reasoned not from theory but from empirical fieldwork. In Latin America, South East Asia, Africa and Southern Europe she found a third alternative to managing common resources, and doing so more sustainably than either states or markets most often do. She found that **communities managing their commons successfully had developed social norms and institutions that could adapt to the seasonal variations and circumstantial changes of the natural resource.** Rather than being guided by individual self-interest as Hardin and other economists had assumed, Ostrom brought to light that a commoner's individual behaviour was not that of a rational egoist but rather that of a conditional co-operator.[39] In her analysis she stressed the importance of institutions and social relations in organising collective action for the interest of the many.

Under Ostrom's perspective, what Hardin described in 1968 was not a commons. He was describing a scenario in which there were no boundaries to the grazing land, no rules for governing it, and no community of users. He was focused on describing a resource open to "free-riders", with no institutional structure for its management; an open-access regime, a "free-for-all in which everything is free for the taking".[40] Instead, according to Ostrom, a commons has a community of users that sets boundaries, defines rules of use, monitors resource usage, enforces sanctions for overuse and follows social norms. A commons includes a community that benefits from the resource and is willing to act as its steward. That is, a commons is not a resource in itself. It is a resource, plus a community of commoners, plus the governance rules and norms the community implements to manage the resource system.[41] All three – resource, community and governance institutions – form an integrated whole; they go together and do not make sense as isolated parts.

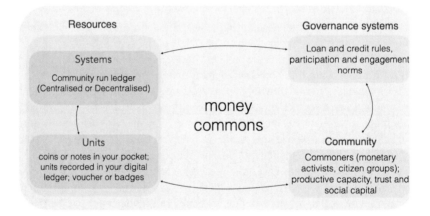

Source: Adapted from Ostrom (2009)

It is in this line of thought that monetary activists, citizen groups and community organisers are starting to remake the communal relations and governance rules of the money commons. Reasoning along Elinor Ostrom's lines, these practitioners and activists set out to create their own monetary systems and put them at the service and management of communities. Following her advocacy for direct participatory governance, locally adapted rules, and social and environmental justice, they went beyond reconceptualising money as a commons and onto embedding the creation and governance of the new monies in the communities that use them. Indeed, understanding money as a commons affects the way communities remake money and manage the money commons.

Remaking money: Design features for a money commons

Money as a commons sheds light on the fact that there is more than one way to design our monetary architecture – ways beyond the prerogative of bankers and incumbent financial actors. From Spain to the US in the Global North, from Eastern Africa to Latin America in the Global South, citizen groups, activists, and community organisers are reclaiming the power to create money by designing, organising and implementing local complementary currencies.[42] Money-making empowerment notwithstanding, the question is how to align the interests of those producing money with the interests of those using it, along with a vision of an equal, inclusive and environmentally sustainable future. Designing a money commons is not simply about introducing an alternative currency. The new currency must relate to the entire ecosystem – the *resource system* we need to manage, the *community* of users it is to serve, and the *governance* rules that steer the allocation of *resource units* and the coordination of the community.

Such a redesign of money requires us to challenge not only our thinking of money but, even more importantly, its internal architecture. For, if money is designed upon the same features underpinning today's official money, we risk reproducing the same mistakes. Our chance to build monetary systems that advance inclusive and sustainable futures resides in the new producers and users of money overcoming dominant patterns of thought and practice, acting not only as if they were already free but truly freeing themselves from today's monetary dogma. In the conviction that we need not only subvert our patterns of thought but also to quickly build a solid alternative, we will focus the remainder of the chapter on the design traits of those complementary monies truly freeing themselves from conventional thought and practice.

1. Complementary: Overcoming the conflict between money functions

Typically, the three functions of money – as a unit of account, as a means of exchange, and as a store of value – are fulfilled by a single national currency. Yet, we saw above, the latter two functions foster contradictory individual behaviours, resulting in dynamics that entrench inequality and reduce overall resilience. There is however no need to force all three functions onto one single currency. We can have a multiplicity of currencies.

Grassroots and community currency practitioners argue for the separation of functions into special purpose currencies. Their suggestion is to have the national currency serve as the unit of reference and store of value, and the complementary or community currency to work as a means of payment, the functions of 'store of value' and of 'means of exchange' never competing for the use of any particular currency.[43] Functional *complementarity* of multiple currencies, it is suggested, can make the system as a whole more robust and resilient, potentially contributing to the overall performance of the national currency.[44]

2. Interest-free: Eliminating the possibility of rent-seeking

Interest paid on money holdings encourages savers not to part from their money, or to part only at a price higher than the interest they receive on their holdings – a behaviour that constrains access to money to commoners or investors. Interest, that is, hampers the circulation of money, thus reducing its capacity to act as a medium of exchange.

To prevent local complementary currencies from acting as a store of value and inhibit commoners from hoarding the currency, grassroots communities are creating money free of interest. Even for those communities funding trade through debt creation, the commitment to repay the monetary units recorded on a debtor's account is for repayment of the principal alone. No interest ticking each month; no promise to pay back an amount that is larger than what one received; debts designed to be re-payable. Such a system makes money accessible, its supply directly tied to the original purpose of the complementary currency – satisfying community needs – rather than to the speculative and hoarding behaviours that interest encourages.

3. Non-convertible to a national currency: Disabling commodification

The possibility to guarantee conversion of the local complementary currency into the conventional national currency is a design feature of heated debate. Proponents argue the feature makes the currency attractive to a larger number of users who want a guaranteed value in their national currency and is thus key to scaling up these complementary monies (e.g. Berkshares). Opponents argue that convertibility – fixed or floating – is both practically problematic and conceptually traps us into a commodity understanding of money, thus reproducing some of the problems of today's national monies.

Among the practical challenges of convertibility, the most salient are constraints to the supply of the local currency and the difficulty to manage exchange rates. First, the currency supply. Currencies that are 100% backed and redeemable at a fixed exchange rate are scarce by design because the supply of national currency limits the supply of the local currency. Even if the local currency is only fractionally backed, there is the possibility of a 'bank run' which would make the currency disappear. Second, the exchange rates. Most cryptocurrencies adopt a flexible exchange rate or market approach, which opens up for speculation on market value appreciation. While this may promote adoption, at least when prices are rising, conversion at variable exchange rates makes the local currency vulnerable to price volatility and 'currency runs'. Such currencies end up downplaying the usefulness of money, diluting their commons-based values.

Conceptually, convertibility amounts to selling the local complementary currency for the national currency, thus commodifying the complementary currency and promptly restoring its function as a store of value. Given the possibility to trade the local currency for one that serves a wider regional area and is used for general purposes, users have a larger incentive to accumulate the local currency for exchange to the national one (as observed in some of the Kenyan community currencies).[45] Encouraging hoarding and speculation, convertibility takes the complementary currencies out of local circulation, limiting the currency's ability to easily flow within the community. Convertibility also opens a door for capital to leak out of the community, depleting the supply of local currency and further worsening the currency's capacity to function as a means of payment. And yet, as we saw, these complementary monies aim to work as means of payment. It is for this reason that many community currencies refrain from conversion to national money.

4. Clear boundaries: Demarcating exchange circuits

A focus on facilitating the circulation of money with a view to make it flow rapidly among the commoners' demands for money constrained locally. Not for the sake of regionalism or autarky. But, rather, for the same reasons as for precluding conversion and for separating the functions of money. Money with a jurisdiction as large as the national it is intended to complement would leak out of weaker local communities towards economic hubs and financial centres, thus hampering local access to money, inhibiting local economic activity, and maintaining long supply chains.[46] Further, serving a similar territory and a comparable general purpose would make the alternative and national currencies compete as means of exchange – a Hayekian market of currencies where the stronger currency is bound to end up substituting the weaker ones.[47] With substitution, the functions of money collapse, once again, into a single currency, leading us back to a currency that can be hoarded out of circulation.

For a real chance to advance a sustainable and inclusive future, complementary currencies need to be properly demarcated, either territorially or functionally, or both.[48] Most community currencies are regionally delimited. Others are circulated nation-wide yet limited to a particular purpose. Such is the case of the Fureai Kippu in Japan, which focused on rewarding caring for the elderly, and could be used by the commoners for future elderly care.[49] Another example is the WIR, which circulates only among small and medium-sized businesses in Switzerland (not other countries, not among large companies, and not in financial markets). Clearly delineated currency jurisdictions hamper the leakage of currency and powers its ability to perform as a means of exchange for the commoners.

5. Democratic: Bringing issuance closer to the users

As already discussed, money creation today is carried by a variety of banking and financial actors in a hierarchy, each layer building on and expanding from the previous. At the pyramid's apex lies the Central Bank (creating cash and reserves), followed by private commercial banks and the bank deposits they produce. The lower layers are constituted by various credit instruments issued by private third-party non-bank financial institutions. Crushed by the pyramid, and without any possibility to issue any official form of money themselves, are the commoners. In pyramidal monetary architectures where money is supposed to trickle from the top down, workers, citizens and households at the bottom are excluded from the possibility to create and govern money.

But issuance and governance of a currency can be brought closer to the commoners in at least two ways. The first design makes local authorities and municipalities the issuers of a local complementary currency. The second turns money users into currency issuers.

Among the first, we find local authorities issuing local monies or voucher systems aiming for some form of local economic development. Some of these municipal monies are backed by national legal money, the aim usually being to temporarily confine the circulation of money in the local economy, activating local markets and increasing the spending multiplier effect (i.e. more income and jobs). This is the case of the Mumbuca currency in Maricá prefecture (Brazil), the Youth Basic Income in Gyeonggi-do province (Korea), the Sol-Violett in Toulouse (France), or the Grama in Santa Coloma de Gramanet (Spain). Other local municipal monies derive their value instead from acceptance in payment of certain municipal services or fees. These are designed to encourage particular desirable behaviours. For example, the E-portemonnee rewards eco-friendly behaviours in nine Belgian municipalities in exchange to access to leisure and cultural centres; the municipal coworking Sinergics in Barcelona (Spain) facilitates the exchange of office space for community work; the public policy in Curitiba (Brazil) exchanges correctly separated waste in recycling centres for public transport tickets; or the Torekes in Ghent (Belgium) exchanges gardening plots for civic engagement.

T=0	Previous amount	Change	Current amount
Omar	0	0	0
Teresa	0	0	0
Sara	0	0	0
Emily	0	0	0
Total	0	0	0

T=1	Previous amount	Change	Current amount
Omar	0	-60	-60
Teresa	0	0	0
Sara	0	+60	+60
Emily	0	0	0
Total	0	0	0

Teresa rents out her car to Omar for 100 CC.

Omar sells apple-pie to Emily for 30 CC.

T=2	Previous amount	Change	Current amount
Omar	-60	-100	-160
Teresa	0	+100	+100
Sara	+60	0	+60
Emily	0	0	0
Total	0	0	0

T=3	Previous amount	Change	Current amount
Omar	-160	+30	-130
Teresa	+100	0	+100
Sara	+60	0	+ 60
Emily	0	-30	-30
Total	0	0	0

Source: Own elaboration

A second way to democratise money creation turns commoners into issuers of the currency. Mutual credit currency systems rely on the logic of clearing to redress the current power imbalance between money users and money issuers. If the buyer has a positive balance (such as Anna in table 1 in the image below where she buys something from David), then that buyer will use her balance to make an exchange with a seller. However, if the buyer's balance is negative or zero, buyers can issue money (within a limit set by the commoners) to pay for the goods as the case of Barbra in Table 2 illustrates, where she buys something from David. A central book-keeping system records a negative entry on the buyer's balance and an equal positive entry on the seller's balance – negative balances thus signalling the buyer's commitment to contribute to the community as much as s/he took (bought) from it. Balances are cleared out as buyers with positive balance pay for goods from sellers with negative balances. The clearing logic enables users to issue money as they need it, overcoming scarcity and automatically adapting the money supply to the community's trading needs. Indeed, operating as a counter-cyclical force, mutual credit currencies such as the Sardex in Sardinia (Italy) and the WIR in Switzerland have proven to help small and medium-sized businesses in particular during economic recessions.[50]

While mutual credit systems reach deeper in its democratic creation of money, both municipal currencies and mutual credit currencies bring money issuance closer to the commoners. This enables the continuous adaptation of these local monetary systems to the changing circumstances and needs of its ultimate users. Proximity to the place where money is created also enables commoners to increase their knowledge of how money works and how it is used for the service of the community.

In combination, the design features that municipalities and the grassroots are putting forward are slowly suggesting a commons-based multi-currency monetary system; monetary plurality at local, regional, national and international levels; a landscape of local currencies each adapted to the priorities, needs and resources of the communities behind them.[51]

Rethinking and remaking money for an inclusive and resilient future

"We cannot solve our problems with the same thinking we used when we created them." Attributed to Albert Einstein in answer to the prevention of future world wars, this quote points to where to start if our aim is systemic change. Not in the tweaking of regulations. Not in gradual adaptation. But in radically recasting the patterns of thought that guide our relation to the 'thing' organising what we want to change. If we want to change how the economy works – or, if you prefer, if we want to change how we produce and consume – then we need first to change the way we conceive and relate to money.

It is here, in our conception of money, that the work of remaking money for a sustainable future needs to begin. It is possible for communities to create their own special purpose money, and to design it radically differently from most national monies. The most decisive step in this direction is for community architects to abandon an understanding of money as commodity. Money as commodity infers scarcity and a zero-sum distribution where some have it and others don't. Scarcity leads to competition and then to an incentive of leverage and reselling; money accumulated to make more money, diverting it from its social role of organising the production and distribution of wealth in a manner desirable by its participants. The deficiencies of today's conventional national monies – from the possibility to leverage and expand money to the possibility of its indefinite accumulation – are rooted in our incapacity to tell money from commodity.

Ultimately, the five monetary design features identified among local complementary currencies highlighted above recast our conception of money from a commodity and towards a social organising tool for the commons. They understand money as a relation of trust and mutual responsibility among community members, money as a social infrastructure for the coordination of communal contributions and appropriations.[52] Credit money created not with an end to be sold for other forms of money or financial assets – as it is the case with today's national currencies – but with an end to build a productive community. Money acting as a giant spreadsheet for the recording and settlement of individual contributions to and appropriations from the community.

Herein, we believe, resides the most radical proposition of community currencies. With many such projects failing to last, their promise, so far, lies not in building a stable monetary system that can become an alternative to the current one.[53] Rather, their promise lies in teaching the general public that a different money is possible; in reminding the co-responsibility we all share in building healthy real local economies; in helping to develop communal socio-economic practices. In other words, their potential lies in how these local complementary currency initiatives inspire us to move away from a pattern of thought that sees money as a thing, towards one that puts relations and the commons centre stage.

References

1.   Tobin, J. (1972). *Inflation and Unemployment. American Economic Review*, 62, pp. 1-18.

2.   Chertkovskaya, E. and Paulsson, A. (2021). *Countering corporate violence: Degrowth, ecosocialism and organising beyond the destructive forces of capitalism. Organization, 28*(3), pp. 405-425.

3.   Schumacher, E.F. (1973). *Small Is Beautiful: Economics as if people mattered.* Harper Perennial.; Jackson, T. (2009). *Prosperity Without Growth*, London. Earthscan.

4.   Cheney, G., Santa Cruz, I., Peredo, A.M. & Nazareno, E. (2014). *Worker cooperatives as an organizational alternative: Challenges, achievements and promise in business governance and ownership. Organization, 21*(5), pp. 591-603.; Azzellini, D. (2018). *Labour as a Commons: The Example of Worker- Recuperated Companies. Critical Sociology, 44*(4-5), pp. 763-776.; Souleles, D. (2019). *Another Workplace is Possible: Learning to own and changing subjectivities in American employee owned companies. Critique of Anthropology, 40*(1), pp. 28-48.

5.   Reichel, A., De Schoenmakere, M. and Gillabel, J. (2016). *Circular economy in Europe: Developing the knowledge base. European Environment Agency Report 2/2016.*; Korhonen, J., Honkasalo, A. & Seppälä, J. (2018). *Circular Economy: The Concept and its Limitations. Ecological Economics, 143*, pp. 37-46.

6.   Kennedy, M. (1995). *Interest and inflation free money: Creating an exchange medium that works for everybody and protects the earth.* Stranger Journalism.; Greco, T. (2009). *The end of money and the future of civilization.* Chelsea Green Publishing.; Lietaer, B., Arnsperger, c., Goerner, S. & Brunnhuber, S. (2012). *Money and Sustainability: The Missing Link.* Report from the Cub of Rome.; Arnsperger, C., Bendell, J. & Slater, M. (2021). *Monetary Adaptation to Planetary Emergency: Addressing the Monetary Growth Imperative. Institute for Leadership and Sustainability (IFLAS) Occasional Papers, 8.* University of Cumbria.

7.   Ingham, G. (2004). *The Nature of Money.*

8.   Bollier, D. and Conaty. P. (2015). *Democratic Money and Capital for the Commons: Strategies for Transforming Neoliberal Finance Through Commons-Based Alternatives.*; Slater, M. and Jenkin, T. (2016). *The credit Commons: A money for the solidarity economy.* Published at www.creditcommons.net.; Barinaga, E. (2020). A route to commons-based democratic monies? *Embedding the governance of money in traditional communal institutions. Frontiers in Blockchain, 3*, p. 50.

9.   Lietaer, B. (2001). *The future of money.* Century.

10.   Ryan-Collins, J., Greenham, T., Werner, R., and Jackson, A. (2014). *Where Does Money Come From?: A Guide to the UK Monetary and Banking System.* New Economics Foundation.; Jackson, A. and Dyson, B. (2012). *Modernising Money: Why our monetary system is broken and how it can be fixed.* Positive Money.; McLeay, M., Radia, and Thomas, R. (2014). *Money creation in the modern economy. Bank of England Quarterly Bulletin.*; Dyson, B., Hodgson, G., and Lerven, F.V. (2016). *Sovereign Money.* An introduction.; Pettifor, A. (2017). *The Production of Money: How to break the power of bankers.* Verso.; Desan, C. (2020). *The Key to Value: The Debate over Commensurability in Neoclassical and Credit Approaches to Money. Law and Contemporary Problems, 83*(2), pp. 1-22.; Arnsperger, C., Bendell, J. & Slater, M. (2021).

11.   Mehrling, P. (2013). *The Inherent Hierarchy of Money. Social Fairness and Economics: Economic Essays in the Spirit of Duncan Foley.* Routledge, pp. 394-404.; Gabor, D. and Vestergaard, J. (2016). *Towards a Theory of Shadow Money. Institute for New Economic Thinking, INET Working Paper.*

12. Mehrling, P. (2013).

13. Gabor, D. and Vestergaard, J. (2016).

14. McLeay, M., Radia, and Thomas, R. (2014).

15. Graeber, D. (2011). *Debt: The first five thousand years*, New York. Melville House.; Amato, M. and Fantacci, L. (2012). *The End of Finance*. Polity Press.; Desan, C. (2014). *Making money: coin, currency, and the coming of capitalism*, USA. Oxford University Press.; Martin, F. (2014). *Money: The unauthorized biography*, New York. Alfred A. Knopf.

16. Minsky, H. (1986) *Stabilizing an Unstable Economy*, New York. McGraw-Hill Professional.

17. Sacks, J. (2002). *The Money Trail: Measuring your impact on the local economy using LM3*. New Economics Foundation.; Palley, T.I. (2011). *The contradictions of export-led growth: Public Policy Brief*, New York. *Jerome Levy Economics Institute of Bard College, 119*.

18. Palley, T.I. (2011).

19. Graeber, D. (2011).

20. Keynes, J.M. (1936). *The general theory of employment, interest and money*, New York. Harcourt, Brace.

21. Robinson, R.I. (1966). *What should we teach in a money and banking course?. The Journal of Finance, 21*, p. 341.

22. Graeber, D. (2011), p. 213.

23. Desan, C. (2014).

24. Lietaer, B., Arnsperger, c., Goerner, S. & Brunnhuber, S. (2012)

25. Kaufman, F. (2020). *The Money Plot: A History of Currency's Power to Enchant, Control and Manipulate*, New York. Other Press.

26. Dillard, D. (1980). *A monetary theory of production: Keynes and the institutionalists. Journal of Economic Issues, 14*(2), pp. 255-273.; Ülgen, F. (2013). *Coordination in economy. An essay on money. New Contributions to Monetary Analysis: The foundations of an alternative economic paradigm.* Routledge, pp. 172-187.

27. Wray, L.R. (2012). *Modern money theory: A primer on macroeconomics for sovereign monetary systems.* Palgrave Macmillan.; Kelton, S. (2020). *The Deficit Myth: Modern Monetary Theory and the Birth of the People's Economy*, New York. PublicAffairs.

28. Benes, J., and Kumhof, M. (2011). *Risky bank lending and optimal capital adequacy regulation. IMF Working Papers*, pp. 1-27.

29. Jackson, A. and Dyson, B. (2012).

30. Ussher, L. (2016). *International Monetary Policy with Commodity Buffer Stocks. European Journal of Economics and Economic Policies: Intervention, 13*(1), pp. 10-25.

31. Hardin, G. (1968). *The Tragedy of the Commons. Science, 162*, pp.1243-1248.

32. Ostrom, E. (1991). *Rational choice theory and institutional analysis.* Toward complementarity, p. 30.

33. Hess, C. and Ostrom, E. (2003). *Ideas, Artifacts, and Facilities: Information as a Common-Pool Resource. Law and Contemporary Problems, 66*, pp. 111-146.

34. Ostrom, E. (1991), p. 30.

35. Hardin, G. (1968).

36. Barinaga, E. (2020). A route to commons-based democratic monies? *Embedding the governance of money in traditional communal institutions. Frontiers in Blockchain, 3,* p. 50.

37. Hayek, F.A. (1990). *Denationalisation of money: an analysis of the theory and practice of concurrent currencies,* London. 3rd edn. Institute of Economic Affairs.; Gladstein, A. (2021). *Financial Freedom and Privacy in the Post-Cash World. Cato Journal, 41*(2).

38. Benes, J., and Kumhof, M. (2011). *Risky bank lending and optimal capital adequacy regulation. IMF Working Papers,* pp. 1-27.; Jackson, A. and Dyson, B. (2012).

39. Ostrom, E. (2000). *Collective Action and the Evolution of Social Norms. The Journal of Economic Perspectives, 14*(3), pp. 137-158.

40. Bollier, D. (2020). *Commoning as a transformative social paradigm. The New Systems Reader.* Routledge, p, 5.

41. Ostrom, E. (2009). *A General Framework for Analyzing Sustainability of Social-Ecological Systems. Science, 325*(5939), pp. 419-422.; De Angelis, M. (2017). *Omnia sunt communia: On the commons and the transformation to postcapitalism.* Zed Books.

42. Lietaer, B. (2001).; Kennedy, M., Lietaer, B., and Rogers, J. (2012). *People money: the promise of regional currencies.* Triarchy Press.

43. Greco, T. (2009).; Kennedy, M., Lietaer, B., and Rogers, J. (2012).; Lietaer, B. (2001).

44. Amato, M. and Fantacci, L. (2012).; Vallet, G. (2016). *A local money to stabilize capitalism: the underestimated case of the WIR. Economy and Society, 45*(3-4), pp. 479-504.

45. Kiaka, R., Barinaga, E., and Oloko, M. (Under review). *Gaming the system: How communities strategize around currencies, convertibility and cash transfers in Kenya.*

46. Ward, B. and Lewis, J. (2002). *Plugging the Leaks: Making the most of every pound that enters your local economy.* New Economics Foundation.

47. Hayek, F.A. (1990).

48. Blanc, J. (2011). *Classifying "CCs": Community, complementary and local currencies' types and generations. International Journal of Community Currency Research.*

49. Hayashi, M. (2012). *Japan's Fureai Kippu time-banking in elderly care: origins, development, challenges and impact. International Journal of Community Currency Research, 16*(A), pp. 30-44.

50. Stodder, J. and Lietaer, B. (2016). *The Macro-Stability of Swiss WIR-Bank Credits: Balance, Velocity, and Leverage. Comparative Economic Studies, 58,* pp. 570–605.; Lucarelli, S. and Gobbi, L. (2016). *Local clearing unions as stabilizers of local economic systems: a stock flow consistent perspective. Cambridge Journal of Economics, 40*(5), pp.1397-1420.

51. Gómez, G. (2018). *Monetary Plurality in Local, Regional and Global Economies.* Routledge.

52. Slater, M. and Jenkin, T. (2016). *The credit Commons: A money for the solidarity economy.* (www.creditcommons.net).; Bollier, D. and Conaty. P. (2015). *Democratic Money and Capital for the Commons: Strategies for Transforming Neoliberal Finance Through Commons-Based Alternatives.*

53. Gomez, G.M. and Dini, P. (2016). *Making sense of a crankcase: monetary diversity in Argentina (1999–2003). Cambridge Journal of Economics, 40*(5), pp. 1421-1437.; Alves, F.M. and Santos, R.F. (2018). *A literature review 2010-2016. International Journal of Community Currency Research, 22*(Summer), pp. 4-15.

Dodo, Phoenix or Butterfly?

Why it's time for TrAdaptation

Professor Rupert Read[1]

[1] This piece has my name on it. But much of what is in it is a direct product of the TrAd collective. I want to especially thank Oona Menges, Simon Be, Skeena Rathor, April Griefsong, Ruth Allen, Scott Henery, Morgan Phillips and Rachel Bailey, for co-thinking that has made this piece *possible*.

I have argued for several years now[1] that our civilisation faces a choice between three possible futures:

1. Complete, terminal collapse.
2. Collapse, followed by a new civilisation.
3. Transformation – arriving at a new civilisation through deliberate, intentional change.

You'll notice that I do not consider the continuation of the current civilisation as an option. It is now clear that not only is such continuation undesirable – as our current civilisation *is* the sixth mass extinction (besides being socially inequitable) – but it is also impossible.[2] The only way we can get through this is by way of massive change, intentional or otherwise.

There is room for differences of opinion as to the likelihood of these three options occurring. I now regard (2) as by far the most likely.[3] But such differences do not alter the *logic* of the situation. If one accepts that we face a choice between these three possibilities, it is clear we ought to aim towards Butterfly (option 3), but also at making Phoenix (2) as good as possible, as an 'insurance policy' against becoming the Dodo (1).

Phoenix is obviously immeasurably better than Dodo. But we should be clear that Phoenix comes on the back of immense suffering and difficulty: a phoenix rises *from ashes*. That is why Butterfly is clearly the option to aim at, so long as there is any chance of it. But, given Phoenix's immeasurable superiority to Dodo, we also have a strong responsibility to place plenty of effort at avoiding Dodo and at least enabling Phoenix. In this chapter I will explore how Transformative Adaptation (or 'TrAd) distinctively aims at Butterfly, and represents the most likely way we can — via Butterfly or (more likely) Phoenix — avoid becoming Dodo.

---

1   See e.g. my 'viral' talk given at Cambridge University, "This civilisation is finished". See also my 2019 book of that name that Samuel Alexander edited.

2   For justification of this claim, see e.g. Tim Jackson's Post-Growth. See also Green House's books, The post-growth project and Facing up to climate reality.

3   For my reasoning as to why I think this, consult my book This Civilisation is Finished.

   As I'll explain below, my colleague Jem Bendell regards (3) as impossible. I regard it not as impossible (I don't think we can know the future *that* much), but as now sadly very unlikely. But it is still that for which we should *aim*: that is a key distinguishing feature of TrAd (from Deep Adaptation).

Figure 1: The Dodo   **Figure 2:** The Phoenix   **Figure 3:** The Butterfly

What is Transformative Adaptation?

Transformative Adaptation [TrAd] is based on the awareness that climate disasters are here, and are going to get worse. We need to *adapt* to this new reality, but we need to do so in a way that rises up to meet it, which is *transformative* of our existing failed institutions. TrAd is thus a set of responses to our declining climatic and ecological reality that is simultaneously profoundly realistic and seriously transformational in intent.

Part of such realism is acknowledging that these necessary changes are unlikely to be undertaken sufficiently by governments. **The Glasgow CoP is going to fail us:** that is virtually certain. So we must mainly undertake TrAd *for and by ourselves,* modeling the future that we want to see, and hoping thereby to spawn a positive power of imitation. TrAd is going to mean things like growing our own food, and (more generally) insisting upon whatever is necessary in order to do that safely for the long term. This is non-negotiable: if the law gets in the way of this, then it is the law, and not us, that will need to give way.

TrAd is how we get to aim at Butterfly-style transformation without collapse, while simultaneously minimising the chances of becoming the Dodo. Thus TrAd involves preparing for Phoenix too (as opposed to letting Dodo in the door, through acting like ostriches!).

A very brief history of Transformative Adaptation

For many years, the main emphasis in climate-discourse has been on 'mitigation' – prevention and reduction of harm from emissions. 'Adaptation' to the problem has largely been frowned upon as a kind of giving up.

But, with the anthropogenically-triggered weirding of global weather in recent years, there has been growing awareness that adaptation cannot be avoided. The UN and a few isolated academics first came up with the idea that, if there is to be adaptation, it should typically be *transformational* in intent, not merely incremental. Academics have developed this further with a series of case studies of 'transformational adaptation'; some historical, many for the global South. Usually, such adaptation is practiced when it is clear that continuing with any kind of 'business as usual' is no longer an option.

The concept of transformational adaptation is too good a concept not to make the most out of. It is as inspiring as it is necessary. Green House, the radical thinktank that I co-founded a decade ago, decided in 2015 to make its big project the pursuit of transformative adaptation to emerging dire climate reality across the spectrum of policy. This culminated in Green House's book, 'Facing up to Climate Reality'.[4]

More recently still, a group of activists – most of whom have been connected to Extinction Rebellion – decided that the banner of transformative adaptation makes sense (as the next move on from the dying hope for sufficient 'mitigation'). This is the TrAd collective (www.transformative-adaptation.com). Much of what is in this piece, I owe to our collective work together.

It is true that the 'adaptation' part of TrAd contains something 'negative': a ruthlessly honest admission that it is now too late to think primarily in terms of mitigation alone. It has positive dimensions too, such as a serious (re-) localisation agenda. The 'transformative' part of TrAd is obviously positive, going beyond talk of 'transition' to embrace the need for system-change. In this way, as I'll explain in more detail below, TrAd is very different from Incremental Adaptation, which is negative in the sense that it merely tries to preserve the current system. TrAd also differs from Deep Adaptation, insofar as DA risks giving up on the prospect of transformation and so can seem to tend towards taking collapse as inevitable. I am fully with Jem Bendell in regarding our current civilisation as not one that can be sustained, but I continue to hold out some hope that it might be transformed without us having to endure a collapse event.

Tradition is a powerful part of TrAd. TrAd aims at a survivable future, in many ways a flourishing one. But it does so in full awareness that we will not survive, let alone flourish, without giving full due to the past. To wisdom traditions. To crop varieties in their splendid manifoldness. To how Indigenous civilsations and some peasant civilisations successfully sustain a way of living that is genuinely light upon the Earth.

In this way, TrAd is rooted in our history.

TrAd also offers a new hope, after the abandonment of present forlorn hopes (basically, of hopes for the perpetuation of our current way of life). And I'd rather a thimbleful of real authentic grounded hope than a barrelful of fake put-on-a-happy-face ignorant pseudo-hope. Climate-despair is less likely to *take* us than it is to take those who are Polyannaishly avoiding the real need for TrAd, and who are pretending that we can go on with a reformed version of business as usual.

---

4   Foster (ed), London Publishing Partnership: 2019. https://www.greenhousethinktank.org/facing-up-to-climate-reality.html

Fundaments of Transformative Adaptation

The TrAd collective has thought together for a long time about the basic elements of what is being talked about here. We suggest that there are three fundaments of TrAd: Land, Community and Transformation.

Land

We mean by this not only the land, but the water and the air. And we mean *place*: land is not just – as economics has wrongly claimed it to be – a transferable commodity; it is typically unique. *What* the land **is** depends partly on *where* it is, and on its *history*. And much land is or should be a commons. It is not separate from the communities that depend upon it and that guard it. Let's do a brief comparison between how the present system deals with land and how TrAd would be different. For example: community allotments on derelict land vs. the same land being fenced off for years and then paved over for an office parking lot whose staff commute from many miles away. Under TrAd, if the council doesn't facilitate such creation of allotments, people would just go ahead and pop them up anyway, then seek to defend them.[5] People need land. Land typically needs people. And land carries *meaning*. Part of Transformative Adaptation is without doubt going to be returning land to people.

Community

There is a great hunger at this time for a rebirth of real community. That means different things to different people: for me, it means things like sitting around fires and singing together. And not just for me: fire is primal, as is song, dance, rhythm. But whatever the resurgence of community means to you, my bet is that you are hungry for it. Absolutely fundamental to TrAd is just such an assertion of the importance of and non-negotiability of real community – which means, most importantly, actual geographic community, collectivity

---

5   I.e. Transformative Adaptation (TrAd), as reconceived and emboldened by the TrAd collective, breaks new ground (relative to the Transition Towns movement, and to the academic/institutional conception of Transformational Adaptation) in being willing to use non-violent direct action as a tool where appropriate and necessary – one (key) tool among others.

of people in a place[6] – over the pseudo-individualism that dominates the popular image of our culture, and (as can be witnessed very clearly in relation to Covid, but is equally true in relation to climate) is killing us.

Community requires *connection*: with each other, and also with the Earth and its many other beings. It requires *co-liberation*: our freeing ourselves, together. Ultimately, it requires *common democracy*: this is a crucial part of what we want to achieve (and, where feasible, it is also a great way to *achieve* it). People's assemblies, citizens' assemblies and the like are both an aim of TrAd and a potential vehicle towards its realisation.

Transformation

As mentioned in the previous section of this paper, the TrAd vision values tradition. It values age-old wisdom, and does not fetishise 'progress'. But the vision is clear-seeing that we cannot now survive, let alone flourish, without transformation. Transformation *is coming*; our current system and civilisation are finished, and attempts to prolong them further will only worsen a crash (thus bringing about a *brutal* transformation). The transformation that is *needed* is one that is intelligent and deliberate, recognising this truth about the best-before date on our current way of living. Such transformation will be about going back to the land *and* moving forward into a new future (a future where we will use less energy, but probably most of the energy we use will be genuinely renewable). The existing system is unlikely to facilitate such transformation.[7] *This is why*, while we should aim to get transformation happening through governments, local authorities, the United Nations (etc), where possible, we should also be realistic enough to recognise that most of it will probably have to be led 'bottom-up'. And it may well require civil disobedience to be made possible at scale, and certainly in the cause of specific necessary pieces of TrAd-in-action.

To sum up the story so far: We can only expect people to care about our shared global environment by taking care of their *fundamental* needs – for meaning, for connection, for food and drink. TrAd aims directly at satisfying these needs.

---

6   I.e. 'Online communities' cannot be enough.

7   If you disagree with this assessment, consider how little official support there has been for the Transition Towns Movement. Very often, the authorities have served as bars to the Movement, rather than as facilitators to it. And now we are out of time.

TrAd in our current movement-moment

Extinction Rebellion [XR] has done fantastic work moving the dial on the ecological emergency. Meanwhile, the Transition Towns movement, regenerative agriculture and permaculture have long been working on the ground to seek the changes we need, from the bottom up. *The question arises: Is there a way to bring these two approaches together?*

XR's approach to the long quasi-permanent emergency we're stuck in, like virtually everyone else's in the 'environmental' movement, has focused to date on so-called 'mitigation': reducing climate/eco damage (ideally, to zero) by cutting emissions and stopping habitat destruction, through Government action. To this end, it aims to put pressure on the government. However, this is no longer tenable as the sole objective, simply because XR's demands are not going to be attained. Too little time is left (three of the seven years from the foundation of XR to its chosen date for reaching carbon zero have passed!), and the British Government (together with the economic system) is too profoundly resistant to doing the right thing. Trying to fill the jail cells (with a diminishing number of rebels who are willing to do so) isn't enough. And 'mitigation' in its technical sense is not a sufficiently encompassing objective; it is time for adaptation to join the party.

Many of us have been aware of this for some time; the awareness can no longer be kept at bay.

The 'Theory of Change' that XR has been using is not enough. *We need to* **embody** *the transformation that we aim to bring. We need to be fully addressing the crisis, which has gone too far to be addressed through 'top-down' measures alone, and which requires us to accept the bitter harvest of the failures thus far.*

Three kinds of adaptation?

When I talk about adaptation, it is important to bear in mind that it can mean different things. We can group adaptation into three types:-

- *Shallow adaptation.* This involves no significant psychological change: just business as usual while trying to cope with a deteriorating world. [The IPCC calls this 'incremental adaptation' – it includes such things as building higher sea walls and flood-proofing buildings.]

- *'Transformative Adaptation'.* This requires a willingness to undertake major psychological adjustments away from what has been 'normal; i.e it is based on fundamental systems change. [The IPCC calls this 'transformational adaptation', though what is meant by this phrase is often more modest than what we have in mind as TrAd'. Part of the motivation for organising through the lens of 'Transformative Adaptation' is to turn this inspiring phrase into a reality worthy of it. Examples encompassed by the TrAd vision include restoring wetlands and mangroves and kelp forests, using appropriate technology, agriwilding, living closer to the land, and localised food production.]

- *Deep Adaptation*. DA is based upon preparing for a future where our existing society is going to be swept away. It requires massive psychological adjustments. [I am strongly in favour of Deep Adaptation, and co-edited with Jem Bendell the first book on it.[8] It is a beautiful vision for Phoenix; a vital part of avoiding Dodo. But alone it is not enough; it might even run the risk of seeming to some to be a self-fulfilling counsel of doom.] For those who accept the need for DA, self-sufficient communities and totally different economic models are some of the things seen as necessary.

Looking at these three types of adaptation, I'd argue that shallow adaptation is worse than useless, on its own, because it pretends we can keep this civilisation stumbling on without real change. We can't. The longer we try to do so, the further we go off the cliff. Shallow 'adaptation' is *resistance* to change. It's a new climate denialism. Consider for instance the revealing fact that Scott Morrison, Australia's Prime Minister, last year leapt straight from old-fashioned climate-denial to a shallow-adaptation-only agenda, bypassing prevention and mitigation altogether![9] This implies directly that shallow, incremental adaptation only actually is real adaptation at all in the broader context of transformation. I mean: sometimes we do indeed need to strengthen some conventional flood defences, etc. But if we do so without having a joined-up plan for systemic change to tackle the causes too and to look to the long term – a plan for a transformed way of living which accepts reality and tries where feasible to stop it from getting worse – then we aren't really adapting. Merely Canute-ing...

On the other hand, Deep Adaptation (DA) is necessary, but arguably it should be viewed as an insurance policy against worst-case scenarios – not as the whole goal. In particular, it risks a debilitating assumption that collapse is *definitely* coming. DA works best if conceived rather as in alliance with TrAd; it then represents a way of taking precautions against a possible/likely (not certain) collapse.[10] The difficult truth is that the general perception of DA is that it assumes that collapse is inevitable (and within the decade). Because that's what its founder Jem Bendell thinks and what his viral paper asserts. So there is, in effect, an ambiguity within the term 'Deep Adaptation'; does one mean the concept, the movement, the paper, or the views of its founder?

---

8   https://jembendell.com/2021/02/23/deep-adaptation-the-book/

9   See https://independentaustralia.net/politics/politics-display/morrison-now-demands-we-adapt-to-climate-change-catastrophes,13509 & https://slate.com/technology/2020/02/scott-morrison-australia-fires-climate-change-adaptation.html .

10   I return to this point below. It is possible for there to be a full-scale rapprochement between TrAd and DA, if we don't assume collapse. Given that Bendell has actually defined DA more recently as including those who think collapse to be already unfolding, inevitable *or ['only']* likely, then the door is open for this to occur.

One of the hopes that Jem and I have for the book on *Deep Adaptation*[11] is that, partly by virtue of having me as co-editor, and partly through the *various* voices within it being signed up to different levels of collapse-anticipation, we'll be able to correct the misperception of DA as a concept/movement that requires commitment to the belief that collapse is inevitable within the short to medium term.

Both Transformative and Deep Adaptation make it essential that we confront what I call 'the great sorrow'. This stems from a realisation that a 'great turning' of thought and action, hoped for by my teacher Joanna Macy,[12/13] is not enough; that it's too late to accomplish such a turning even on an emergency basis in a way that will obviate great suffering. Great suffering is coming.

In summary: there are only actually two forms of adaptation possible: Transformative and Deep. For, as explained above, incremental, defensive 'adaptation' *is not really* adaptation *at all*. It does not genuinely adapt; it is a way a form of ongoing denial, pretending that system-change is not coming, whether we like it or not.

The difference between TrAd and DA is *partly* a matter of emphasis and rhetoric. My belief is that TrAd will appeal to many who, however mistakenly, consider DA a form of 'doomerism'. TrAd can function as what I call a *moderate* flank to XR: in that it doesn't aim at arrest, and thus, with its positive vision, and in a way slightly less-demanding methods, it attracts some who XR puts off. Somewhat similarly, TrAd can function as *a moderate flank* to DA, in holding the coming end of this civilisation as not one that will inevitably occur by way of *collapse*. Transformative and Deep Adaptations in fact overlap substantially. We might think of them as potentially unifiable: Transformative And Deep Adaptation – TADA. Like a magician pulling out their rabbit from the hat -"Tada!"

The real, profound opportunity here, then, is simply to frame adaptation adequately. Because be certain: there *will* be more talk of Adaptation coming. Adaptation will be done, as things unravel, and it will be partly up to us whether that adaptation is shallow (maladaptation)[13], deep and/or transformative. The stakes are very high, because in this emerging contest there will be lots of 'bad adaptors'. Recall once more the way the Australian Government sought to pivot straight from climate-denial through to 'incremental adaptation', bypassing 'mitigation' altogether.[14] Against the deadly nonsense of such pseudo-adaptation, we need to counterpose the case for TrAd, as including 'mitigation' (i.e. pro-active emissions reduction, etc.) and as entirely serious about profound change.

The concept of adaptation cannot be left to malevolent actors such as the Australian government. It's our moment, to make adaptation focal, and in effect to *define* it. As, with any luck, I'm doing – with your help, reader – here!

---

11   Polity Press, 2021.

12/13 In her essay in our book on Deep Adaptation, Macy herself bravely admits this.

13   The matter of maladaptation is explored in Great Adaptations by Morgan Philips (2021, Arkbound Foundation).

14   See https://slate.com/technology/2020/02/scott-morrison-australia-fires-climate-change-adaptation.html .

Our vision

Such is the urgency of the predicament our species faces – with a defining aspect of that urgency being precisely that most people and governments have not fully appreciated it – that there's practically no level of rhetoric that would count as 'extremist'. Because what's *happening* – the extreme Arctic temperature rises, the experiencing recently in the Middle East of some 'wet bulb' temperature conditions[15] that will rapidly kill humans exposed to them, the terrifying unprecedented 'heat dome' that formed over western Canada in June 2021, the increase in methane emissions, the worse than-'worst-case' scenario glacial melt, devastating wildfires across the globe, and much more – is already 'unbelievable'. Increasingly, unliveable.

This is the context in which sounding the alarm is as necessary as ever, and in which a steadiness under pressure and a realism about what we can now hope for are essential complements.

But of course: actions speak louder than words. When we start to *act* on the kind of vision implicit in this paper, we take back the power. One of the features of TrAd that many find attractive is exactly its refusal to take no for answer. The determination to put this vision into action, no matter what the obstacles.

Without vision, the people perish. We must always match awareness of and honesty about our intense vulnerability[16] to a vision that can rise to meet it.

As explained at the opening of this chapter, some kind of civilisational 'decline' and probable 'fall' – the ending of this civilisation – is now inevitable. The future is already here, only it's not evenly distributed, yet. Some parts of the global South are already experiencing collapse. *The extremely hard task is to help each other morph gracefully into a better civilisation as we undergo energy descent*, the inevitable reduction of the amount of energy-use and material through-put that makes possible our extreme civilisation. That process (which is very likely at some point to proceed via civilisational collapse but doesn't yet have to) will primarily be a process of adaptive relocalisation, a process that may have been jump-started by Covid. This is transformative adaptation. TrAd is a win-win-win: we mitigate the effects of dangerous climate change, we work with nature rather than against her, and we transform society in the direction it needs to transform anyway. TrAd enables us to cope with the deterioration that is already baked in while potentially improving our society and our future.

Why have so many, including climate activists, resisted the adaptation agenda, to date? It's perplexing, because, unlike 'mitigation', adaptation offers direct advantages to those engaging in it. It delivers returns selfishly and not just altruistically.

Perhaps the reason for this resistance to adaptation is that, once we talk/do adaptation, *we can no longer pretend to ourselves and each other that the climate*

---

15 See https://www.cbc.ca/news/science/how-hot-is-too-hot-for-humans-understanding-wet-bulb-temperatures-1.6088415 .

16 See my "Theses on Corona" for an understanding of our vulnerability for our time, the time of corona: https://medium.com/@rupertjread/24-theses-on-corona-748689919859 .

and ecological crisis is not deadly real. And yes, nearly all of us still want to pretend this, most of the time.

But once we take the plunge, dropping this insupportable pretense, we overcome the huge collective action problem notoriously making climate a 'wicked problem'. Because, as I say, adaptation can offer real advantages to those undertaking it, and without having to wait a generation or more for the advantages to start to be delivered.

Once more though, it makes it absolutely critical that we get the right kind of adaptation happening. What we absolutely don't want to do is to provide succour to those who would only do stupid short-term things like (only) make the sea walls and the levees higher. If we manage to accomplish TrAd without collapsing altogether, then we get to be Butterflies emerging from the earlier stage of munching through our ecosystem like there's no tomorrow. We get to *keep the best of what we have (including global communication and inter-connectivity) while rebuilding community and insuring ourselves against over-dependence on long, uncertain, polluting supply lines.* With TrAd-centred 'glocalisation', our world can be the best of both worlds. As hinted earlier, TrAd goes 'back to the future': it returns us to aspects of traditional life that should never have been abandoned, while keeping those features of life today that should not be lost, and that are compatible with one-planet-living.

If necessary, we can do this for ourselves.
We have to try.

How is TrAd different from the Transition Towns movement?

It isn't. We're natural allies. But this needs to be both realised and 'real-ised'. To achieve TrAd will involve politics in the broad sense of that word; ultimately, as I've said, it will at times potentially require serious non-violent direction action (NVDA): guerrilla gardening *at scale* and pop-up allotments that *we defend.* Or taking back land for the landless. These ideas and starting to implement them are something that the experience of XR (including learning from its blunders) can bring to the likes of the Transition Movement.

Let's delve a little more into thinking Transformative Adaptation alongside its *allies* and fellow travellers.

TrAd is an approach, a concept to be put into practical action. A practical philosophy. Many elements of it are already being enacted. Here are some of the organisations already engaging in activities that are compatible with the TrAd vision:

> Green House, the Glacier Trust, Trust The People, Climate
> Emergency Centres, The Land is Ours, The Land Workers
> Alliance, Collapsology & Deep Adaptation (especially
> insofar as they don't presume collapse is certain), as well as,
> of course, the Transition Towns Movement...[17]

It is time the adaptation movement embraces the tools of non-violent direct action, too. Doing so can give us our best shot at transformatively adapting to a world on the brink of climate and ecological collapse – giving us our best shot at becoming Butterfly, while simultaneously preparing to survive the likely future relatively well as a Phoenix.

A way forward: a 'rebel alliance'?

We need then an *alliance* between the likes of XR and the likes of the Transition Towns movement and permaculture. If someone wants simply to go and grow food and create a community, great — but lots of people were of course doing that before XR. And what Transition folk have found again and again is: the powers that be stymie change at the point where something genuinely radical was being considered. It's time to stop letting such 'No's be taken for an answer!

We have an opportunity here *to unite many of the hitherto-separate movements seeking to model and create a healthy planet. That is the golden thread.* It is why we seek out actions which embody the story of system-change via an alternative system that we model **and** that challenge the existing system at the same time. A transformed, adapted future, if it is to be made manifest, is going to require localisation **and** civil disobedience. What will be truly transformative is if these get done *simultaneously.*

Conclusion: the beginning is here

I opened this paper with three 'options'. The 3rd, 'Butterfly', was of wise pro-active societal transformation. This is the dream that motivates TrAd, alongside the need to prepare together for something significantly less smooth.

But as I've also hinted, we need to transform civiliZation *so that it's truly worth saving.* At present, it's ecocidal. Which is not just self-undermining, but horrible. In fact, evil.

If we only talk/do DA, we'll be accused of giving up. A gulf will open up between the localisers/'crusties' and the 'political'/activist types. But why can't great, unprecedented strength be found if we were to really bring these two distinct types together? TrAd is a way to do that. It's never been done before

---

17 Key intellectual 'mentors' of TrAd include Wendell Berry and William Ophuls. In terms of
    contemporary like-minded voices, Chris Smaje's work on A Small Farm Future is crucial.

at scale. Now is the time.

Our climate is breaking down. But we can put breaks on the breakdown. *We should drop much of what we think we know: including the rash assumption that we know what the future will hold.* A humble, precautious, unknowing attitude to the future is exactly what TrAd cultivates. The future could be wonderful or terrible beyond imagination – or both. We need to move into an uncertain future in a way that does not presume, in the manner that our arrogant civilisation at present does, that we know that the future will be good – or bad. TrAd *protects against the worst — while inviting and seeking to manifest the best.* It could enable us to transcend the 'environmental' movement — and start to build an eco-logical future.

TrAd actions are likely to be most effective if they are the change we want to see in the world. If they are beautiful and powerful; if they make sense to people; if they try to create something and not just hold it back. The most obvious ways of narrating TrAd will involve the growing of food or activities similarly fundamental to our lives, *starting to make possible a vision of a good future, despite everything.* Ergo, TrAd combines the practical goals of permaculture with the methods of XR. To embody senseful acts of beauty.

Tragically, our best hope now is probably to get hit hard but not *completely* devastatingly by climate disasters, fairly soon.[18] (For such disasters will be probabilifying TrAd, without delivering collapse first.) Otherwise we are very unlikely indeed to achieve Butterfly, and can hope for Phoenix at best.

'Dodo', by the way, doesn't necessarily mean that humanity goes extinct. It's more like the scenario that Lovelock famously sees as likely: *civilisation* goes extinct. Humanity survives probably, but clinging to the wreckage, without any Phoenix in sight. It could see the *Mad Max* future of our nightmares.

Instead: picture a future in which we respond pro-actively to the coming disasters by shortening supply lines. Picture a new civilisation in which we live much more lightly on the land. A future in which we get to realise 'the leisure society' – while finding meaningful work, close to where we live, producing more of what we really need. A future in which we flourish – and maybe even manage to head off collapse, even as planetary conditions get harder, as for a good while to come they are now certain to do.

Picture this, and *you are picturing transformative adaptation.*

Prof. Rupert Read is co-editor with Jem Bendell of Deep Adaptation (Polity Press, 2021), and is the author of Parents for a Future (www.parentsforafuture.org). You can find out more about

---

18   See https://ueaeprints.uea.ac.uk/id/eprint/63743/1/Accepted_manuscript.pdf for detail on this point.

Transformative Adaptation or get involved at http://www.transformative-adaptation.com.

References

1. Read, R., 2020. *What if we looked down?*: Rupert Read XR talk, on Youtube live [Video]. [Online] Available at: https://www.youtube.com/watch?v=wKv5IlmLv-c [Accessed July 2021].

2. Read, R., 2019. *This civilisation is finished: Conversations on the end of Empire – and what lies beyond.* s.l.:Simplicity Institute.

3. Jackson, T., 2021. *Post Growth: Life after Capitalism.* s.l.:Polity.

4. Green House, 2014. *The Post-Growth Project: How the End of Economic Growth Could Bring a Fairer and Happier Society.* s.l.:London Publishing Partnership.

5. Green House, 2019. *Facing up to Climate Reality; Honesty, Disaster and Hope.* s.l.:London Publishing Partner.

6. Bendell, J., 2020. *Deep Adaptation: A Map for Navigating Climate Tragedy.* s.l.:s.n.

7. Withers, R., 2020. *The Great Australian Cop-Out.* [Online] Available at: https://slate. com/technology/2020/02/scott-morrison-australia-fires-climate-change-adaptation. html[Accessed July 2021].

8. Phillips, M., 2021. *Great Adaptations.* s.l.:Arkbound.

9. Prévost-Manuel, J., 2021. *How hot is too hot for humans? Understanding wet-bulb temperatures.* [Online] Available at: https://www.cbc.ca/news/science/how-hot-is-too-hot-for-humans-understanding-wet-bulb-temperatures-1.6088415[Accessed July 2021].

10. Read, R., 2020. *24 Theses on Corona.* [Online] Available at: https://medium.com/@rupertjread/24-theses-on-corona-748689919859 [Accessed July 2021].

11. Smaje, C., 2020. *A Small Farm Future: Making the Case for a Society Built Around Local Economies, Self-Provisioning, Agricultural Diversity and a Shared Earth.* s.l.:Chelsea Green Publishing Co.

12. Read, R., n.d. *On preparing for the great gift of community that climate-disasters can give us.* [Online] Available at: https://ueaeprints.uea.ac.uk/id/eprint/63743/1/Accepted_ manuscript.pdf [Accessed July 2021].

Figure 1: Ballista, CC BY-SA 3.0 <http://creativecommons.org/licenses/by-sa/3.0/>, via Wikimedia Commons

Figure 2: https://i.pinimg.com/originals/f1/ca/01/f1ca010558af7adff602d2fe7d69a083.jpg

Figure 3: Photo by Tina Nord from Pexels

Conclusion

The challenge before us is immense. On the one side, the collapse of society and an irreversible mass extinction event that will affect the global biosphere for thousands of years. On the other, a vertical climb towards a fundamental socio-economic transition on a scale that has never been seen before.

We need to change how we act, but just as importantly we need to change how we think. The idea of the world serving as some human life support system, 'as a machine designed to produce and sustain life'[i], needs to be dropped. This book has sought to prevent deep alternatives, both in terms of preparing and responding to climate change, as well as reversing its structural causes.

In Section 1, we have seen the nature of the emergency facing us, while covering the unique impacts to the biosphere and oceans. As an inherently civilisational problem, being caused in large part by our socio-economic model, it has been explored how alternative ways of living can address the situation and pave the way to a better future. Here, one of the book's main themes is introduced: that of localisation; a shift from globalised supply chains built upon environmental destruction and social exploitation, towards sustainable networks rooted in communities.

Following on from this, Section 2 examined some of the existing impacts and responses to climate change – from shifts in Nepalese agriculture and the personal story of Fazeela Mubarak in Kenya to Brazilian methods of adaptation and the impact of community gardens in London at the height of COVID-19. Throughout the stories and case studies, people and communities (often from their own initiative) have striven to adapt to climate change in a democratic and resilient fashion while making major shifts towards a zero waste, zero emissions society.

Section 3 delves further into the subject of major structural transition, challenging the dogma of unlimited growth and other destructive myths. The authors highlight the role of self-sufficient communities and ecovillages, with a counterpart look at alternative economic models and localised currencies. The final chapter shows how the methodologies of diverse climate groups like Extinction Rebellion and the Transition Towns movement can join together to help society make a necessary transition – as opposed to completely collapsing.

Throughout these chapters we have uncovered examples of local people rising up in the face of immense challenges to forge a new future. In many cases, they have to ignore or outright break the processes of government and market forces in trying to make their communities more resilient to climate change. In many ways, what we seem to be seeing is a failure of larger organisations, alongside regional and national government structures, to not only tackle the climate crisis but to act in the interests of their citizens' wellbeing. At the same time, many of these structures are indirectly or even directly hindering grassroots efforts to take the initiative through the way they prioritise and subsidise the initiatives of big corporations, to expansive bureaucracy and outright prohibitive laws.

This is not to say that national governance is, by default, doomed to failure: multiple countries – Sweden, Bhutan, Denmark and New Zealand –

---

i   Daniel Quinn (1992) 'Ishmael', Bantam Publishers

have proven otherwise. Similarly, the importance of international bodies cannot be overstated: it is only thanks to the efforts of the United Nations, for example, that we are making any organised multi-lateral progress towards tackling the climate emergency at all. And yet, for as long as most governments follow the same economic model of 'endless growth' (defined by GDP), the kind of transformative changes required will remain out of reach [See Box X]. As noted by the United Nations:

> 'Protecting life on Earth, including human life, requires actions that are significantly more effective than those taken thus far. Action to halt the loss of biodiversity and land degradation, avoid dangerous climate change and keep the effects of chemicals on the biosphere within tolerable limits must be coordinated to be effective. All these forms of degradation are primarily driven by the unsustainable level of consumption by the well-off, while the poor are left behind, characterizing contemporary civilization. Achieving transformative change requires that the fundamental drivers of overconsumption are addressed, through changes in personal values, norms, economic and social operating rules, technologies and regulations.'[ii]

Key areas for transformative change

1. Paradigms and visions of a good life: move towards paradigms that emphasise relationships with people and nature over material consumption, including many existing visions of good lives as those lived in accordance with principles and virtues of responsibility to people and nature.

2. Consumption, population and waste: reduce the negative global effect of human needs and demand – a function of consumption and production rates, population size and waste – by reducing per capita consumption and production in some regions and human population growth in others.

3. Latent values of responsibility: unleash existing capabilities and relational values of responsibility to enable widespread human and organisational action.

4. Inequalities: Systematically reduce inequalities in income and other forms, including across gender, race and class.

5. Participation in governance of environmental action and resource use: practice justice for and inclusion in decision-making for those most affected by it, especially Indigenous peoples and local communities.

---

ii   This is from the UNEP report (2021) *Making Peace with Nature.* https://wedocs.
unep.org/xmlui/bitstream/handle/20.500.11822/34948/MPN.pdf

6. Externalities: understand and internalise the distant, delayed and diffuse negative effects of actions, including economic activity.

7. Technology, innovation and investment: transform regimes of investment and technological and social innovation, such that technologies and their use produce net-positive impacts on people and nature (for example, by transitioning to a circular economy and eliminating waste).

8. Education and knowledge generation and sharing: promote the broad base of knowledge and capability that is fundamental to well-functioning and just societies, and increase and spread knowledge specific to sustainability.

Source: UNEP (ibid)

The fact is, even if a miraculous agreement emerges from the COP26, and countries swiftly implement every aspect they commit to, climate change is going to remain with us. All the carbon and methane emitted today will still be around years and indeed decades later. The present temperature rise of 1.4°C will be higher and, as things stand, that increase will entail widespread instability and risks. Humanity has stretched the planet to its limits, thus far avoiding the consequences of this in many places, but soon we will all have to face up to them. Any allusions to technological quick fixes are red herrings to the deep and long-term structural changes that are required. Adaptation needs to go further than simply building flood defences and storm-proofing homes.

Hope from Glasgow...?

As this book goes to press, the COP26 Climate Summit takes place in Glasgow. We could choose to examine the nature of the UN climate negotiations and potential methods of implementation, although given that subject has been dealt with elsewhere,[iii] it seems pertinent, as a Glasgow based organisation, to take a look at the city itself. Within it are lessons about wider society and the prospects of effective climate action.

Glasgow, once second only to London at the height of the British Empire, has profited from a variety of exploitative and extractive industries – from slavery to fossil fuels. Times have changed; docks and factory chimneys have been replaced by modern buildings. And yet, despite the shiny green of the COP26 SSE Hydro venue, the city around is decaying: treeless central streets speckled with litter sit beneath corporate offices and hotels, while outlying

---

iii   See, for example, Vesselin Popovski (2019), 'The Implementation of the Paris Agreement on Climate Change', Routledge

areas lie wasted from their own past developments. Public venues and services are shut and curtailed by budget constraints, even as their senior executives pocket six-figure salaries. Fast food joints, takeaways and pubs succour the needs of the rest. And yet, for a city where a 5 minute bus journey on the main private company Firstbus costs £2.50 or more, it is not much different from other cities – at least in the UK. As with so many other places, there are pockets of difference – from the lush parks of Kelvingrove and Glasgow Green, to community gardens and the organic, 'zero waste' food stores. And yet these are always the exceptions: for every cycle lane and planted tree there is a maze of congested roads and concrete. The island of 'civilisation', formerly existing in an ocean of nature, has swapped place with the ocean.

The façade and decay of modern urban cities? Above from top left:

1. SSE COP26 Hub: modernistic and green, the setting of the COP26 venue in Glasgow stands like an island from most other parts of the city, echoing how efforts that try to truly tackle climate change are the exception across the world.
2. Argyle Street: an example of a standard shopping/commercial district, with not a tree in sight.
3. Derelict area of land near Dalmarnock: formerly a plot for lorries to unload, surrounded by other vacant plots, covered in concrete and tarmac.
4. The Peoples Palace and Gardens: closed since 2018 due to concerns around the type of glass used, with a £5 million renovation cost cited despite no quotes being obtained (per Freedom of Information Requests 2020-2021). Now the once tropical biome lies untended and dying.

What would it take to turn a 'first world' northern European city like Glasgow around? There are many possibilities. For example, a 'corp' of people from all backgrounds could systematically go from one side of the city to the other, creating community gardens and planting trees on the many derelict sites; public transport could serve the interests of the public rather than generating a revenue for wealthy owners; roads and buildings alike could be converted to meet the needs of a planet that cannot cope with a continuing dependency on fossil fuels. The solutions are neither complex nor out of reach. But, under the current economic system, it seems delusional to expect such things from being implemented any time soon – let alone within the short window of time we have available.

This is just one city – a relatively wealthy one, within a highly developed country. Given this, just imagine the challenges that face cities in poorer nations – to say nothing of outlying towns and settlements. Taking this further, it seems reasonable to conclude that some kind of societal collapse – spurned by the climate crisis – is very likely. At best, as Professor Read explored, we can aim for a fundamental transition. But, either way, we must adapt – behaviourally, structurally and cognitively. This book has sought to present the extent of that challenge, as well as the opportunities arising from it.

A final thought

We have been confronted many times with the presence of humans being a negative impact on other species and the delicate web of life itself. No other species has wrought such destruction – spanning the atmosphere to the oceans and being responsible for a host of (on-going) extinctions. It would be easy to conclude that the demise of humanity would result in a much needed reprieve for other life. At the same time, the fact remains that humans are part of the web of life. It is only in the last 200 years that wide-scale and escalating damage has been caused. Before that, Indigenous peoples lived sustainably with other species and preserved their environment, rather than exhausting it. Some pockets of this way remain, while in other places we are attempting to 'relearn' how to live in harmony with nature.

If we understand the problems of over-exploitation, extraction, dominance and destruction to have arisen more from our socio-economic system than some innate biological characteristic, then there is hope. More than that, we can envisage a situation where humanity becomes a force of good – preserving and spreading life, rather than destroying it. The fact remains that, whether or not we remain on Earth, every species faces inevitable extinction. Our changing solar system – with a star destined to become 10% brighter in 'only' 1 billion years – means that Earth will mutate into a planet similar to Venus. The oceans will boil and the atmosphere become a toxic soup, with temperatures hot enough to melt metal. Going the opposite direction – the Earth's inner core is an internal 'dynamo' of magnetism, shielding our planet from harmful solar radiation that would otherwise strip away the atmosphere. It is slowly cooling, destined to eventually become dormant, and there's no known technology to halt that process. Whichever way we want to imagine it, all life on Earth will come to an end. But there is a species with the intelligence to sustain it beyond the planet – perhaps fulfilling a larger purpose that goes beyond our own survival.

When we embrace such possibilities, rather than surrendering to hopelessness and the sense of deserved doom, the future is a little bit brighter. We cannot remain blind to the challenges ahead, but history has shown how the spirit of human ingenuity and perseverance can overcome what were once thought of as impossibilities. We are part of life, perhaps unique in our ability to understand what lies ahead, and we can choose to take a separate path.

Let's do it – for the chance won't come again.

About the Arkbound Foundation

The Arkbound Foundation is a small literature charity based in Bristol and Glasgow. Our aim is to support people from a range of diverse and disadvantaged backgrounds to publish books that cover important social and environmental themes. Alongside book publishing, the charity delivers mentoring, workshops and events.

Since being founded, the Arkbound Foundation has made strong environmental commitments, ranging from using the most environmentally friendly printing methods to planting 1000 native oak saplings. Our aim is to continue being a carbon negative organisation (meaning we take actions and support initiatives that absorb more carbon than we produce), while highlighting the importance of environmental justice.

If you would like to find out more about us, please visit www.arkfound.org